D1205189

A FAR-AWAY WAR
Angola, 1975-1989

Editors

Ian Liebenberg
Jorge Risquet
Vladimir Shubin

Co-editors

Gert van der Westhuizen
Hedelberto Lopez Blanch
Gennady Shubin

A Far-Away War: Angola, 1975-1989

Published by SUN MeDIA Stellenbosch under the SUN PRESS imprint
All rights reserved

Copyright 2015 © SUN MeDIA Stellenbosch and Authors

First edition, September 2015

ISBN 978-1-920689-72-8
ISBN 978-1-920689-73-5 (e-book)

Set in 12/15 Dante MT
Cover design and typesetting by SUN MeDIA Stellenbosch

Cover image © Cuban Military Archives, Havana

SUN PRESS is an imprint of AFRICAN SUN MeDIA. Academic, professional and reference works are published under this imprint in print and electronic format. This publication may be ordered directly from www.sun-e-shop.co.za.

This publication has been peer reviewed by specialists in the field.

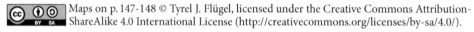
Printed and bound by Creda Communications, Cape Town.

This publication can be ordered from:
orders@africansunmedia.co.za
Takealot: bit.ly/2monsfl
Google Books: bit.ly/2k1Uilm
africansunmedia.store.it.si *(e-books)*
Amazon Kindle: amzn.to/2ktL.pkL

Visit africansunmedia.co.za for more information.

Contents

Acknowledgements

The editors and authors would like to thank the many people from various backgrounds who have shared their views, thoughts and reflections on the Angolan War before and since 2000. We thank the numerous South African ex-national servicemen who have shared their experiences with us collectively and individually over many years. The same applies to Cuban volunteers in and out of uniform, Angolan (in this case MPLA) combatants and Russian (then Soviet) veterans.

Well-deserved gratitude goes to George Risquet from Cuba, the Cuban Military Archives and the helpful staff there, Hedelberto Lopez Blanch from *Journal Juventad*, Vladimir and Gennady Shubin from the Africa Institute in Moscow, Igor Maidanov and Andre Tokarev (Moscow), Clara Pulido, David Gonzales and Silvio Baro from the (previously) Centre for African and Middle Eastern Studies in Havana (CEAMO), Emeritus Prof Phil Eidelberg (previously Unisa), General Paulo Lara and various senior Angolan officers and MK cadres who served in Angola between 1979 and 1989. The previous ambassadors of Cuba, Mrs Armenteros and Mr Angel Villa also deserve special thanks for their generous support and continued assistance, sometimes on short notice and with little guarantee of a concrete outcome, as at the time of the start of the project there was no publisher, nor any real funding available – only the wish to contribute other perspectives and real-life experiences to the multi-layered story of the Border/Bush/Angolan War. Many of those with whom we have interacted since 1975 will remain anonymous, but the valuable, emotional, existential and sometimes life-changing experiences that they shared with us are deeply appreciated and added much value to our (and we trust, the reader's) understanding of this particular "small and far away war" with its lasting legacy.

Friends, colleagues, co-workers, former students and institutions helped to form thoughts around this work. There are far too many to name. Some are: Gen (ret) Solly Molo, (the late) Rocky Williams, Mandla Seleoane, Robin Lloyd-Jones, Francois de Wet, Francois Vreÿ, Abel Esterhuyse, General Paulo Lara, Brig Gen L. Yam (previously Commandant at the South African Military Academy), Ian van der Waag, (the late) Elize Botha, Fankie Monama, Dries Liebenberg, Godwin Ayribi, Deon Visser, Tjaart Barnard, Evert Kleynhans, Herman Warden, Audrey Lawrence, Benjamin Mokoena, Thean Potgieter, Con Visagie, Godfrey Ramuhala, Martin Mendelsohn, (the late) Ruhr Martin, (the late) Jacques Liebenberg, André Groenewald, Col (ret) Johan Potgieter SADF, (the late) Ronnie van Rooyen, H.W. Short, Prof André Wessels, General McGill Alexander, Calvin Manganyi and (the late) Leo Barnard.

During the course of research, members of the research team travelled all over South Africa, Namibia, Angola, Cuba and the then Soviet Union (today Russia). During these travels, especially to other countries and continents, we encountered only hospitality and care, as well as an immense measure of readiness to assist and much goodwill. We thank the people involved, although they will remain nameless because recalling all of them would be well-nigh impossible.

The editors would like to extend their appreciation to the Office of the Dean, Faculty of Military Science, Prof Sam Tshehla and the Office of the Commandant of the Military Academy, Brig Gen L.K. Mbatha for their support as well as to Colonel M. Vena at the Military Academy. Also to Ina Botes, Chief Librarian at the Military Academy Library, Saldanha and the always friendly and helpful library staff, the staff and colleagues of the Centre for Military Studies (CEMIS), Andries Fokkens, Faculty Manager of the Faculty of Military Science, Stellenbosch University, Saldanha, and Betty Russel-Smith for her professional language editing. During the initial phases of this project the support of the then Dean of Social Sciences at Unisa Professor Mandla Makhanya, current Rector and Vice Chancellor of Unisa, was crucial.

As editors we express our gratitude to Johannes Richter from SUN MeDIA for his always helpful, professional and friendly assistance throughout the publication process. Likewise we extend our appreciation to Tyrel Flügel, School for Geospatial and Information Studies, Faculty of Military Science, Stellenbosch University, for his kind assistance with the generation of various maps for this publication.

Lastly we are grateful to the two assistants in the Centre for Military Studies, Audrey Lawrence, office coordinator and junior researcher, and Dawn Rakumakoe, post-graduate student.

The above-mentioned should, however, not be blamed for the interpretation of the information shared with the reader, nor the opinions held by the editors, advisors or contributors to this work.

THE EDITORS
Saldanha, 1 September 2015.

Dedication

It is with deep regret that we learned on the 5th of October 2015 that Jorge Risquet has passed away. He will be remembered not only for his role in Cuban politics, but also as civilian representative of the Cuban Republic in Angola during 1975/1976, and as chief negotiator of Cuba during the tripartite negotiations of 1988 to end the conflict in Angola. His role to achieve lasting peace in southern Africa will be remembered.

Tienie du Plessis (1949-2015), a close friend and colleague, was intimately involved with the history of this publication. As a veteran of the border war (Operation Savannah, 1975/1976), astute political and historical observer and publisher, his support for this work was invaluable.

This book is dedicated to their memory.

Contributors

Ian Liebenberg
Director Centre for Military Studies, Faculty of Military Science,
Stellenbosch University (Military Academy).

Phil Eidelberg
Prof (emeritus), formerly of the Department of History, University of South Africa.

Jorge Risquet[†]
Cuban Civilian Mission in Angola (1976) and member of the Central Committee of the
Comunist Party of Cuba. Chief Cuban negotiator during the Tripartite negotiations, 1988.

Vladimir Shubin
Prof (emeritus), former Deputy Director of the Institute for African
Studies, Russian Academy of Science, Moscow.

Gennady Shubin
PhD History, Senior Research Fellow, Centre for Southern African Studies,
Institute for Africa Studies, Russian Academy of Sciences, Moscow.

Hedelberto López Blanch
Journalist, historian and author, Havana, Cuba.

Klaus Storkmann
Major Dr, German Armed Forces Centre for Military History and Social Science, Potsdam, Germany.

Ulrich van der Heyden
Professor, Dr, Dr, University of South Africa, Pretoria.

Tienie du Plessis[†]
Publisher, Pretoria.

Gert van der Westhuizen
Journalist and historian, Johannesburg.

List of abbreviations

AFVs	Armoured fighting vehicles
ANC	African National Congress
APCs	Armoured personnel carriers
ARMSCOR	Armaments Corporation of South Africa
ATA	Afrikane teen Apartheid
BDK	Be-eindig Diensplig Kampanje
CAR	Central African Republic
CEAMO	Centre for African and Middle Eastern Studies in Havana
CIA	Central Intelligence Agency
CIR	Revolutionary Instruction Centre
COSWAR	Committee on South African War Resistance
CPSU	Communist Party of the Soviet Union
DRC	Dutch Reformed Church
DTA	Democratic Turnhalle Alliance
DTFPF	Defence of Tradition, Family and Property Foundation
ECC	End Conscription Campaign
EDV	Eindig Diensplig Veldtog
FAPLA	People's Armed Forces for the Liberation of Angola (Forças Armadas Populares de Libertação de Angola)
FAR	Revolutionary Armed Forces (Cuba)
FLEC	Front for the Liberation of the Enclave of Cabinda
FNLA	National Front for the Liberation of Angola (Le Front National de la Libération de l'Angola)
FRELIMO	Mozambique Liberation Front (Frente de Libertação de Moçambique)
GDR	German Democratic Republic
GOC	General Officer Commanding
ICJ	International Court of Justice
IDASA	Institute for Democracy in South Africa
IISS	International Institute for Strategic Studies
IRC	Indian Reformed Church
MIA	missing in action
MININT	Ministry of the Interior (Cuba)

MK	Umkhonto weSizwe
MMCA	Cuban Military Mission in Angola
MPLA	Popular Movement for the Liberation of Angola (Movimento Popular de Libertação de Angola)
MRL	Multiple rocket launcher
NP	National Party
NSF	National Students Federation
NUSAS	National Union of South African Students
OAU	Organisation of African Unity
PAC	Pan Africanist Congress
PKI	Indonesian Communist Party
PLAN	People's Liberation Army of Namibia
RSA	Republic of South Africa
SAAF	South African Air Force
SACBC	South African Catholic Bishops' Conference
SACC	South African Council of Churches
SACP	South African Communist Party
SADF	South African Defence Force
SANDF	South African National Defence Force
SDS	Studente vir 'n Demokratiese Samelewing
SSC	State Security Council
SUCA	Student Union for Christian Action
SWA	South West Africa
SWAPO	South West African People's Organisation
SWAPOL	South West African Police
SWATF	South West African Territorial Force
UDF	Union Defence Force
UN	United Nations
UNICEF	United Nations Children's Fund
UNITA	National Union for the Total Independence of Angola (União Nacional para a Independência Total de Angola)
UNTAG	UN Transition Assistance Group
USA	United Sates of America
USSR	Union of Soviet Socialist Republics
VSF	Verenigde Stellenbosche Front

Introduction

The fog of war and the dust of many conflicts tend to obscure truth. Truth is, indeed, the first casualty of war. During 2015 all those involved in this extensive conflict will commemorate the fortieth year since South Africa invaded Angola for the first time. Thereafter the South Africans maintained a semi-permanent presence in Angola, which led to immense suffering amongst Angolans and destroyed infrastructure for many years. The South Africans had to withdraw from Angolan territory, having been driven back in 1976. In the extensive battles of Cuito Canavale (1987/1988) the South African military and politicians, not heeding earlier experiences, withdrew in a less than dignified manner despite their generals still claiming a victory in Angola. The editors of this work cannot claim ownership of the truth about the war in Angola. We consciously allow different voices to speak and other views to be heard about an era of war in southern Africa. We cannot get closer to understanding what really happened if we are not perceptive to other perspectives and the ways in which other people experienced and interpreted their experiences. The average conscript and lower-ranking soldier that fought, albeit on different sides, had similar experiences. The bane of being a soldier, whether friend or foe, frequently leaves mirror images and similar pains, joys, fears, successes and failures – for those in the field and their loved ones at home. In the trials and tribulations of war, there seems to be a deep human universality.

Although breaking new ground, this is not a definitive work. It is exploratory, deploys multiple perspectives and voices, and invites further multi-partnership research and dialogue. The work shares with the reader previously unpublished (photographic) material. Many works on the war have appeared in South Africa since the 1990s. Unfortunately, the majority of these works with a few exceptions, including websites on the war, entertain only a South African perspective.

Since 2000 there has been a virtual explosion of works on the Bush War/Border War/ Angolan War (*Bosoorlog/Grensoorlog/Angola-oorlog*). Numerous works have appeared and are appearing in Russia and Cuba as well. On the Namibian war of liberation, which had been ongoing since colonial times, numerous works have seen the light, not all of them well known – or rather they have been lesser read because of the selective memories of South Africans. Due to language differences, authors' – and perhaps readers' – preferences, these works do not "talk" to each other and perspectives from Namibia, Russia (then the Soviet Union), Angola and Cuba are less known and read in South Africa (in some cases the perspectives from the "other side" are not known at all, or, because of ideological convictions, not considered at all). Keeping in mind that more than half a million South African men served in the military during the era of the Border War, this is regrettable.

Information that was denied these men has also influenced, and is still influencing, their relationship networks and their wish to know more about a "past up there".

The Border War lasted from 1966 to 1989. It included South African trans-border operations into Angola between 1975 and 1988 and influenced the lives of many. South African security forces were semi-permanently involved in Angola (mostly the southern part, but also as far north as Cabinda) through more than a hundred operations, which ranged from those that were strictly limited to those on a large scale. The outcome of the war is still controversial, as it was then, with all sides claiming victory. While lives were lost by all involved, the Angolans and Namibians, at the centre of this protracted conflict, suffered the most. The war is deeply etched in the memories of the civilians and (para-)military personnel who were affected by it. Many southern African societies still live on a day-to-day basis with the "walking wounded". This group contains ex-military personnel from all participating countries, but the civilians of the Frontline States who suffered during apartheid's wars of destabilisation and were never compensated, are far more numerous.

Some of the major actors in this war were the People's Liberation Army of Namibia (PLAN), the military wing of the South West African People's Organisation (SWAPO), the Angolan Movement for Popular Resistance of the People (MPLA) armed forces (FAPLA), the South African Defence Force (SADF), the Cuban forces and Russian advisory components as well as the South West African Territorial Force (SWATF), which acted as a Namibian-based proxy for the South African security forces. Others who took part included UNITA, a guerrilla movement led by Jonas Savimbi, which, before 1975 had close ties with the Portuguese colonial forces, and after 1975, was supported by the South African government and intermittently also by the Central Intelligence Agency (CIA) of the United States of America (USA). Earlier the FNLA of Holden Roberto, funded by the CIA and operating from Zaire as a proxy of the USA, also played a role. Other participants were the ANC cadres deployed in Angola. As trainees, some of them were deployed with the Angolan and Cuban forces and their training camps were strafed by the South African – even at times the then Rhodesian – Air Force, and they were also targeted by special force operators.

The war and its impact are clearly still much-debated and controversial subjects. The last of the debates is far from being concluded. The twentieth anniversary of the battles of the Lomba River, Tumpo Triangle and Cuito Cuanavale were in 2008. In 2009 it was 20 years since the first democratic elections in Namibia. And in 2010, with the FIFA World Cup soccer tournament being held in South Africa, Namibia celebrated the twentieth year of its independence, which followed the implementation of UN Resolution 435. In 2011 it was 30 years since the Angolan government implemented conscription to bolster its forces in its struggle against the SADF and UNITA. The centenary of the Union Defence

Force (UDF), precursor to the South African Defence Force (SADF) and the South African National Defence Force (SANDF), was celebrated in 2012. When South African soldiers died in a battle in the Central African Republic (CAR) during 2013 after a controversial deployment, it recalled contacts of thirty, forty years earlier when South African forces engaged SWAPO and FAPLA in southern Angola, two countries far from their own. And 2015 marks the fortieth year since South African forces invaded Angola with the tacit support of the USA (for the Cubans this would become the "first war in Angola"; for the Angolans it was to mark the beginning of their "second war of liberation").

In South Africa many works by retired generals, or people of higher rank attached to the permanent force or specialist forces, have been published. Some works have also been written by people who could be called "embedded journalists" or "sympathetic academics". More recently works have appeared that attempt to tell the story of more junior officers, or the normal soldier, many of them conscripts.[1] These works are important because erstwhile South African conscripts are now telling their own stories. These are not the stories told by generals and colonels, using only South African documents and claiming that they know best because "they were there".

In this work new voices are heard and other views on the Border War / Bush War and its outcomes in Angola are expressed.

We do not forget the South African conscripts. Nor do we ignore the role of objectors to apartheid military service. The torturous years of internal and external conflict saw many tensions, clashing views and socio-political paradoxes, if not outright contradictions. We also allow more voices to be heard and images to be seen. The book includes a variety of photographs and illustrations, posters, maps and other imagery. It brings the story closer to home and provides a broader "feeling" of what happened then.

As a result of the conflict in northern Namibia and Angola, and the wish to uphold a non-democratic government at home, the South African government in time increased national service for conscripts from three months to two years. Around 600 000 young South African men underwent training. The majority of them did not serve on the border or experience actual combat. But they played an important, if not crucial, role in Pretoria's show of strength in south and southern Africa, especially in occupied Namibia and in Angola. They were a ready answer when the ruling government was questioned by its own citizens, and many served in the townships during the 1980s. Some of them returned from the "war up there" in body bags, others were wounded, died in accidents far away or at home, some committed suicide or became emotionally scarred. These young men were trained for war and kept prepared in order to provide a reservoir of bodies (or rather numbers) to be used if necessary.

South African losses during the Border War, according to official information, were around 2 000 (excluding losses by the South West African Territorial Force (SWATF), created under SADF auspices). Losses by UNITA will perhaps never be known. Roughly 300 000 Cubans of both genders in and out of uniform served in Angola between 1975 and the Cuban withdrawal at the end of 1990. Cuban losses numbered 2 077 killed and missing in action, according to Cuban statistics. Full clarity on FAPLA's losses are unlikely to be gained as the first invasion of Angola by South Africa and her allies coincided with a change of state in Luanda after colonialism. There were no new structures of administration in place and for decades thereafter the country experienced conflict and levels of disorganisation which was exacerbated by the planned destabilisation of the Pretoria government.

The war caused extensive social disclocation in Angola. Hundreds of thousands of Angolans were displaced and some estimates put the number of refugees as high as 3 000 000. Angola was forced to institute conscription in 1981/1982 in an attempt to guard against South African cross-border operations, infiltration by special force units aimed at the destabilisation of the Angolan infrastructure, and regular UNITA activities with the support of South Africa and, at times, the USA. Northern Namibia was also the scene of large-scale dislocation of communities. Angola's infrastructure was destroyed and the civilian population has to deal with the deadly legacy of thousands of unmarked landmines that still claim, and will continue to claim, scores of innocent victims.

Our stories – or the voices offered here – tend to be different. It is not a story told by South African generals and officers. It tells the stories of Cuban, Russian and East German involvement in the war for southern Africa and also touches on the anti-war movement in South Africa. The stories are told from the point of view of Russians, Cubans and East Germans; not by South Africans influenced by the "Total Onslaught"-ideology who tend to turn erstwhile opponents into stereotypical "Rooi Gevaar"-ideologues. Perhaps most importantly, we also offer people a rare glimpse into photographs from the Cuban and Russian archives.

The work does not argue that those who killed the most enemies and their associates were victorious. It does not try to suggest that the apartheid forces were not at times tactically very apt and held a superior advantage in several operations. The South African politicians set out on a conflict where they could not maintain a strategic advantage, simply because Pretoria upheld a perspective that misread the reality of national struggles for liberation and of international opinion, because they were blinded by an ideology which, in turn, undermined their effectiveness on other levels in the long run. This work also does not try to prove who won the Battle of Cuito Cuanavale, the Tumpo Triangle and Lomba River, some of the turning points in the conflict that escalated before the withdrawal of South African forces from Angola. Over time the political and militarist masters in

Pretoria realised that you cannot hold on to or dominate territory that does not belong to you, irrespective of the fact that you are the dominant regional power.

As resistance to an unjust war and unjust means to wage a war was a serious concern in South Africa, and war resisters frequently described as part of the "enemy" by apartheid politicians and their political generals, notes on conscientious objection and political objection to the war waged inside South Africa, Namibia and Angola are included. Objectors frequently questioned the use of the military to uphold apartheid in South Africa. They were small in number, but were a constant irritant to the militarists in South Africa. Unlike the stereotypes of apartheid propaganda, these resisters were not only English speaking or fearful; nor were all of them people with no military experience, as some were deployed in Namibia (*Suidwes-Afrika*) and Angola. Falling back on their personal conviction and principles, with unique moral fibre they challenged the conscience of hawk-like politicians and generals and their academic advisors. Their principled stand against violence in service of a minority regime which upheld racial discrimination had far more influence than the apartheid leaders were prepared to admit.

This illustrated work concludes with a comprehensive bibliography on the Border War, apartheid South Africa's foreign policy and military destabilisation in the region, as well as the effects of militarisation during the 1970s and 1980s on our own and surrounding communities.

We trust that this publication will contribute to a wider understanding of a war in which many partook and a conflict that has some lasting consequences which are still felt today in South and southern Africa. If this publication contributes to the ongoing socio-historical dialogue and its outcomes for all those involved, the editors and contributors would be satisfied with their contribution to this multi-layered discussion. And hopefully it will leave the future generations of our country and in the region with a broader understanding of a conflict that should never have been.

IAN LIEBENBERG
September 2015

Notes

1.   Consult the extensive source list/bibliography at the end of this work for publications relating to this war.

On our Borders
Namibia seeks its own Destiny

Ian Liebenberg

The Namibian people fought for many years for their independence against foreign occupation. Their wars for liberation started before Karl Marx's voluminous writings on workers' exploitation reached Namibian shores, and preceded "The Cold War" mythology, even paranoia, advocated in the United States' newspapers and pro-government media in South Africa at the time of the Border War.[1] Namibians, indeed, fought foreign occupation long before they were called terrorists or there was a perceived "Total Onslaught".[2] Much was to happen and endless rivers of blood were to be spilled between the arrival of German Imperial Commissioner, Heinrich Goering (father to Herman Goering, the WW I fighter pilot and later Nazi leader) and the hoisting of the Namibian flag in Windhoek on the 21st of March 1990.[3] In October 1885 Heinrich Goering requested Berlin to provide German military protection[4] to German business interests such as the German Colonial Company for South West Africa.[5] Extensive conflict was to start that saw violent mutations in the Border War at Cassinga and Cuito Cuanavale a century later.

The Namibian struggle was complicated by the Cold War mentality and racist agendas between 1950 and the withdrawal of the South African occupying forces. Resistance against colonialism and forces of occupation started early with the Nama, Damaras, Herero people and the Bondelswarts resisting German colonial occupation. The Bondelswarts later on also put up resistance against Jan Smuts' Union of South Africa government and were defeated by land and air forces from South Africa (South Africa took over the trusteeship of South West Africa as a Class C mandate following the surrender of Germany after the First World War).

At the turn of the previous century the Herero revolt had been brutally suppressed under German rule, leading to the genocide of more than 70% of the Herero people. Although genocide is a contested term, it is widely recognised that that was done to the Hereros.[6] In 1904 Chief Samuel Maherero and his chiefs, resisting the looting of their land, cattle and the cruelties visited upon workers and peasants, decided on rebellion. Von Trotha, as German Military Governor and Supreme Commander of the German forces in the *Shutzgebiet*, issued a *Vernichtungsbefehl* (extermination order) that was to lead to the merciless extermination of the Herero survivors, old and young, male and female, after the initial resistance faltered – though not before a second battle at Oviumbo brought German forces near to disaster and caused outrage amongst the political leaders in Berlin.[7]

Schutstruppen on camels. SOURCE: *Die Kampfe der Deutschen Truppen in Südwestafrika*, Berlin, 1906, Ernst Siegfried Mittler und Sohn.

Namibians taken prisoner by German troops during the Herero War. SOURCE: Jeremy Sarkin. *Germany's Genocide of the Herero: Kaiser Wilhelm II, His General, His Settlers, His Soldiers*. Cape Town: UCT Press/James Currey, 2010. p. 121. A variety of photos relating to the same subject can be found in David Olusoga & Casper W Erichsen. *The Kaiser's Holocaust: Germany's Forgotten Genocide and the Colonial Roots of Nazism*. London: Faber and Faber, 2010.

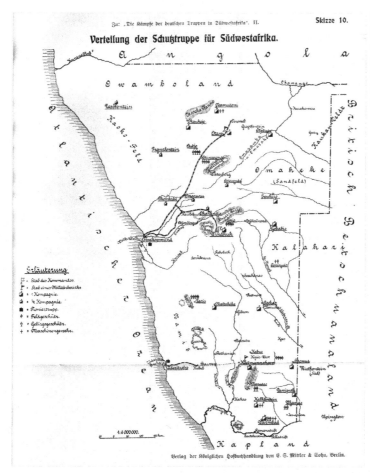

With the outbreak of the Herero uprising the Nama and other peoples adopted a fatal "wait-and-see policy".[8] Months later the Namas revolted and through swift, elusive commando raids by Witbooi and others such as Cornelius and Morenga, the war took on a guerrilla dimension.[9] Despite bold resistance the Nama population was to be halved through a policy of extermination.[10]

It was but a harbinger of what was to come. Soggot argues: "Foreshadowing the ambitions of the twentieth century totalitarian regimes, the authorities set out to divest the survivors of the social and cultural fabric which had nurtured [these] people. In the last resort the planners in Berlin and Windhoek sought to fashion the residual human material in their possession in a singly anonymous malleable working class which understood the iniquity of idleness and the indissoluble link between their welfare and the well-being of their masters."[11]

This domineering mentality of the ruling elite was to remain largely intact after the departure of the German rulers and the Union government, as new master of the territory, took control. The territory was referred to as a mandate (Class C) by the League of Nations that was established after World War 1.[12]

The wish of Namibian people to be free did not disappear once the Union Government uprooted German rule. From 1915 to 1920 the Union Defence Force (UDF) continued its policing role of the indigenous population. A South West African Police force was also formed. In the southern part of Namibia the Bondelswarts, who were defeated in the war of 1903–1906 by the Germans, remained restless.[13] Change from one ruler to another ruler and occupier was not to be taken without determination to achieve political freedom. Tensions rose in the southern territories and by April/May 1922 came to a zenith when some farms were raided by the Bondelswarts. With the use of machine guns, mountain guns and air raids, the Bondelswarts were eventually defeated.[14] Within two years the newly formed South African Air Force (SAAF) was used twice; once against its own citizens in the mining strike in the Transvaal, and the other against the Bondelswarts in "the mandate".

The next incident was the Rehoboth (Baster) uprising in 1924 and 1925. Here the issue was, apart from land, again that of having a political say and sovereignty/self-governance. Initially the Baster community followed a campaign of peaceful resistance organised by the Majority Party of Samuel Beukes.[15] In 1925 the resistance was crushed, among others by a show of force from the SAAF.

Another incident was the action taken against Chief Ipumbu of the Ukuambi people in Ovamboland. When the chief refused to abide by an ultimatum that he pay an outstanding fine, an uneasy period followed. Ipumbu himself was a restless and authoritarian character and this did not help in the context.[16] Following the use of armoured cars, aircraft and ground forces, Chief Ipumbu was eventually captured and sentenced in 1932. However, peace was not to last forever in Ovamboland and this relatively small incident would later be overtaken by another "small war" of some magnitude that spilled far wider.

Through their persistent, even if less successful resistance, Samuel Maherero, Jacob Marengo, Jonker Afrikaner, Hendrik Witbooi, Jacobus Christiaan, Abraham Morris, Simon Koper[17] and others were to become revered names in the history of the desolate, sunburnt land that is now called Namibia.

Under Smuts, H.F. Verwoerd, John Vorster and P.W. Botha white Namibians, loyal to the leadership in South Africa, started referring to Namibia (then known as South West Africa – SWA) as South Africa's "fifth province". But in spite of this, Namibian people persevered in their attempts at independence, combating superior armed forces from South Africa who believed SWA was rightfully theirs to be ruled as they saw fit, despite international objections.[18] As in South Africa, territorial segregation between "ethnic" groups was envisaged and South African legislation, including security laws, applied in the territory.[19]

Despite resistance by trade unions, fledgling rebellions, and some protest by African states, Namibia's status remained that of a mandate.[20] The International Court of Justice (ICJ) ruled in 1966 that Liberia and Ethiopia did not have any legal rights or interest in the matter of SWA. For a brief moment, South Africa's mandate over Namibia was confirmed. For the South West African People's Organisation (SWAPO) the ruling confirmed their need to fight back by means of an armed struggle. In a way many Namibians felt that their long (since at least 1903) struggle for self-determination in their chosen homeland had been betrayed by the International Court and the richer nations of the world (some of them represented in the UN Security Council).

The first clash between South African forces and SWAPO guerrillas took place on the 26th of August 1966 at Ongulumbashe in Ovamboland. Two guerrillas were killed and eight captured, while six escaped.[21] On the 27th of August, the pro-government mouthpiece, *Die Burger*, shared with its readers that "Everything points to it that the situation in Ovamboland is under control."[22] This statement was to become a fascinating piece of understatement, if not a misreading of what was to come in the next decades. Ongulumbashe was the first of many skirmishes, or "contacts" as the South Africans referred to them. SWAPO continued its struggle, despite the numerically superior "killing rate" regularly achieved by the South African forces. By 1972 northern Namibia was engulfed in "low intensity guerrilla warfare".[23]

SWAPO supporters in Windhoek   *Photo: SWAPO*

In 1967 the Ovambo leader Mr Herman Toivo ja Toivo was sentenced to life imprisonment and fourteen others to lesser sentences.[24] The offences for which they were found guilty were related to the Terrorism Act and the Suppression of Communism Act of South Africa as applied in Namibia.[25]

In December 1971 and January 1972 Ovamboland and the rest of Namibia experienced extensive labour unrest.[26] The Tanga Consultative Congress in Tanzania in December 1969 and January 1970 resulted in increased SWAPO activity. Infiltration of guerrillas, agitation and labour unrest made the point: Namibians were poised to fight rather than to submit.[27]

SWAPO supporters in Windhoek, December 1978   *Photo: SWAPO*

South African authorities responded with strict emergency regulations. Large-scale security operations and detentions followed and South African security laws were adopted. International criticism increased, but South Africa maintained its position. The UN Security Council confirmed the revocation of South Africa's mandate in Namibia and by 1971 the ICJ had re-affirmed that South Africa was illegally occupying Namibia and that the occupation was in contravention of international law.

The Evangelical Lutheran Church of Owambo-Kavango and the Evangelical Lutheran Church in South West Africa protested to South African Prime Minister John Vorster about apartheid policies in Namibia.[28] These churches were in support of the advisory opinion adopted by the ICJ in 1971 that South Africa's mandate over Namibia was invalid. The open letter from the church leadership in Namibia to the South African leader B.J. Vorster received scant attention.[29] In 1974 the UN adopted the name Namibia for South West Africa, a year after the UN General Assembly declared SWAPO the sole and authentic representative of the Namibian people.

When Portuguese colonial forces withdrew in a hurry from Angola after the coup against the Caetano government in 1974 in Lisbon, three liberation movements vied for power (actually only one was a liberation movement, as one, UNITA, was implicated in earlier dealings with Portuguese security forces, and the leader of the other one, the National Front for the Liberation of Angola (FNLA), was hardly on Angolan soil and was in the pay of the USA's Central Intelligence Agency (CIA). The Popular Movement for the Liberation of Angola (MPLA) had significant support in urban areas, including workmen's associations/unions and since 1954 had demonstrated their ability to fight and survive in the field, despite setbacks.[30] UNITA and the FNLA received Western/US backing (Earlier on UNITA also had some backing from the people's Republic of China). South Africa invaded Angola from the south in support of UNITA and supplied hardware and advisors to the FNLA guerrillas and government troops from Zaire in the north. South Africa's involvement in Angola in 1975/1976, to bolster the "anti-communist" forces of the rebel movements FNLA of Holden Roberto and UNITA of Jonas Savimbi, heightened tensions. During Operation Savannah, as the incursion into Angola was called, losses, according to the then Chief of the South African Air Force, were "28 SA men killed in action and about 100 wounded".[31] In the future, South Africa would enter Angolan territory regularly on numerous operations and with virtual impunity. South Africa made several hot pursuit raids into Angola. At the end of 1979 (October) the General Officer Commanding (GOC) of South West Africa Command (SWA Command), Jan Geldenhuys, suggested that the effective SWAPO fighting forces, estimated at between 6 000 and 8 000 had been diminished by 2 000 as a result of South African military action. It was suggested that SWAPO deaths increased from 10 per month to 80 per month between 1978 and 1979. The SADF claimed that the killing rate was 33 guerrillas for every member of the South African security forces that was lost.[32] Much more was to come in the next decade ...

The SADF took full responsibility for counter-insurgency operations in Namibia. André du Pisani, a Namibian scholar, argued in 1988 that "from the perspective of a frontier army, it is important to reiterate that the SADF was introduced into an already highly charged political arena".[33] In Western Europe, the Scandinavian governments and other countries recognised SWAPO as Namibia's sole representative.[34]

A United Nations publication argued in 1974:

> No people can win freedom by outside action alone... the scope of the [Namibian freedom fighters' activities] ... [are of such a nature] as to require a permanent state of alert from the occupying power ... they [SWAPO] show that they are not

waiting passively on what the international community can do for them. For them the United Nations is a factor, admittedly an important one, but their hopes and aspirations are not totally dependent on goodwill from the outside.[35]

The former Secretary-General of the UN viewed the situation as "one of the gravest challenges to the authority of the United Nations" and called for united action. His successor, Kurt Waldheim, in his special report on Namibia for 1973 emphasised the "special responsibilities of the international community towards the Territory and the people of Namibia", and urged the United Nation's organs, and the Security Council in particular, "to seek effective approaches to bring about a solution based on the inalienable rights of the Namibian people to self-determination, national independence, and the preservation of the unity and territorial integrity of Namibia".[36]

Such statements were a reminder of Toivo ja Toivo's words during his "terrorism" trial of 1968: "We are Namibians, not South Africans ... Only when white South Africans realise this and act on it, will it be possible for us to stop our struggle for freedom and justice, in the land of our birth."[37] At the time few realised that Toivo said, "Namibian" and not "communist", and that the (national) struggle for liberation from foreign domination was but a continuation of what the Herero people and Hendrik Witbooi had stood for many years before – Toivo's statement was a golden thread in a historical quest for Namibia's own destiny.

For the Namibian people in the land of their birth, the government in Pretoria had other plans. The South African Odendaal Commission (1962–1964) made it clear that "a policy of differentiation must be followed here" and that "ethnic groups are [to be] basic units of development".[38] In the eyes of many this was a further attempt to structure Namibia along the lines of apartheid. This commission and subsequent political restructuring took place despite the visit of a UN Special Committee for South West Africa to Namibia to which Pretoria reluctantly agreed. The two members of the Committee, Victor Carpio (Philippines) and Martinez de Alva (Mexico) pointed out that clearly the Pretoria government was intent on the subordination of the people of Namibia to their own likes (1962). Pretoria forged ahead with its own designs.[39]

Only three per cent of Namibians voted in local government elections arranged by the occupying power in 1973. This underlined the perception that South Africa was illegally occupying Namibia. South Africa's later invasion of Angola with the support of the USA and its use of Namibia as a springboard for regional destabilisation, only added to this view. South Africa's (Pretoria's) attitude and actions escalated the regional cycle of violence with increasing military involvement, including involvement from non-African states. The consistent build-up of South African forces led to an arms race in southern Africa, but even if they had combined their resources, the Frontline States could not match the military power of South Africa. South Africa's aggressive posture forced the Frontline States to spend money on arms, rather than much needed development.

In 1978 the UN adopted Resolution 435. This time the so-called Western Five – the USA, Britain, the Federal Republic of Germany, Canada and France – temporarily agreed that Namibia should be granted independence and that a UN Transition Assistance Group (UNTAG) was to assist in the process to ensure free and fair elections. Yet covert support to South Africa continued, notably from the USA and Britain.[40] And SWAPO continued the armed struggle ...

Boere on horseback killing **SWAPO**. SOURCE: ComOps poster SADF (1979) from author's archive.

A South African attempt at an internal settlement that excluded SWAPO, failed. The *Turnhalle Beraad* (Turnhalle Convention) was a failure despite the fact that someone like Dirk Mudge had left the National Party to establish the Republican Party among Namibians. Participants in the Turnhalle Convention, which evolved into the Democratic Turnhalle Alliance (DTA), became fragmented. It was clear that South Africa's involvement in Namibia, despite a tug of war between internal parties, overshadowed the internal wish to solve the differences between Namibians. A Namibian-based journalist interviewed in 1984 in Windhoek pointed out how the South African government had abused the DTA, especially the Republican Party of Dirk Mudge, for its own ends. One view had it that Mudge himself was deeply dissatisfied with the apartheid government for not ushering

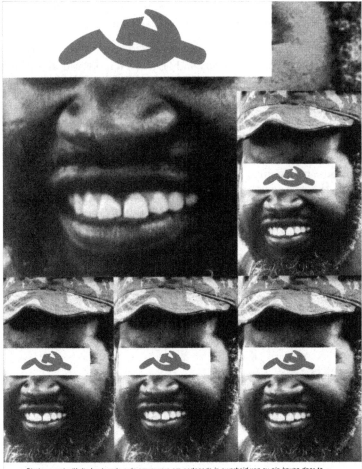

South African government propaganda against "terrorism" circa 1983.
SOURCE: Author's archive.

Die insurgent will die bestaande orde omverwerp om sodoende 'n owerheid van sy eie keuse daar te stel. Dit maak nie vir hom saak hoeveel lewens in die proses verloor word nie.

in a political settlement. Mudge suggested that SWAPO might have to be a part of the eventual political solution. He used simple, but striking logic: "You cannot win a guerrilla war. If you win it [the guerrilla war] by 51 per cent, still 49 per cent of the people will continue to fight. If you have [... an election] ... and you end up with these percentages [normal] politics can continue." Mudge made it clear that the National Party did not have support in Namibia, despite what Pretoria said. He predicted that the National Party, like smaller ethnic parties, would end up with little influence in future Namibian politics. Thirty odd years later, Dirk Mudge was proved correct.[41]

At the time Mudge and the DTA were, partially as result of the manipulation and abuse of the "internal leaders" such as the DTA and Republican Party by Pretoria's leaders, tainted and not seen as legitimate internationally. Despite this the DTA did gain representation as the largest opposition grouping in the Namibian parliament after the first free and fair elections in Namibia, thereby playing a role in a new multi-party (albeit a dominant party) democracy and the non-racial politics of an independent Namibia.

As a war against occupying forces, the resistance had the characteristics of an anti-colonial war. Namibians were conscripted and recruited by the South African army to fight against the liberation movement. For some, this had some elements of a civil war.

In 1980 the South African government created the South West African Territorial Force (SWATF) and conscripted Namibians. Pretoria's rulers also inaugurated the South West African Police (SWAPOL) in 1981 to assist South African forces in maintaining "law and order".

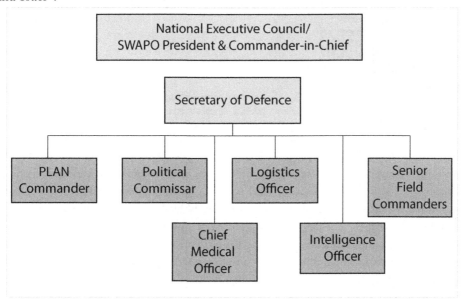

SWAPO's Political and Military Structure: From the time of the first battle between SWAPO guerrillas and South African security forces in the 1960s, the organisation honed itself for the armed struggle which was to last until 1989. The military wing, People's Liberation Army of Namibia (PLAN), operated under its political leadership. SOURCE: www.mod.gov.na.

During the 23 years of war, some of SWAPOL's sections operated in northern Namibia as paramilitary counterinsurgency units, rather than as a regular police force. The activities of Koevoet, the police counterinsurgency unit, created mistrust, fear and animosity. Koevoet operations, it was said at the time, accounted for up to 80 per cent of war deaths in Ovambo and Kavango. SWATF units, such as 101 Battalion, and 32nd Battalion, consisting of ex-Angolan guerrillas under white leadership, contested Koevoet's supremacy and claimed greater efficiency in the war against "terrorists" and the race to bring home "ears" (the success of operations were measured by "kills" or bringing "ears" home).

First multi-party elections in Namibia 1989.
SOURCE: Author's archive.

Many civilians and the media did not distinguish between Koevoet, special forces (recces), 101 Battalion, airborne soldiers and the conscripts deployed in northern Namibia. Moonlight operations were frequently undertaken in Ovamboland and Angola by South African Special Forces, 32 Battalion and parabats, as the airborne soldiers were known in South African parlance. Abuses were frequently blamed on all uniformed members, including conscripts. The current South African government has not yet released or declassified documents relating to civilian losses in northern Namibia. Even if documents are eventually declassified, unmanaged-, under-reporting at the time will remain another problem and the specific number of civilian deaths due to operations by South African forces is unlikely to be known.

Many Namibians fled their homes during the war. Some went to Angola, where the situation was not much better because of South African and UNITA activities in large parts of southern Angola. Estimates on the number of Namibian refugees range from 50 000 to 70 000. Refugees were airlifted back to Namibia on 452 flights in 1989. A total of 42 736 people of all ages returned during the final stages of the UN airlift.[42] This number excludes people who made their own way home.

Thousands of Namibians, mainly Ovambos, were forcibly removed from a strip of land between one and four kilometres wide along the border between Namibia and Angola to create a no-go zone (*kaplyn*). A dawn-to-dusk curfew was imposed and civilian people who disregarded it were sometimes killed.

SADF incursions frequently forced refugees to flee again; Operation Reindeer (Cassinga) being one example. People forced off the land by the raging war in northern Namibia (Ovamboland), had to choose between becoming permanent refugees and being forced into sub-standard urbanisation in sprawling townships in northern Namibia, nominally under the "protection" of the occupying forces. Lack of services increased the occurrence of typhoid, tuberculosis, measles and other diseases. At one stage, shanty town dwellers accounted for more than 200 000 people in the immediate areas of Ondangwa and Oshakati, nearly a quarter of the Namibian population.[43] In Angola the situation was hardly better. The United Nations Children's Fund (UNICEF) estimated that as result of operations in the early 1980s, 160 000 Angolans were left homeless and that up to 100 000 Angolans died as result of war-related famine between 1981 and 1985. UNICEF also estimates that up to 33 000 children died of unnatural causes between 1981 and 1988.[44]

"No elections in Africa have been so thoroughly prepared, so meticulously covered and carefully monitored as these."[45] Despite the large territory, Namibia was sparsely populated and apart from the liberation struggles fought against colonial/occupying forces, Namibians themselves, though culturally different, for the most part were not a deeply divided society, which probably assisted in the process once the occupier and common enemy had left. The

Poster distributed in preparation for UNTAG-supervised elections 1989. SOURCE: Author's archive.

United Nations Transitional Assistance Group (UNTAG) consisted of 4 650 soldiers, 1 000 police and a large number of civilian administrators and volunteers. SWAPO won 57,3 per cent of the vote (41 out of 72 seats) and the Democratic Turnhalle Alliance 28,6 per cent (21 seats).[46] The smaller parties such as the United Democratic Front, the Action Christian National, Federal Convention of Namibia, the Namibian National Front and the National Patriotic Front of Namibia, divided the few remaining spoils.[47] The elections took place in November 1989, the constitution was drafted within two months and Namibians became independent with festivities held in Windhoek on the 31st of March, attended by Western and non-aligned glitterati alike. A war that could have been prevented as early as 1946 came to an end after much blood had been spilt.

Both Namibia and Angola, but especially Angola, were to suffer for decades after the destabilising conflicts that they had experienced. This multi-layered and torturous conflict and its roleplayers are discussed from different viewpoints in the chapters that follow. These chapters may not heal the pain and destruction, but hopefully they will, to an extent, lift some of the dust hanging over numerous battlefields and so contribute to a better understanding of this "far-away" war and the effects it had – and indeed still has ...

Notes

1.   The deeply entrenched Cold War mythology changed in a socio-political myopia that is still prevalent in memoirs of South African generals and colonels, military authors and even some historians (The works by Magnus Malan, Jannie Geldenhuys, Helmut Römer-Heitman and Leopold Scholtz being examples).

2.   Consult André du Pisani, *SWA/Namibia: The Politics of Continuity and Change* (Johannesburg: Jonathan Ball, 1985), 21ff; Horst Drechsler, *"Let us Die Fighting": The Struggle of the Herero and Nama against German Imperialism (1884–1915)* (Berlin: Akademie-Verlag, 1966); Peter H. Katjavivi, *A History of Resistance in Namibia* (London: James Currey, 1988) 8ff. An innovative earlier compilation edited by Christopher Saunders, *Perspectives on Namibia: Past and Present* with contributions by Neville Alexander, Keith Gottschalk, Ottillie Abrahams and André du Pisani is also relevant (Centre for African Studies, Occasional Paper No 4, University of Cape Town). Also see David Soggot, *Namibia: The Violent Heritage* (London: Rex Collins Publishing, 1986). A recent well-researched work published by a South African historian is also worthy of consulting. See Louis Bothma, *Vang 'n Boer: Die stryd tussen Boer en Ovambo* (Langenhovenpark: L.J. Bothma, 2012). Bothma's work in Afrikaans is one of the very few non-fictional works published by South African authors since 1990 (26 years since the withdrawal of South African forces from the war following the Cuito Cuanavale battles) that broke through the biases – and in cases myopia – of numerous works by South African authors on the border war. It indeed provides a fresh perspective on a contemporary war fought on the wrong premises. Bothma's work has both done the South African readership, academic and military expert-practitioners a favour and set an example of telling history both in context and in drawing telling historical parallels.

3.   As Herbert Wieland has it: "The end to thirty-one years of German and seventy-five years of South African rule." Weiland, "Namibia: A fresh deal", *International Affairs Bulletin* 14, no.1 (1990): 22.

4.   For the strong elements of racism and (violent) paternalism inherent in the German dealings with the peoples of Namibia, consult Soggot,4ff. For the justification of the then German colonial mentality consult Paul Rohrbach, Deutsche Kolonialwirtschaft: Südwest-Afrika, Band 1, Berlin-Schöneberg: Bundverlag der "Hilfe", 1907.

5.   Soggot, 3.

6. See Jeremy Sarkin, *Germany's Genocide of the Herero: Kaiser Wilhelm II, His General, His Settlers, His Soldiers* (Cape Town: UCT Press, 2011), and David Olusoga and Casper W. Erichsen, *The Kaiser's Holocaust: Germany's Forgotten Genocide and the Colonial Roots of Nazism* (London: Faber and Faber, 2010). To read the German viewpoint/justification of the time, see *Die Kampfe der Deutschen Truppen in Südwestafrika* (Berlin: Ernst Siegfried Mittler und Sohn, 1906). On Herero genocide also consult Bothma.

7. Soggot, 8ff.

8. Ibid., 11.

9. Ibid., 11.

10. Ibid., 11. See also Henning Melber, *Our Namibia* (London: Zed Press, 1986), 81.

11. Soggot, 12–13.

12. Which explains why workers in Namibia consistently resisted exploitation. Compare Richard Moorsom, *Walvis Bay: Namibia's Port* (London: International Defence and Aid Fund (IDAF), 1984), 41–42; Cronje and Cronje, *The Workers of Namibia* (London: IDAF), 77ff; A.W. Berkhof, *Gewapend Geweldloos: Over de Bevrijding van Zuidelijk Afrika* (Utrecht: Werkgroep Kairos, 1984), 49. For more on how foreign companies assisted Pretoria's government in the exploitation of Namibians, consult *Allies in Apartheid: Western Capitalism in occupied Namibia*, ed. Allan. D. Cooper (London: MacMillan Press, 1988); Ann and Neva Seidman, *US Multinationals in Southern Africa* (Dar es Salaam: Tanzania Publishing House, 1977), 162ff.

13. Andries Fokkens, "The Suppression of Internal Unrest in South West Africa (Namibia), 1921–1933", *Scientia Militaria* 40, no. 3 (2012): 116.

14. Ibid., 117–121, 126.

15. Ibid., 128.

16. Ibid., 132, 134, 137.

17. Simon Koper's exploits made him famous for some, notorious for others. Forced into the eastern parts of south Namibia to Grootkolk (Geinab) at the juncture of the South African, Namibian and Botswana borders (the northern part of the Kalahari-Gemsbok Park) he continued his guerrilla campaign. "Driven eastwards into the dune country Cooper [*sic*] fought on desperately and skilfully" (Lawrence G. Green, *To the River's End* (Cape Town: Howard B. Timmens, 1947), 26. Koper's killing of captured German soldiers at the Geinab outpost in an eye-for-an-eye approach towards the end of the 1904–1907 guerrilla campaign is mentioned as an example of Koper's notoriety by Green. At the time the Herero population had already been largely decimated by the German forces of Von Trotha.

18. For a lengthy saga on objections from Namibian people, international leaders, the UN and even attempted interventions by the South African white opposition leader, Sir de Villiers-Graaff against top-down rule by Pretoria in Namibia, consult *A Trust Betrayed* (United Nations Office of Public Information, 1974) 6ff, 25ff, 35ff, 42ff.

19. Annette Seegers, *The Military in the Making of Modern South Africa* (London: I B Tauris, 1996), 135.

20. See again *A Trust Betrayed*, 6ff.

21. *Die Burger*, 27 Augustus 1966; *Rand Daily Mail*, 27 August 1966; *Rand Daily Mail*, 29 August 1966 (Newspaper Compendium, Pretoria University).

22. *Die Burger*, 27 Augustus 1966: "Alles dui daarop dat die toestand in Ovamboland onder beheer is na gisteroggend se geveg tussen die Suid-Afrikaanse polisie en 'n bende gewapende guerrilla vegters wat die gebied oor die grens binnegekom het." Note the term guerrilla fighters used here. In an increasing state of political mobilisation and propaganda SWAPO guerrillas were soon referred to as terrorists and not guerrillas. The same applied to the South African liberation movements the ANC, PAC and others.

23. On low intensity guerrilla war in northern Namibia see Muriel Horrel, *Race Relations as Regulated by Law in South Africa, 1948–1979* (Johannesburg: South African Institute for Race Relations, 1982), 316.

The part by Horrel dedicated to developments in Namibian politics discusses in great detail the apartheid legislation and corollary security legislation in Namibia: 285ff, 302ff. See especially: 315–316.

24.   Horrel's figures differed from another publication which mentions that of the 34 defendants two were acquitted. Nineteen were sentenced to life imprisonment and the others received terms of up to twenty years. See United Nations, *A Trust Betrayed*, 31.

25.   Horrel, 316.

26.   Cronje and Cronje, 77ff.

27.   Ibid. See also Katjavivi, 38ff.

28.   The role of religion and churches in Namibian history, colonialism and liberation deserves far more than can be dealt with here. As far as the post-1950 liberation struggle in Namibia and the role of the churches are concerned, consult among others Werkgroep Kairos, *Kerk en Bevrijdingsbewegingen* (Utrecht, 1981), 40ff, 69ff.

29.   Werkgroep Kairos, *Kerk en Bevrijdingsbewegingen* (Utrecht, 1981), 56–57.

30.   Ian Liebenberg, "Talking Small Wars in Far Away Lands: Three Incidences in Angola's 'Second War of Liberation'" in *Regions, Regional Organisations and Military Power*, ed. Thean Potgieter, Abel Esterhuyse and Ian Liebenberg (Stellenbosch: Sun Media, 2008), 66–68.

31.   Horrel, 317. Unita and FNLA losses were not mentioned, nor the lives lost by pro-Western/RSA mercenaries during the campaign.

32.   Ibid., 318.

33.   André du Pisani, *Beyond the Barracks: Reflections on the Role of the SADF in the Region* (Braamfontein: The South African Institute of International Affairs (SAIIA), 1988), 14.

34.   Ibid., 14ff. See also Andre du Pisani, "South Africa in Namibia: Variations on a Theme, "*International Affairs Bulletin* (South African Institute of International Affairs, SAIIA) 10, no. 3 (1986): 6ff for an earlier assessment.

35.   United Nations, *A Trust Betrayed*,40.

36.   Ibid., 42.

37.   Ibid., 42–43.

38.   Ibid., 22–24.

39.   Ibid., 21.

40.   See John Stockwell, *In Search of Enemies: A CIA Story* (London: Andre Deutsch, 1978), 272–273; Robert S. Jaster, *South Africa in Namibia: The Botha Strategy* (Lanham: University Press of America, 1985), 92, 114; Namibia Support Committee, *Namibia 1884–1984: Readings on Namibia's History and Society*(Lusaka: United Nations Institute for Namibia, 1988), 698, 699–701; Ian Liebenberg, "From Racialism to Authoritarianism: South Africa, Militarised Politics and the Implosion of State Legitimacy under Apartheid," in *Changing Security Paradigms and South Africa after the Cold War*, ISPAIM Occasional Paper (Bucharest: Military Publishing House 10, no. 16 (2011): 72–73.

41.   Transcript of interview (masked), undated (personal collection, Liebenberg).

42.   United Nations, *UNTAG in Namibia: A New Nation is Born* (Windhoek: John Meinert, 1991), n.p.

43.   South African Catholic Bishops Conference (SACBC), Special publication on Namibia, 1989.

44.   Also compare A. Vines on the consequences of the extended conflict in Angola. *Track Two Occasional Paper* 8, no. 2 (2006): 3, 6. Covert assistance to Unita by the USA amounted to US$250 000 000 between 1986 and 1991, making it at the time the second largest United States covert programme followed by support for the Afghan *mujahedin*. Vines, 3, 6.

45.   Weiland, 22.

46.   Ibid.

47.   Ibid.

Namibia: From Colony to Independent State

1858	An early attempt at peace and nation-building: The Treaty of Hoachanas, an agreement for peace and friendship signed by Jonker Afrikaner, Kido Witbooi, Paul Goliath, Willem Swartbooi, Amraal, David Christian and Tjamuaha (Chief Maharero and Griqua delegates from the Northern Cape were present but did not sign).
1884	Adolph Lüderitz and Heinrich Vogelsang acquire land in dubious deals around Lüderitz (Angra Pequena) from Joseph Fredericks of the Bethanie people. Witbooi protested against these deals with little effect.
1885	German Imperial Commissioner Heinrich Goering appealed to Berlin for a military presence to protect German business interests. Missionaries play a dubious role.
1890	Windhoek occupied despite protests from Maharero, supreme chief of the Herero people.
1893	The Germans attack Witbooi.
1894	German Major Theodor Leutwein, the third of the Reich's supreme officials, took control of the territory. Colonisation became violently explicit. Leutwein's rule is marked by a carrot-and-stick approach and Namaland was conquered (temporarily). The Herero people's land became the next objective.
1895	Leutwein determines to use force against the Hereros and reports to the German Imperial Chancellor that war against the Hereros may be economically beneficial to Germany.
1903	Large tracts of land and livestock brought under German control. Settlers move in widely. Bondelswarts uprising takes place.
1904	Herero Revolt, extermination order and genocide under Von Trotha.
1905–07	War of resistance continues.
1908	Discovery of diamonds in southern Namibia.
1915	South African occupiers take over from the German colonisers. (The South African flag now flies in Windhoek.)
1917	South African forces kill King Mandume.
1920	Mandate of Namibia handed to the Union of South Africa by the League of Nations.
1922	Bondelswarts rebellion crushed by the Union Government.
1925	Baster rebellion crushed by Union Government.
1932	Ipumbu's rebellion crushed in Ovamboland.
1944–45	The United Nations is established.
1946	South Africa refuses to submit Namibia mandate to UN Trusteeship.
1948	National Party take power in South Africa.
1949	South Africa refuses to submit reports on the Namibian territory to the UN. Namibians request self-rule.
1954	"Native Affairs" in Namibia placed under direct control of Pretoria.
1958	Ovamboland People's Organisation formed.
1960	SWAPO established.
1962	Odendaal Commission appointed by Pretoria. (Report that recommended Bantustans for Namibia appears in 1964.)
1963	SWAPO started training cadres for armed resistance.

Namibia: From Colony to Independent State   (continued)

1966	UN General Assembly ends South Africa's Mandate over Namibia (Resolution 2145). The first skirmish between guerrillas and the South African Police takes place on 26th of August 1966 in northern Namibia. Prime Minister B.J. Vorster subsequently declares that "everything is under control". The Swedish Foreign Minister Torsten Nilsson asked the United Nations to annul South Africa's mandate over South West Africa/Namibia. International Court's "Non-Decision" on the issue.
1968	SWAPO leaders convicted in treason trial. SWAPO's position in exile therefore strengthened.
1969	Swapo guerrillas active in four regions, namely Ovamboland, Okavango, Kaokoveld, the Caprivi Strip and as far south as Grootfontein/Tsintsabis.
1970	UN Security Council declares South Africa's hold on Namibia illegal.
1971	Open letter from Namibian church leaders to President B.J. Vorster condemning South Africa's occupancy of Namibia and political repression of Namibians.
1972	The International Court confirms the UN Security Council's decision to be legitimate. Large-scale labour unrest manifests itself in Namibia. South African security legislation applied to Namibians. South African military cooperation with Portuguese colonial authorities in Angola stepped up. South African society increasingly militarised.
1973	SWAPO recognised as representative of the people of Namibia. Pretoria's local government elections (self-governance/local authorities as key concepts) in Namibia draw little support.
1974–76	The Carnation Revolution in Portugal topples the authoritarian Caetano government. Angola and Mozambique become independent. South Africa, with CIA assistance, invades Angola. Soweto rebellion takes place in South Africa.
1977	Turnhalle (internal) constitution in Namibia accepted in whites-only referendum. Democratic Turnhalle Alliance founded.
1978	The Cassinga raids (Operation Reindeer).
1979–88	Regular South African Defence Force raids into Angola translate into semi-permanent presence in Angola. Destabilisation of Frontline States that support the ANC or SWAPO becomes commonplace. Regular raids into Angola, Mozambique, Zambia, Botswana, Lesotho, Swaziland and Zimbabwe take place. Large-scale covert support rendered to UNITA by South Africa and the USA (USA policy of "constructive engagement"). The US policy of constructive engagement plays a major role in escalating conflict, furthering destabilisation and extending human suffering in southern Africa, especially in Angola and northern Namibia.
1988	South Africa's military adventures in Angola come to a standstill.
1989	Elections in Namibia under UN supervision of Resolution 435 (UNTAG).
1990	Namibia becomes independent in March.
2001	President Sam Nujoma of the ruling party SWAPO announces that he will not stand for a third term as President of the Republic of Namibia.

This chronology is derived from, among others: Henning Melber, *Our Namibia* (London: Zed Books, 1983); Horst Drechsler, *"Let us Die Fighting": The Struggle of the Herero and Nama against German Imperialism (1884–1915)* (Berlin: Akademie-Verlag, 1966); *Namibia: Past and Present*, Ed. Christopher Saunders, Centre for African Studies, Occasional Paper 4, University of Cape Town (1984): 7ff; David Soggot, *Namibia: The Violent Heritage* (London: Rex Collins); Peter Katjivivi, *A History of Resistance in Namibia* (London: James Currey, 1988); United Nations: Office of Public Information, *A Trust Betrayed: Namibia* (New York: 1974); Division Liason Services, Department of Governmental Affairs, Election '89 (Windhoek: 1989*); UNTAG, A New Nation is Born*: *UNTAG in Namibia* (Windhoek: United Nations, 1990); Andries Fokkens, "The Suppression of Internal Unrest in South West Africa (Namibia), 1921–1933", *Scientia Militaria 40*, no. 3 (2012): 109–146; *Rand Daily Mail*, 27 August 1966; *Rand Daily Mail*, 29 August 1966.

Tempest in a Teacup?
The Angolan War as Cold War Template, 1975–1989

Phil Eidelberg

The term "Angolan war" is controversial. The motives of some of its main foreign participants, such as Cuba and the Soviet Union, have often not been fully understood. Did the USSR enter the Angolan war during the mid-1970s from a position of relative strength or relative weakness? Was the balance of power between the USSR and the USA shifting towards or away from the Soviet Union by 1975?

Things are seldom as simple as they look. Mention must be made of the Soviet "perception around 1970 of a shift in the global 'correlation of forces' at the expense of the West".[1] According to this view in the US and Western Europe, the shift was due to the impressive increase in Soviet armaments during the previous fifteen years, including the achievement of nuclear parity with the United States and the growth of the Soviet navy into a world-class actor. The decline of the United States was demonstrated by its humiliating defeat in the Vietnam War between 1968 and 1975.[2] Viewed within this context, the Soviet involvement in Angola from 1975 was one more phase of its expansionist ambitions, now extended to Africa. The United States' withdrawal from the Vietnam War at the end of 1975 would appear to be a mirror image of its final military defeat in Indo-China.

On the other hand, was the USSR really growing as a world power and at the expense of the US at the time? And was Moscow's intervention in the Angolan civil war a sign of strength? If the Soviet empire was at the height of its powers during the 1970s, why then did it precipitately decline and eventually disintegrate during the 1980s and early 1990s? Why was its leadership at times so cautious in intervening aggressively in Africa?

When the Soviet Union entered the Angolan conflict, it had had a series of foreign policy and internal setbacks during the decade and a half since the late 1950s. In 1958, their communist post-World War II ally, China, had broken with Moscow. While Peking regarded Washington as a menace as grave as Moscow, changes took place. This led to a dramatic rapprochement by the early 1970s and ultimately full diplomatic relations in 1979 between China and the US. By the time the Soviet Union was getting involved in the Angolan civil war in 1975, her strategic military power and political position within the USA-USSR-Communist China triangle had weakened.

The United States' withdrawal from Vietnam was softened by an improvement in relations with Communist China that made up for the loss of Indo China. Furthermore, the presence of large-scale US military involvement in South Vietnam from 1965 may well have encouraged the mass destruction of the Indonesian Communist Party, the PKI, during late 1965–66 by the Indonesian army. The PKI was at the time the largest non-ruling communist party in the world and its destruction was possibly a setback for Moscow's international ambitions. Indonesia, after all, was a far more important country economically and strategically than South Vietnam.

A number of African political leaders who were inclined towards the Soviet Union were overthrown, killed or died in the 1960s: Patrice Lumumba in the Congo in 1960, Ahmed Ben Bella in Algeria (1965), Kwame Nkrumah in Ghana (1966), Sukarno in Indonesia (1967), Modibo Keita in Mali (1968); Gamal Abdel Nasser in Egypt (1970), Anwar Sadat of Egypt and Salvador Allende in Chile (1973). These lost allies were succeeded by heads of state more interested in improving their ties with the capitalist West, notable amongst these were Hosni Mubarak of Egypt. In West Africa, Thomas Sankara's regime was belatedly toppled in 1988 because of his critical stance against the West, especially France. The next incumbent proved more accommodative to the West. As a result, the Soviet Union seemingly developed a policy of encouraging friendly Third World regimes no longer simply through diplomatic and economic support, but by actively supporting them militarily. Ironically, this change of policy towards military intervention made the USSR appear increasingly similar to Western neo-colonialist and imperialist powers. The more optimistic policy of Nikita Khrushchev (1955–1964), who saw Third World regimes as independently able to move towards socialism, was dropped. Instead, under Leonid Brezhnev (1964–1982), Soviet military intervention was at times actively pursued.

The failed Czech defection from the communist camp in 1968 was perhaps an even greater sign of weakness than the previous Hungarian revolution attempted in 1956. The Hungarian revolution after all, from the Soviet perspective, had been an unfortunate by-product of the previous three years of political and economic reforms known as "de-Stalinisation". De-Stalinisation gave political space for an anti-centralist uprising in Hungary. People thought that the reforms would allow for independent state-building alongside the USSR. This was not to happen. The unrest in Hungary, established less than a decade before, could be treated as "growing pains" afflicting the young communist regime. The Czech defection of 1968, on the other hand, occurred two decades after the establishment of communism in a country seen as the industrial showcase of communist Eastern Europe.

In the context of international political economic trends, the defections were perhaps not a symptom of short-term growing pains. They were rather a symptom of longer-term economic decline. The communist USSR-led regimes had had twenty years to produce a viable dynamic economy and had failed in the eyes of the defectors. The USSR was confronted with a vote of no confidence, not so much from anti-communist forces, as in

Hungary, but from within the party itself. While the Soviet Bloc was catching up to the West militarily during the decade preceding the Angolan war, it was falling behind economically.

The Soviet military involvement in Angola can be seen as an example of a post-Khrushchev policy and a result of a decline in status of the Soviet Union. Moscow no longer saw the change in the balance of power in favour of the socialist camp as natural and inevitable. Expensive investments, including military support, which the Soviets could ill afford, were an attempt to uphold international status. The Cubans provided troops to aid the beleaguered MPLA in Angola, while the Soviets provided much-needed weapons and equipment as well as non-combatant personnel. This included personnel who, as the war dragged on, acted as military advisors and sometimes determined FAPLA strategy for offensives against the contending UNITA guerrilla forces based in south-eastern Angola.

The Soviets would gain little from their involvement in Angola. Not only did they obtain no naval bases, but Luanda maintained strong economic ties with the West. Angola's oil-rich Cabinda exclave continued to host major petroleum companies such as Elf Aquitaine (France) and Gulf Oil (USA). This indicated the continuing hegemony of capitalism's economic power across the globe, even in the face of the Soviet armed intervention at the time.

Soviet involvement in Angola during the mid-1970s and well into the 1980s provided a potential threat to the West's oil supplies in the eyes of the USA and its allies. By placing their armed forces in proximity to some of the capitalist world's main sources of oil, the Soviets, with the help of their Cuban allies, perhaps hoped to use this as leverage in any future diplomatic negotiations. Moscow had already been applying this tactic to Eastern Europe through the region's dependence on Soviet oil and gas.

Soviet intervention in Angola can be better understood if seen within the context of Moscow's simultaneous intervention in Somalia and Ethiopia. The parallels between Ethiopia and Angola are striking. Just as Soviet intervention in Angola was triggered by the Portuguese decolonisation in 1974 it would ultimately be helped in Ethiopia by the overthrow of the pro-American Emperor Haile Selassie in the same year. Soviet support of the new Dergue military regime in Addis Ababa paralleled support of the MPLA in Angola. In both cases, the Soviets concentrated their influence largely on the military.

Simultaneously, Soviet involvement in the Horn of Africa, first in Somalia between 1971 and 1976 and subsequently, in late 1976 and early 1977 in Ethiopia, permitted the Soviet Navy to become an actor in the Indian Ocean. Access to naval bases in Ethiopia placed the Soviets in proximity to key ocean routes linking the US, Western Europe and Japan to the oil deposits of the Persian Gulf. Moreover, the Soviet military presence in Ethiopia placed the USSR relatively close to the vast oil fields in the Arabian Peninsula just across the Red Sea. The Soviet navy had already significantly increased its presence in the Indian

Ocean since 1968. Its direct military involvement in the Horn of Africa in the early and mid-1970s would further buttress this presence. As in Angola, so in Ethiopia, the Soviets provided advisors and weapons while it was the Cubans who provided the actual combat forces against neighbouring Somalia. This worried the USA and its allies.

During the late 1980s, the Soviets and Cubans began to disengage militarily from Ethiopia, parallel to their seeking a political settlement in the Angolan war. But unlike in Angola, where the MPLA regime was able to survive Soviet and Cuban disengagement, the pro-Soviet regime in Ethiopia could not.

The many striking parallels between Soviet and Cuban involvement in both Angola and the Horn of Africa, particularly Ethiopia, suggest that the Soviet Bloc's involvement in the Angolan war was not spontaneous or accidental. It may well have been a coordinated effort to acquire strategic influence in areas which were important sources of oil, such as Angola's Cabinda province and the Arabian Peninsula. The shortcoming of this grand design was that it was too ambitious. The military and political involvements in both Angola and Ethiopia placed the Soviet Union within reach of major sources of oil for the US, Western Europe and Japan, but also stretched its resources. In the long run, the Soviet Union lacked an economic infrastructure robust enough to make this strategy a successful one. On the contrary, the geopolitical military strategy would backfire in that it helped severely weaken the Soviet Bloc's economic potential at an earlier time than the one that now befalls the rapidly declining economy of the US.

The US Clarke amendment, cutting off further American aid to the UNITA guerrilla forces (19 December, 1975), initially forced the South Africans to discontinue their raids into Angola. These raids were soon resumed with great vigour and at regular intervals. Cross-border operations, some conventional in nature by the SADF, became a regular occurrence and the USA would enter the picture once again. Jonas Savimbi's UNITA, a proxy/ally of South Africa, controlled diamond-rich areas and was able to pay for assistance from South Africa through natural resources. And South Africa gained from this cooperation. South Africa could not resist the revival of resistance against Luanda. The South African penetration into Angola during 1975 and 1976 and South African military action on a regular basis thereafter, in turn, further encouraged the Soviet and Cuban build-up of FAPLA, the MPLA's military wing. Apart from arms imports Angola, in an attempt to curb UNITA and SADF operations, introduced military conscription in 1982.

The two interrelated conflicts in Angola and Namibia became more intense and served as catalysts for each other. In Angola one civil war flowed into another and anti-colonialist wars in the region were transformed into a war between an African country (South Africa) and another African country (Angola) infused by the Cold War syndrome. Civilians were caught in between, as in countless other wars.

In Angola, as in the Horn of Africa, the USSR and its Cuban allies would end up in a series of inconclusive land battles during the late 1970s and 1980s which would sap the economic strength of the Soviet Bloc. In turn these land battles also drained the resources of an increasingly isolated government in South Africa.

Things are seldom as simple as they look. African countries fought against past colonialists and the proxy forces supported by them. For many it was an anti-colonial struggle. One may question whether it was a struggle against capitalism, as many of those countries that liberated themselves today have mixed economies and some embraced capitalism and the free market. The Cold War and clashing perspectives created possibilities for interference. The dragging conflict eventually forced foreign powers to rethink their strategies and Angola maintained its long-fought-for independence like Mozambique. The Frontline States survived. Namibia gained its independence and five years later South Africans experienced their first free elections – Cold War or not.

Notes

1.   Robert G. Patman, *The Soviet Union in the Horn of Africa: The Diplomacy of Intervention and Disengagement* (Cambridge: Cambridge University Press, 1990), xi.

2.   Ibid., 63–65.

The Militarisation of South African Society 1972–1988

Ian Liebenberg

The word "militarisation" is used when a country's leaders depend increasingly on the army and security forces to suppress unrest rather than try to find political solutions through negotiation and diplomacy. Another possible definition of militarisation is the securitisation of state and society; however, some would argue that the mentalities that lead to securitisation of state and society are only a prelude to militarisation and the projection of military force internally and externally by a state. Militarisation frequently occurs when a country, or the ruling section of the population, feels threatened. This leads to a state that depends on military power and one which emphasises state security rather than development projects, education, principled equality of the citizenry, human rights, voting rights, a free media, free movement and association, the right to belong to a cultural or linguistic or religious/non-religious group or orientation and the values of negotiation or democratisation. Some refer to this situation, depending on some qualifications, as a "garrison state", a "security-minded state", a "bunker state", or a "praetorian state".

Militarisation influences domestic policies and foreign policy, and often leads to interference in the affairs of neighbouring states. Internally, militarisation leads to the suppression of political resistance by citizens of the state.[1]

The scene for a security state and later militarisation was set with the National Party's (NP) victory in 1948. Strong-handed government was to escalate from the 1960s until well into the 1980s. The minority government was not popular and had to rely on the police to suppress unrest and protest, while the majority of South Africans requested the right to vote, and after years of peaceful resistance embarked on an armed struggle to attain democracy, Prime Minister John Vorster depended on and made substantial use of the police (especially the secret police) and the Bureau of State Security. P.W. Botha, his successor, came to power with loyal followers and advisors like General Magnus Malan and former Minister Louis le Grange. Botha was more militarily minded than Vorster. Botha and his advisors were soon called "securocrats" – those who favoured hard-handed (military) options.

From 1948 the "black problem" plagued the NP government. As only white people had voting rights in South Africa, agitation for equal rights for all South Africans, including black people, increased a fear of the "Black Threat" or *Swart Gevaar*. The "Red Threat" or *Rooi*

Gevaar (communism) also figured. Liberalism was also unpopular with the government and its supporters and apartheid laws later prohibited open political discussion and mobilisation, while the liberals advocated an open society free of racial discrimination.[2] For a while, when the People's Republic of China was on a friendly footing with the Soviet Union, the fear of Chinese Communism ("ChiCom") was also prevalent (this may have been partly due to Chinese support for the Vietnamese liberation struggle that ended in the defeat and embarrassment of the occupying US force).[3] After the Soweto uprisings in 1976 and with increasing activity on the northern boundary of Namibia, one of the hotspots being Ovamboland, or Sector 10 – a "red zone" in the military language of that time – the military and related forces were increasingly called upon to safeguard the Republic of South Africa (RSA) from a perceived communist threat in the north. Those fighting national struggles for liberation (and frequently liberals or pacifists) were seen as part of a communist onslaught of a total nature. One cannot expect all politicians to have read history, and even if they did, personal interests and power will interfere. In the case of South Africa, virtually all struggles aimed at national and personal freedom were equated with communism or worse, "anarchy and chaos" (by implication they were also frequently labelled as anti-Christian by those in power, an idea propagated in attempts to indoctrinate their followers).

The Cold War syndrome was exploited as an excuse for maintaining the *status quo* in South Africa and Namibia.[4] Western and South African media endlessly provided examples of how the Soviet Union supplied arms to all and sundry. Needless to say, there was a counter side to this coin, which is seldom considered – even in current publications on the Border War/Angolan War. South Africa under apartheid rule often worked covertly with the North Americans, while Britain, France, Belgium and Germany supplied arms to the apartheid government at various stages. Britain provided South Africa with Vampire fighter jets, later Canberra's (B1, 12 and T-4s) and Buccaneer bombers (S-50s), Shackleton (MR3) long-range maritime patrol aircraft and Wasp helicopters. Ferret reconnaissance cars and Saracen armoured personnel carriers (APCs) were also acquired from Britain. France provided Mirage fighters (Mk IIIs and F1s), Puma, Super Felon and Alouette helicopters (first Mk IIs followed by the famous Mk III) that would play an important role in the Bush War. Earlier on South Africa had also acquired Harvard aircraft for training as well as Sabre fighter aircraft from the United States of America.

At one stage, Belgium provided FN rifles, later manufactured in South Africa under licence and named the R1 (as a semi-automatic rifle it was designated R-3). Spain exported small arms ammunition to South Africa, while Italy first provided training and close air support aircraft and later provided licences for the construction of the Impala (Aermacchi 326), produced here as the Impala Mk 1 and Impala Mk 2. South Africa and Israel (later Chile, Argentina, Uruguay, Paraguay and Taiwan as well) began working closely together on a security level. These Latin American countries were ruled by military dictatorships or *juntas* guilty of serious human rights abuses. These states also received large-scale military and economic aid from the US. South Africa also bought naval strike craft of the Reshef class from Israel and then produced them locally.

South Africa also worked on developing its nuclear capability with Israel and France, and had earlier engaged in nuclear technology exchanges with the US and West Germany. France provided Daphné class submarines, which ensured that South Africa was the only country in sub-Saharan Africa that boasted a submarine capability.

When international sanctions and the arms embargo tightened in the 1970s, South

Mirage FIs, compliments of France, in flight. As the war in Angola escalated various forms of camouflage were introduced. SOURCE: *Scope*, Defence Force Supplement Part 3, 9 December 1977.

Africa began to develop its own weapons technology with the aid of foreign knowledge. The time of armoured vehicles such as the Marmon-Harrington, Ferret and Panhard armoured cars and APCs such as the Saracen was disappearing. The Eland armoured car (an adaptation of the French Panhard) was produced under licence and the Ratel infantry fighting vehicle was developed following the experience gained during the first invasion of Angola. South Africa started the development of uniquely adapted landmine-resistant vehicles from earlier experiments based on Land Rovers and Unimogs. Soon a variety of anti-landmine vehicles were produced and upgraded continuously. From the early Hyenas and Hippo APCs (the latter based on a Bedford chassis) new models followed as did the *Buffel* (Buffalo) land-mine resistant APC and Caspir (various models).

Large numbers of Impala Mk I and Mk II, based on the Italian Aermacchi 326, were built. The development of the G-5 and G-6 artillery systems and Valkiri multiple-rocket

Display of air power by the South African Air Force (SAAF) in the 1960s. Seen here are Sabre Mk VIs, Mirage IIIs, Canberra and a Buccaneer S.Mk 50. SOURCE: David Becker, *On Wings of Eagles: South Africa's Aviation History*, 1995, Durban: Walker-Ramus Trading, p. 186.

South African imports came mostly from Western countries (NATO). The UK, France, Belgium, Canada, the Federal German Republic and later Italy were the main suppliers. Western-aligned countries such as Israel, and Latin American military regimes such as Argentina and Chile, served as conduits.

launchers also followed. The infantry assault rifle used by South African troops, the R4, was an (improved) copy of the Israeli Galil. The R4, which replaced the FN and R1/R3 during the 1980s, followed the trend of using a smaller calibre, namely 5,56 mm, rather than the previous NATO standard 7,62 mm calibre ammunition.

By 1972, a State Security Council had been established in South Africa and the South African Defence Force (especially the army) stepped increasingly into the limelight. The defence budget increased annually, although by 1972 the RSA was already militarily stronger than all the other sub-Saharan African states combined. Due to South Africa's large-scale weapons procurement programme in the late seventies and early eighties, this gave rise to an arms race in southern Africa, especially among countries suffering under South Africa's military involvement, such as Angola. Because of growing South African operations in southern Angola after Operation Savannah (1975/1976), which had a destructive impact on the Angolan infrastructure, Angola started to arm itself and implemented conscription in 1981 and 1982. Apart from hard arms, Angola imported soft-skinned and light vehicles from various countries such as Portugal, Japan, Canada and Spain, to bolster its forces.

Cadets: More than 600 schools took part in the cadet system where learners from Grade 8 (Standard 6) to Grade 12 (Matric) were prepared for military service with drill and field exercises.
SOURCE: *The Cadet*, an insert to *Uniform*, SADF publication, 1985.

Girls participated in cadet drills on a voluntary basis. SOURCE: *The Cadet*, an insert to *Uniform*, SADF publication, 1985.

Government expenditure and Defence expenditure, 1962–1990[5]

Year	Government expenditure in R(000)	% change in government expenditure	Defence expenditure In R(000)	% change in defence expenditure	Defence expenditure as % of total government expenditure	Government expenditure as % of GDP
1962	647 434		71 865		11,1	16,6
1963	698 419	10,7	124 697	73,5	17,9	17,2
1964	782 104	12,1	115 304	-7,5	14,7	17,2
1965	1 007 866	22,4	189 243	64,1	18,8	19,2
1966	1 097 566	8,9	179 004	-5,4	16,3	19,3
1967	1 657 325	15,1	212 437	18,7	12,8	20,2
1968	1 889 350	11,4	242 192	14,0	12,8	20,2
1969	2 078 285	1,1	236 987	-2,2	11,4	18,9
1970	2 464 846	18,6	258 372	9,0	10,5	19,8
1971	2 711 330	11,0	251 632	-2,6	9,3	20,1
1972	3 524 729	30,2	315 253	25,3	8,9	23,5
1973	3 810 232	8,1	327 285	38,2	8,6	22,3
1974	4 549 417	19,4	425 317	30,0	9,4	21,2
1975	5 659 474	24,4	696 914	63,9	12,3	21,9
1976	7 040 387	24,5	1 087 213	56,0	15,5	24,4
1977	8 547 029	21,4	1 384 427	27,3	15,0	26,3
1978	9 401 732	10,0	1 605 700	16,0	17,1	26,0
1979	10 595 752	12,7	1 669 495	4,0	15,8	24,9
1980	12 110 944	14,3	2 133 903	27,8	17,6	23,3
1981	14 351 470	18,5	2 514 084	17,8	17,5	21,4
1982	17 193 060	19,8	2 871 464	14,2	16,7	22,4
1983	20 580 094	19,7	3 194 861	11,3	15,5	23,4
1984	23 934 649	16,3	3 385 523	6,0	14,1	23,7
1985	29 248 141	22,2	3 997 821	18,1	13,7	24,8
1986	35 273 259	20,6	4 475 035	11,9	12,7	26,1
1987	43 068 649	22,1	5 814 407	29,9	13,5	26,9
1988	50 907 143	18,2	7 064 025	21,5	13,9	27,2
1989	61 037 664	19,9	8 542 159	20,9	14,0	27,0
1990	70 986 803	16,3	10 258 858	20,1	14,5	26,5

NOTE: The defence budget at the time excluded the budget for the South African Police. It also does not necessarily include secret funding for various internal and external activities. Secret funding came from various sources, depending on the perceived needs. See among others, James Sanders, *Apartheid's Friends: The Rise and Fall of South Africa's Secret Services* (London: John Murray, 2006).

Examples of armament and estimated numbers*

Year	Tanks	A/Cars	AFV	APC	Aircraft	Helicopters
1969/70	200	Several hundred?*	None	250	185	80+
1973/74	120	900	None	250	100*	80+
1984/85	250	1 400	1 200	500+	304	90+
1985/86	250	1 600	1 500	1 500	356	90
1988/89	241	1 600*	1 500*	1 500	324*	78*

NOTE: The figures above are based on estimates by the International Institute for Strategic Studies (IISS) in London for the years 1969 to 1989. *Useful, more detailed statistics are provided by André Wessels in *Scientia Militaria* 40 (3), 2012, pp. 222–249 and in *Journal for Contemporary History* 38 (1), 2013, pp. 221–254. For example, Wessels for the year 1988/1989 puts armoured cars at 1 200 and armoured fighting vehicles at 1 300. In terms of aircraft for the year 1973/1974, the numbers are higher than those indicated in the IISS table. The number of aircraft in 1973/1974 is higher than the number indicated in the table while he suggests far higher numbers of aircraft for 1988/1989, and mentions that there were 317 combat aircraft , more than 130 basic trainers and ±170 transport and other aircraft of all types. For 1988/1989 Wessels suggests that ±187 helicopters were still In service. Following the Second World War, South Africa's armoured capacity was limited to some tanks (i.e. Sherman, Stuart, Comet and some Centurions) and armoured cars such as WW2 vintage Mk IVs (a local product) and 65 Lynx armoured cars of which not all were serviceable. A number of light Ferret armoured cars were also imported from Britain. Armoured personnel carriers (APCs) were introduced in the 1960s. Initially, Saracens imported from the UK were used and later local products such as the Hippo and Buffel. Armoured fighting vehicles (AFVs) came into service late in the 1970s following the Angolan experience of 1975/76. The result was the locally produced Ratel, which appeared in different variants. At some stage, South Africa sold off some Centurion tanks, while Comet and Sherman tanks went out of service. Centurions were then again acquisitioned to be modified as the Olifant (various models) of which some were deployed in Angola during 1987/1988. (In Israel, upgraded Centurions were initially called the Ben Gurion and were produced in various models.) Figures for aircraft are somewhat difficult to interpret because various models were used over time and not all listed were fighter aircraft or bombers, while the Aermacchi 326 (Mk II) was used for training and operational deployment. Vampires and Sabres went out of service, some Harvards and smaller numbers of Alouettes were sold or on semi-permanent loan (some to Portugal [for use in Angola and elsewhere], some to Zimbabwe – then called Rhodesia), and Mirage F1s, apart from various models of the Mirage Mk 3, came into service. Some Mirages were later upgraded to the Cheetah which, according to some, resembled a similar Israeli upgrade of the Mirage dubbed Kfir. While technology exchange did take place between South Africa and Israel, the Cheetah and the Kfir demonstrated important differences. There were, however, some similarities in the broad design approach. In the late 1980s, some aircraft were still "on the books" but became unserviceable following use in the Bush War. South African sources admitted to 22 aircraft and helicopters lost in battle between 1974 and June 1988. Others were lost due to training accidents or becoming unserviceable, and some were cannibalised. The real figures for aircraft lost or no longer serviceable may be higher. Losses of Impalas, light aircraft and "choppers" (helicopters) during training and the Border War mainly contributed to these figures. The drop in number of aircraft (table above) between 1985/1986 and 1988/1989 may well relate to losses during the time of the Border War. Losses, however, cannot necessarily be attributed to "lost in combat". Losses of armoured cars, armoured personnel carriers and armoured fighting vehicles between 1979 and 1989 are most likely not indicated as all of these arms were produced locally and relatively speedy replacement was possible.

After the 1970s, South Africa relied more than ever before on the support of the security forces. To ensure national survival, a "total national strategy" was formulated as a counter to the alleged "total onslaught" waged against South Africa. Blacks, Coloureds, as well as Indians, where invited to participate in the war (in 1983, Coloureds and Indians would be allowed to become part of a tri-cameral parliament where the white chamber and the executive State President P.W. Botha would have the final say). Workforce requirements had made it necessary to draft more troops from other ethnic groups, and limited suffrage was one way of doing this.

Die

KAAPSE KORPS - DIENSBATALJON

As the need for manpower as well as to reflect the image of a multiracial society under apartheid rule rose, people of colour were invited into the SADF. Seen here are members of the South African Cape Corps (SACC) in an SADF recruiting flyer, circa 1980. SOURCE: Author's archive.

International sanctions were increasing despite the US and Chester Crocker's policy of "constructive engagement". The Reagan government in the USA argued that South Africa was a historical partner of the US and that the apartheid government should be considered as a legitimate partner to a political solution. At the same time the US provided military support to South African proxy forces such as the rebel movement UNITA in Angola. Constructive engagement allowed the South African government some breathing space for its military engagements in Angola and elsewhere. It also ensured that UNITA, as a proxy force of the United States and South Africa, continued to receive arms from South Africa and the United States of America.[6] US support in the United Nations Security Council ensured that South Africa was not forced to withdraw from Angola and the South African government could tentatively escape international accountability despite widespread calls for more forceful action from the international community and non-aligned member states of the UN.

South Africans of all races started to oppose the regime of P.W. Botha and his generals. Many within the Christian community also opposed Botha's government due to its unreasonable policy. Some conscripts chose to ignore call-ups. The South African economy suffered because of inflation and the cost of the war in Angola.

The war in Angola eventually ended in a stalemate. The South African government had to withdraw its forces from Angola and Namibia. Namibia became independent in 1990, after its first elections in 1989 under UN supervision (UNTAG). Namibians, having started their fight for independence in the 1800s, finally gained their freedom. In Angola, the war lasted much longer as UNITA, headed by Jonas Savimbi, refused to accept election results. The Angolan conflict only subsided after Savimbi's death in 2002. Peace in southern Africa had come at a high price.

Sanctions and an indigenous arms industry

After the Second World War the Union Defence Force demobilised and scaled down to minimal forces, like many other countries. The Second World War, however, propelled South Africa as a developing state into a second industrial take-off stage and proved that the country had the capacity to arm itself if needed. Apart from all sorts of products including sighting pieces, hand grenades, mortars, parachutes, maritime and signal equipment, the Union of South Africa produced nearly 6 000 armoured cars and 600 artillery pieces during the Second World War. The armoured cars produced in six variants saw widespread service, among others in the Far and Middle East, and many were still used in later conflicts. The Union's arms industry included the capability to produce explosives and propellants, the ability to manufacture vehicles, guns, rifles and ammunition of various calibres on a large scale.[7]

The National Party that came to power in 1948 established the Defence Resources Board as a specialist department in the Ministry for Defence in 1949. The Defence Resources Board in turn was succeeded by the Defence Production Office in 1951.[8] When criticised by members of the British Commonwealth for its apartheid policies and hard handedness in maintaining the apartheid system, South Africa left (or rather were expelled from) the Commonwealth and declared itself a (whites only) republic.

When the United Nations in Resolution 161 in 1962 called on member states to stop selling arms to South Africa because of its discriminatory apartheid policies, the Defence Resources Board became the Armaments Production Board.[9] The Arms Embargo declared by the United Nations (Resolution 181 following the Sharpeville shootings) called "on all states to cease forthwith the sales and shipment of arms, ammunitions and all types of military vehicles to South Africa". A December Resolution (UN Resolution 182) also broadened the prohibition of arms-related sales to "equipment for the manufacturing and maintenance of arms and ammunition".[10]

During the last part of Vorster's rule and increasingly under the rule of P.W. Botha, the interests of the Afrikaner politicians, the military and powerful elements of the South African economic leadership merged for political reasons (feelings of isolation and the belief that white South Africa was a stabilising force in an insecure world) and economic reasons (profit sustainability).[11] The South African Defence Budget rose from R327 million in the 1971/1972 budget year to R692 million in 1974/1975. By 1976/1977 (partly as a result of the invasion of Angola) the defence budget was at R1 048 million.[12] Rearmament and a growing arms industry was no longer a question, but from Pretoria's viewpoint, an imperative.[13]

South African Forces in Angola during a cross-border operation. SOURCE: SANDF Documentation Centre, Pretoria

O'Meara argues that the "total strategy" doctrine recognised that economic growth and military preparedness could only be enhanced through the closest possible cooperation between state and the private sector and the "total strategy" doctrine provided a rationale for cooperation between business leaders, military leaders and hawkish politicians.[14]

In 1976 the previous bodies established to procure arms, such as the Armaments Development and Production Board were all amalgamated into the Armaments Corporation of South Africa (ARMSCOR)[15] which was to play an important part in the South African Arms industry for the next fifteen years. By the beginning of the 1980s ARMSCOR was South Africa's third biggest industrial group. O'Meara claims that more than 50 per cent of its manufacturing was contracted out to the private sector to more than 1 200 contractors. About 50 of these were directly involved in manufacturing arms and about 400 to the production of major components.[16] Multinationals such as IBM, Shell, Daimler-Benz and others were involved.[17] In short O'Meara claims that the integrated white economy reached a stage where the system reflected "the nature of a capital intensive, mainly monopoly capitalist (inclusive of) the military apparatus and the political organs of state".[18] But not only hardware was at stake when it came to business. Many textile, mechanical engineering, electronic and building industries and other sectors of the private sector were directly or indirectly involved in this process of militarisation of state and society.[19] Simultaneously conscription, which started off with three months of military service in the late 1960s, was extended to two years by the beginning of the 1980s and the cadet system in secondary schools by now involved approximately 600 white schools. The white civil population were organised into militia known as commandos, while Citizen Force Regiments were amply funded and equipped. For all practical purposes South African society – especially the white sector – became militarised; a nation in arms. (Later on, the South African historian Hermann Giliomee would argue that South Africa was not militarised.[20] He argues that the hawkish General Magnus Malan was a peace builder and reformist, rather than a hawk. Giliomee, inexplicably, did not take into account a whole era in which a garrison society evolved in South Africa and in which violence was exported to southern Africa.)[21]

The invasion of Angola by South African forces in 1975 / 1976 showed up three weaknesses: The lack of an infantry carrying armoured fighting vehicle, long-range artillery and multiple rocket launchers that could counter those in the Angolan arsenal. The South African G-1 and G-2 guns were from World War II origin, namely the 88 mm (25 pounder) and the 140 mm (5,5 inch) guns, both dated and lacking the range for extended artillery duels. The Angolan escapade also emphasised the need for further development and sophistication of mine-protected vehicles, including troop carrier variants. ARMSCOR was instrumental in this. The Ratel Infantry Fighting Vehicle, weighing 19 tons and armed with a 20 mm or 90 mm gun, or alternatively a 60 mm or an 81 mm mortar, and able to transport a section of troops, was produced. The development of the G-5 and G-6 artillery systems and Valkiri multiple-rocket launchers followed.[22] The G-5 and G-6 (the latter a self-propelled artillery piece, versatile, mobile and suitable to African conditions) were important developments and provided the South African Defence Force with sophisticated artillery and a longer range than was available at that stage on the African continent and especially in Angola, where the SADF were consistently operating.[23]

By the end of the 1980s (thus at the start of political transition) the South African arms industry was prominent and some of its products world class. Various projects existed, among others the significant upgrading of the Olifant tank (originally Centurions obtained from Britain, India, maybe Israel, Spain and elsewhere), the development of the powerful and versatile Rooivalk attack helicopter and the artillery systems discussed above. Compared to the quantity of arms in South Africa, the imports of African states in the southern region were in reality no real competitors, and South Africa the main cause of the "arms race" in southern Africa. The "formidable amount of Soviet weapons" received by, for example, Mozambique, was clearly an overstatement by some observers.[24] Soviet veterans deployed at the Lomba River and Tumpo Triangle battles and Cuito Cuanavale, for example, observed that Angola had nothing in its artillery arsenal that could counter the South African artillery, until the South Africans lost air superiority, which tipped the scales rather dramatically.[25]

The Nuclear Option

As in most cases, South Africa's nuclear era started off with the rationale that it was meant for peaceful purposes. Then again, ever since the Manhattan Project and the bombing of Hiroshima and Nagasaki by the USA, societies and people knew instinctively that peace was not necessarily the main intention of nuclear development – especially when you deal with powerful industrial states intent on enforcing their world-view on other peoples. South Africa, compared to other southern African states – even elsewhere on the continent – was an industrial and economic giant with a significant military capacity already. The worldview of the time was one of a deep dislike for communism and a distrust of black people. The "total onslaught" mentality was worsened by the South African political elite (including the so-called *Verligtes* or reformed-minded elite) who uncritically, or perhaps opportunistically, fell for the Cold War mythology propagated in the USA. By adding a nuclear capacity, their intentions were not likely to be peaceful (hardly any African state or for that matter other states, such as the Cubans, Russians or Chinese had a nuclear capacity *in loco*, nor had they the intention to use nuclear arms on the African continent). South Africa was also not regularly threatened, as the USA is currently threatening smaller states such as Vietnam, North Korea and Iran, with full military force. So, unlike these states besieged by a state such as the USA bent on uni-polarism, there was hardly any reason to build a nuclear capability in Africa except to demonstrate dominance over the surrounding territoriums.

South Africa was approached by the USA and the UK as early as 1944 to assist in supplying materials suitable for enrichment to develop a nuclear capacity. With the more-than-ready help of the USA and the UK, the first uranium plant was established at the Wesrand Consolidated mine in October 1952.[26] South Africans had already been under apartheid rule for four years, but this hardly bothered the governments of the USA and the UK.[27] (In 1946 India complained to South Africa about segregationist policies imposed on, among others, South African Indians, and in 1952 the issue appeared on the UN General Assembly's agenda whereafter it was regularly discussed; with the Security Council making little effort to follow the wishes of the General Assembly). By 1955 16 uranium plants existed in South Africa. South African products were a hot hit for the West as South Africa had some of the largest deposits of uranium in the world, then estimated at 625 000 tons.[28]

In 1978 South Africa produced 4 674 tons of uranium oxide with an economic value of R500 million. Most of this was earmarked for export to the USA, UK, France, Germany and Israel (smaller quantities found their way to Taiwan and Japan by 1981).

The Atomic Energy Board announced an enrichment programme in 1970. Within a month after coming to power in September 1978, PW Botha set up a cabinet committee to oversee the military aspects of nuclear devices and it was decided that ARMSCOR, the South African Defence Force and the Atomic Energy Board should work together on a top-secret nuclear weapons programme.[29] By the 1980s the necessary facilities had been erected. Several groups resorting under the "Nuclear Group" (Afrikaans: *Kerngroep*) started with programmes for peaceful and offensive use.[30] In 1973 the search for a test site started. By mid-1977 a test site was completed in the northern Cape Province, a sparsely populated area dependent on agriculture and where most white and Coloured farmers depended on state subsidies to survive. The site was discovered, or perhaps more likely became public knowledge, as a result of discontented farmers expressing their concern, or someone slipping a careless word at a church meeting. South Africa also experimented with a space launch vehicle, of which three versions were developed.[31]

Steyn, Van der Walt and Van Loggenberg are correct in one respect: They suggested that the hysteria about the South African programme was rather hypocritical and that the South African project was small compared to those of the Western nations.[32] This hypocrisy – if not neo-colonial arrogance – still exists today as countries such as Iran, North Korea and Vietnam's projects cannot vaguely weigh up against the offensive arsenals kept by the USA to back up the threats with which they usually conduct their foreign affairs – for the moment only in terms of war talk and techno warfare, and presumably excluding biological and nuclear strikes.

Speculation by theorists such as Spence that South Africa had the "potential to become a nuclear power" by 1982 was wrong. He was right however, in suggesting that South Africa publicly remained ambiguous about its capacity and that it was hardly likely that any other force, even in the midst of the so-called Cold War was to threaten South Africa – let alone attack the country with nuclear power.[33] South Africa was eventually to build six nuclear bombs before it signed the nuclear non-proliferation treaty in the 1990s and dismantled them under the rule of F.W. de Klerk.[34]

Notes

1. For more detail consult Ian Liebenberg and Francois de Wet, "Militarised Politics, Economic Consequences and the Implosion of State Legitimacy in South Africa," in *Reflections on War: Preparedness and Consequences*, ed. Thean Potgieter and Ian Liebenberg (Stellenbosch: Sun Media, 2012), 65–90. See also Ian Liebenberg, "The Arms Industry, Reform and Civil-Military Relations in South Africa" in *South Africa and Romania: Transition to Democracy and Changing Security Paradigms*, ed. Calvin Manganyi, Ian Liebenberg and Thean Potgieter (Durban: Just Done Productions Publishing, 2012), 322–266.

2.   In May 1968 the Liberal Party of South Africa, following the Prevention of Political Interference Bill which prohibited multi-racial membership of political parties, dissolved itself in Caxton Hall in Durban under the banner "FREEDOM FAREWELL". Gert van der Westhuizen argues poignantly: "… there was never again a white controlled party that fought under the banner of true liberalism for the unconditional freedom of all South Africa's inhabitants". Some members (those who were not banned like Patrick Duncan, Joe Nkatlo, Peter Hjul, Randolph Vigne and Jordan Magubane) found their way into the ANC, the SACP, the Armed Resistance Movement (a liberation movement under predominantly white leadership), the Congress of Democrats (COD), and others to centrist white opposition parties such as the later Progressive Federal Party which participated in the white minority parliament. Consult Gert van der Westhuizen, "The Liberal Party of South Africa, 1953–1968," in *The Long March: The Story of the Struggle for Liberation in South Africa*, ed. Ian Liebenberg, Gert van der Westhuizen, Fiona Lortan and Frederik Nel (Pretoria: Kagiso Haum Publishers, 1994), 93.

3.   The fear of Eastern civilisations, especially among Western-orientated South Africans (many of them white at first, but nowadays others as well) is not new. One has to keep a historical perspective about the fear of the Oriental "other" when it comes to the crucial nexus between pre-apartheid colonialist Western thinking, apartheid thinking and the residue of fear that remained post World War ll and was re-vitalised by Cold War propaganda. To quote just one example: "The white races (in South Africa) seem to be tending towards amalgamation and assimilation rather than to further disintegration and divergence, and in view of the possible (future) competition from both the Yellow man and the Black man it is perhaps well that it is so" (W. Bleloch, *The New South Africa: Its Value and Development* (London: Heinemann Publishers, 1901), 216. Thus this statement, to do justice to a historical perspective, was made more than a hundred and ten years ago. In current propaganda the fear of the Oriental "Other" still persists.

4.   The discourse bandied about in the USA at the time greatly assisted the South African government to label their political opponents "terrorists" under the control of Moscow, a superb tactic of labelling legitimate resistance for equality as inhuman and subversive. For an example see Ray S. Cline and Yonah Alexander, *Terrorism: The Soviet Connection* (New York: Crane Russak & Company, 1984), 61: "The terrorist linkages extend from Moscow not only to Korea but as far as the tip of Africa … The presidents of SWAPO and the ANC have repeatedly acknowledged the importance of Soviet support to their organisations." The authors of the same work referred to the armed wing of the ANC (Umkonto We Sizwe) as "the ANC's terrorist wing" (p.62).

5.   "Macroeconomic information", South African Reserve Bank, March 2011, http://www.resbank. co.za/alquery/timeseriesquery.aspx. See Public Finance, 1962–1990, Central government expenditure on revenue account according to class and vote, Pretoria: Government Printers, various publications. Table compiled by Francois de Wet, economist, Faculty of Military Science, Stellenbosch University. See *Reflections on War: Preparedness and Consequences*. Thean Potgieter and Ian Liebenberg (Stellenbosch: Sun Media, 2012), 83.

6.   Simultaneously, South Africa served as a proxy of the United States without realising it, it seems. Few people then realised that the term "useful idiot" was also applicable in this case to the Pretoria government.

7.   Hannes Steyn, Richard van der Walt and Jan van Loggerenberg, *Armament and Disarmament: South Africa's Nuclear Weapons Experience* (Pretoria: Network Publishers, 2003), 47.

8.   Ibid.

9.   Ibid.

10.   Richard Leonard, *South Africa at War: White Power and the Crises in Southern Africa* (Craighall: AD Donker, 1983), 132.

11.   Dan O'Meara, *Forty Lost Years: The Apartheid State and the Politics of the National Party, 1948–1994*(Johannesburg: Raven Press, 1996), 224.

12.   Ibid.

13. In this sense South Africa mirror-imaged the United States of America and benefited from the ideological discourse of a "communist threat" to enhance the sustainability and increase of profit by focusing on an increasingly military industrial complex. Unlike the USA, which maintained theirs after the Second World War, South Africa downscaled and then re-started its arms industry. In both cases these industries became closely connected with an imagined enemy and profit making and, in turn, the exportation of war.

14. O'Meara, 225–226.

15. Annette Seegers, *The Military in the Making of Modern South Africa* (London: I B Taurus, 1996), 216.

16. Ibid., 217.

17. O'Meara, 226.

18. Ibid.

19. Ibid.

20. Hermann Giliomee, "Magnus Malan: Brugbouer na 'n skikking," *Rapport Weekliks*, 24 Julie 2011, p.1.

21. Ibid.

22. A significantly upgraded version of the Valkiri multiple rocket launcher (MRL) was also developed on entering the 1990s. It was called the Bateleur and had an increased effective range and upgraded ammunition.

23. Compare *Bush War: The Road to Cuito Cuanavale*, Louis Bothma (Auckland Park: Jacana Media, 2011), 200.

24. Steyn, et al., 5.

25. Compare Shubin and Tokarev, 2007, 2011.

26. Steyn, et al., 31.

27. Needless to say, it would have bothered the USA and the UK and their satellite states and surrogates if the potential or real holders of a peaceful, defensive or offensive nuclear capacity happened to be in Latin America, or any other society that differed from Christian-Capitalism, and questioned the right of any powerful state to dictate their ideology through a projection of military power over thousands of miles/kilometers once a non-compliant country differed from the core or powerful states' interpretation of the "Liberal Order". In the case of Israel and South Africa it was not a problem. If it was a problem, it was solved through public statements suggesting that it was bad for less powerful communities to have alternative ways of creating natural energy unless "they are our own".

28. Steyn, et al., 31.

29. Ibid., 43.

30. Ibid., 39.

31. Ibid., 58. It is on "record" that the then South African government never tested any of the RSA1, RSA2 or RSA3 potential nuclear carrying missiles – and if they did, never with the supervision and/or advice of the USA, France, Germany or Israel. Compare again the source mentioned in this endnote. But it may depend on which records one depends …

32. Steyn, et al., 63.

33. J.E. Spence, "The Nuclear Option," in *Defence Policy Formation: Towards Comparative Analysis* ed. James M. Roherty (Durham: Caroline Academic Press, 1980), 122.

34. Ian Liebenberg, "Talking Small Wars in Far Away Lands: Three Incidences in Angola's Second War of Liberation," in *Regions, Regional Organisations and Military Power* ed. Thean Potgieter and Abel Esterhuyse (Stellenbosch: Sun Media, 2008), 78–79. Also compare Al J. Venter, *How South Africa Built Six Atom Bombs: And then Abandoned its Nuclear Weapons Program* (Kyalami Estate: Ashanti Publishing, 2008).

The Cubans in Angola, 1976–1990[1]

Hedelberto López Blanch

Cuba had had previous involvements in Africa, but astounded the world, perhaps even its allies, in the middle of the 1970s with its involvement in Angola. Operation Carlota, named after a slave woman who led a rebellion against colonialism in Cuba in the previous century, started in November 1975. The operation marked the beginning of a long-term involvement in Angola. Carlota came into being some months after the USA/CIA, South African and Zairian involvement in Angola started. The events of April 1974, with the overthrow of the Marcelo Caetano dictatorship in Portugal in the "Carnation Revolution", should have opened the way for the independence of Portugal's African colonies, but instead became the harbinger of a destructive, drawn-out see-saw war in Angola.

The Popular Movement for the Liberation of Angola (MPLA) represented the most coherent and inclusive of the Angolan nationalist movements that fought for independence. However, the movement was challenged by the ambitions of two groups supported by the United States, South Africa and Zaire. These were the Angolan National Liberation Front (FNLA) led by Holden Roberto, a Central Intelligence Agency (CIA) collaborator; and the National Union for the Total Independence of Angola (UNITA), led by Jonas Savimbi, at times covert collaborator of the Portuguese secret services and later of the CIA and apartheid South Africa.

Attempts to prevent conflict before Angolan independence led to the Alvor Agreement signed on the 15th of January 1975 after negotiations between the Lisbon government and the MPLA, UNITA and the FNLA. The official date set for the country's independence was November the 11th 1975. The FNLA soon launched attacks against the MPLA. Alvor virtually fell apart as soon as it was signed. By June 1975, an MPLA counteroffensive routed FNLA forces from Luanda.

The FNLA had support from the Mobutu Sese Seko regime, the Republic of South Africa and the United States, with the latter sending weapons and supplies to Kinshasa. (France, having interests in central Africa, also found itself drawn to the FNLA and for some years had good relations with the regime in Zaire.)

The plot was thickening. Two dozen officials, specialists and artillerymen from Pretoria arrived in Kinshasa by plane to join the FNLA troops who would fight the battle for Luanda. The invasion from the north started.

Two battalions of Zairian infantry joined the FNLA in the offensive from the north while South African troops penetrated the south on August the 9th, if not earlier, taking over the Calueque dam inside Angolan territory. On the pretext of securing the water resources at Calueque and Ruacana, the South Africans were soon to advance northwards.

On September the 4th, the FNLA and the Zairians were north of Quifangondo. FAPLA (the military wing of the MPLA) committed their 9th Brigade to battle – actually the only brigade – but so named to confuse the aggressors. The 9th Brigade, which was somewhat under-trained, launched a counter attack. The aggressors retreated in a stampede, leaving cases of ammunition and US-made military equipment in their wake. On the 26th of September the 9th Brigade repelled another attack by the FNLA in Morro de Cal, five kilometres from Quifangondo. The FNLA and its cohorts attacked Morro de Cal with 3 500 men, including 1 200 Zairians on the 23rd of September. The Angolans, together with 40 recently arrived Cuban instructors from the Revolutionary Instruction Centre (CIR) in N'Dalatando, engaged the enemy. In the face of the latter's numerical superiority and weapons, the defenders retreated to Quifangondo. On November the 6th, they repelled an attack on Quifangondo. The enemy tried again.

The last attempt to take over Quifangondo was around the 10th of November, one day before Angola declared its independence. The aggressors assembled a strong attacking force comprising FNLA members, 120 Portuguese mercenaries, two infantry battalions and several armoured battalions of regular Zairian troops. Advisors/combatants from the apartheid regime, led by Ben de Wet Roos and equipped with heavy guns brought by plane from South Africa, were also in the fray. Several CIA agents and USA observers/journalists again accompanied the attacking force. South Africa also supplied planes for reconnoitring FAPLA's positions and attacked Angolan-Cuban positions without success. In the north, the tide was turned. South African military staff was eventually to be extracted once the offensive attempts from the north had failed. The Angolan capital was saved and the enemy scattered. A number of attackers were killed or injured, while armoured and other transport vehicles were destroyed. The FNLA revealed that more than 345 of its troops had been killed, without counting the Zairians or South Africans. As the combat turned into a free-for-all for survival, Pretoria had to finally extricate its isolated forces in the north. Around the 28th of November, a South African frigate lifted the South Africans out of Angola via the port of Ambrizette.

This was one of the first serious setbacks for the joint forces of the FNLA, Zaire and South Africa with their CIA advisors and accompanied mercenaries. In response to the uncontrollable war situation, Portuguese Admiral Leonel Cardoso, Governor of Angola, announced in the name of the colonial power's president that sovereignty was being transferred to the Angolan people without mentioning the MPLA or any other organisation. At 6 pm on the 10th of November he lowered the Portuguese flag in haste and left with the rest of his troops for Lisbon. With the departure of the Portuguese occupying forces, the first war for the liberation of Angola ended and the second war for liberation had already been going on for some months. At midnight on the 11th of November the MPLA announced the former colony's independence to the world. The People's Republic of Angola was born in the midst of another war.

Aggression by apartheid forces continued. On the 14th of October 1975 the SANDF Zulu column (*Veggroep Zulu*) penetrated Angolan territory from occupied Namibia, advancing more than 60 kilometres per day amidst great destruction. The advancing forces took over the towns of Pereira de Eca and Rocadas. Pretoria, with the blessing of the United States, invaded Angola with the aim of neutralising Agostinho Neto's MPLA movement and so pave the way for a proxy regime comprising FNLA and UNITA elements. Battlegroup Zulu was composed of black Angolans who were FNLA guerrilla fighters trained by Pretoria, members of the Flechas, a special unit of Angolans who had fought for the Portuguese regime, Portuguese and other mercenaries combined with South African soldiers and officers.

By late October another battle group Foxbat, had been formed. According to intelligence available at the time, it was made up of at least 100 South African soldiers with 22 Eland-90 armoured vehicles and other war materiel. It was estimated that more than 1 000 South Africans had penetrated Angola and their number was most likely to grow.

Operation Savannah, approved by Prime Minister Vorster in late September 1974, had four phases. The first three were attempts to eliminate FAPLA from the border areas and then from the southwest and central regions. Phase 4 aimed to capture Luanda, or at least cause the fall of it in favour of UNITA and the FNLA. For this reason South African special force operators targeted infrastructure such as pipelines, electrification networks and gas/oil storing installations in Luanda.

Background to the Cuban presence

From June 1975, and possibly much earlier, UNITA and the FNLA were active in Angola with foreign support. In all likelihood the FNLA had had USA support ever since the Alvor Accord. UNITA approached the USA and South Africa for help – in cases through ex-Portuguese security operators. In early August 1975, a Cuban mission led by First Commander Raúl Díaz Argüelles arrived in Luanda and was requested to provide 100 advisors to train MPLA forces. The Cuban government authorised a group of 480 advisors to be sent to train Angolan soldiers over a period of six months. The Cuban arrivals were organised into four units called Revolutionary Instruction Centres (CIR). A group in Luanda was to function as the head of the Cuban Military Mission in Angola (MMCA).

By late September only 50 of the MMCA's members had arrived in Angola. On October the 1st and 3rd two Cuban planes took 142 instructors to Angola. The first airlift was done in virtually obsolete Britannia aircraft that had to "hop" from Havana to Luanda with much-needed stops in between. Between the 16th to the 20th of September the ships *Vietnam*, *La Plata* and *Coral Island* had set sail from the port of Havana with almost 300 men, equipment and provisions for the four instructors groups to be established in Cabinda, N'Dalatando, Beguile, Sarema and the Operations Group in Luanda. The *Vietnam* and the *Coral Island* landed on an uninhabited beach near the port of Amboy in early October, while the *La Plata* docked in Punta Negara, Congo-Brazzaville on the 11th of October. By the third week of October instructors were ready to start training the Angolans. The quickly changing situation soon saw the Cubans becoming involved in battle, rather than undertaking the training of Angolan troops as planned.

South African artillery in action. At the time of the Angolan invasion, the South African arsenal held mainly the 25 pounder (88 mm) seen here and the 5.5 inch (140 mm) artillery pieces, both used in Angola. These models stemmed from Word War II. SOURCE: SANDF Documentation Centre, Pretoria.

On November the 2nd and 3rd FAPLA in Beguile, with 100 soldiers and 40 Cuban instructors, tried unsuccessfully to stop the advance of the South African Zulu column on the town of Cangue. The invaders' casualties included four armoured vehicles and numerous deaths and injuries. Four Cubans were killed, seven were injured and thirteen missing in action (MIAs).

Action in Cabinda

MPLA and Cuban military leadership felt that the greatest danger at the time was the Zairian Army and the Front for the Liberation of the Enclave of Cabinda (FLEC). The Cuban unit there was strengthened by almost 200 men as soon as they became available.

Before November the 11th, unusual movement of regular Zairian troops and the FLEC had been detected. These included forces trained at Zairian bases established in

Quinone and Ethel, joined by foreign mercenaries. In addition, the United States was sending weapons to Mobutu Sese Seko for this invasion. The original plan was for Cuban instructors to train four FAPLA battalions. Training for only one was completed in a hurry. On the 8th of November attacks began against positions defended by 1 000 FAPLA troops and 232 Cubans. The defending forces resisted the attacks. On the 12th of November the defenders went on the offensive. In the contacts that followed more than 1 600 FLEC troops, organised into three battalions and led by 150 mercenaries plus a battalion from Zaire comprising about 200 men backed with tanks, were beaten off. The invading forces fled over the border to Zaire.

Operation Carlota begins

The MPLA government requested assistance. In response the Cuban leadership decided at a meeting held on the 4th and 5th of November to send units of its Special Troops to confront the invaders. Operation Carlota began. The larger-scale deployment came as a surprise to the Soviet Union, but the Cubans had already committed themselves. The first group comprised about 650 men from the Special Troops of the Ministry of the Interior (MININT) and an artillery regiment from the Revolutionary Armed Forces (FAR). These reinforcements were to bolster the Cuban training units in Angola. By this time the Cuban instructors already in Angola were deployed for defence rather than supplying training as originally intended.

On November the 9th, the first reinforcements arrived in Luanda by plane. They were a battalion of MININT Special Troops supported by 82 mm mortar platoons along with limited anti-tank equipment. After participating in the action at Quifangondo, they left for the Southern Front on the 11th of November to face an enemy that was seemingly stronger and more dangerous – and approaching in leaps and bounds.

Reinforcements grew increasingly frequent with the urgency of the situation. The enforcement operation through a convoy of merchant ships that transported armaments and men in sufficient numbers to engage in battle, continued.

The setback at Quifangondo left the FNLA aggressors, Zairians, mercenaries and South African advisors surprised. On December the 5th, the defending forces moved to the offensive on the Northern Front. On February the 26th, the joint Cuban/Angolan forces reached the border with Zaire.

A struggle on the Southern Front

On the Southern Front the Zulu column of the SANDF advanced from Lobito to Novo Redondo with the goal of penetrating towards Luanda. On the 11th of November, Cuban instructors from the Beguile CIR set an ambush for them roughly twenty kilometres south of Novo Redondo. The contact resulted in several casualties for the enemy and temporarily slowed down their advance, while the instructors and FAPLA troops retreated to Novo Redondo. Here combat continued until the South African battle group (Zulu) occupied Redondo on the 13th of November.

The Queue River, which runs between the cities of Novo Redondo and Porto Amboy, was the place chosen to stop the advance of Zulu. In the meanwhile MPLA forces destroyed river crossings and bridges to slow down the South African advance. On finding the bridges over the river destroyed, the South Africans left a small number of their forces in Novo Redondo and the group headed east, looking for routes that would take them to Luanda. Just six kilometres from Ebo, when the South Africans were trying to get to Glabella via one of the embankments, First Commander Díaz Argüelles organised a strategic ambush on a small but very high bridge that crossed the Makassar River. For the South Africans this turned into an ignominious retreat known as the "Ebo gallop".

Casualties for the South African contingent, according to available intelligence information at the time, totalled more than 90, with at least 30 deaths and 60 injuries, and at least eight armoured vehicles lost. In the clashes, the Cubans suffered one dead and five injured, while FAPLA, acting as a reserve echelon, did not enter combat.

In early December the South Africans began an offensive in the direction of Santa Comba-Casamba-Catofe-Quibala, and were able to take over the strategic Morros de Tongo. Meeting rather energetic resistance, South African troops moved further east and took Cariango, Gungo and Tari, and thus threatened the Quibala-Dondo road. After clashes South African forces were halted at the Longa and Pombuige rivers. Another South African force and UNITA troops occupied Luso with the goal of controlling the line from Luso to Zaire. Finally they were also stopped.

Now everyone knows: South Africa is in Angola

On December the 16th four South African prisoners of war who had been captured inside Angola, were introduced to the international media. They were captured on the 13th of December while travelling between Cela and Quibala. In front of the media the South Africans confessed that South African military forces and their cohorts, equipped with modern light and heavy armaments, were participating in the aggression against the Angolan people. Two prisoners of war were taken to Lagos and Addis Ababa where the Organisation of African Unity (OAU) was holding its summit. Two days after the summit ended, the People's Republic of Angola was recognised by the OAU. South Africa's proven involvement in Angola had changed the OAU's mood.

From defensive to offence

With the Southern Front stabilised, Cuban/FAPLA forces moved to the offensive. On the 26th of December an artillery attack from Sanga, Mussende and Cambumbo was launched. On January the 6th, a Cuban-FAPLA column attacked a battalion composed of South African and UNITA forces, killing 30 of them. In South Africa the families of killed soldiers were informed only that they had died in the "operational area" (of Namibia). In the village of Gungo, 70 kilometres from Coerama, three more South African soldiers became prisoners of war.

The city of Huambo was liberated by the Angolan-Cuban forces on February the 8th 1976, followed by Lobito and Benguela on the 10th, Sá de Bandeira on the 16th and Mozamedes on the 17th. Reinforcements arriving from Havana now totalled almost 30 000 men, women (military and civilian) with artillery, armoured vehicles and some aircraft. After the recognition of the People's Republic of Angola by the OAU, Soviet aircraft assisted in the airlift, while delivery by sea continued.

On March the 25th, the SA Defence Minister P.W. Botha announced to the white Parliament that the government had decided that all its troops would get out of Angola by Saturday the 27th of March 1976. South African soldiers thus retreated from Angolan territory.

On the 30th of March 1976 the Cuban-Angolan troops arrived at the Angola/South West Africa border post. On the 1st of April a meeting was held with a South African delegation. First Commander (a Cuban rank of the time) Leopoldo Cintra Frías (Polo) on behalf of the MPLA signed an agreement with the South African military forces aimed at establishing respect for the borders violated by Pretoria. The promises made by the apartheid forces were not kept and cross-border aggression soon escalated.

Preserving Angola's independence

On the morning of the 4th of May 1978 Cassinga, a mining town more than 200 kilometres into Angolan territory with a refugee population of 3 068, suffered heavy bombing. An assault by paratroopers, together with SA ground forces, was made on the surrounding areas. More than 200 paratroopers were dropped from US-made Hercules C-130 airplanes. It became a slaughter. Cuban troops stationed in Chamutete some 15 kilometres away went to the refugees' aid. They were delayed by landmines, ambushes and bombings by South African aircraft which killed 16 of their forces and injured 76 (in the entire war in Angola this was the largest loss incurred by Cuban forces in one day). The South Africans fled in helicopters, leaving hundreds of Namibians dead in their wake, including 300 minors. If Cassinga was a military target as alleged, the collateral damage was immensely disproportionate.

A casevac being transferred to a medical station by Cuban and Angolan personnel following the Cassinga attack on 4 May 1978. SOURCE: Cuban archives.

Another Cassinga casevac being transported to a medical station by FAPLA and Cuban soldiers. The Cuban base Chamutete was roughly 15 km from Cassinga. SOURCE: Cuban archives.

The battles of Cangamba and Sumbe

In the following years Cuban troops and even civilian personnel had to confront and repel numerous attacks by the South African and UNITA forces. After consolidating logistical support bases in the Cuando Cubango region, UNITA forces attacked the village of Cangamba in July 1983 where there was a group of 818 Angolans and 92 Cuban advisors. The defenders resisted all of the enemy's attacks until the aggressors were driven away after some days of heavy fighting. Another unsuccessful attack took place against the city of Sumbe in March 1983.

Cuito Cuanavale: The Second War in Angola

Cuban veterans frequently refer to the "first war in Angola" (1975/1976) and the "second war in Angola" (1987/1988). The Angolans began an offensive called Operation Saluting October towards the south-east to take over UNITA bases in Mavinga on the border with Namibia, but the distance, the region's isolation and an incursion by South Africa caused the Angolan operation to fail, with many Angolan combatants killed.

Cuito Cuanavale was 200 kilometres south-east of Menongue, the last point on the Cuban line, and from there to Mavinga it was more than 250 kilometres, which made it impossible for the Cuban forces to provide any help to the FAPLA forces. Cuban command structures cautioned that if the operation was executed along these tactical lines, friendly forces would be separated from their supply lines. Men and equipment would be worn out and allow the enemy to gain an advantage. After the Cuban-Angolan victory of 1976 it had been agreed that the Soviet Union would deliver modern weapons to FAPLA and that its personnel would advise the Angolan general staff, while the Cubans would train the African nation's officers and soldiers and safeguard the extensive southern border against any deep penetration attacks.

On this occasion South Africans moved against the Angolan troops in three major operations, namely operations Hooper, Modular and Packer. If their assault was successful, the Republic of Angola's government would be effectively destabilised. Angolan President José Eduardo Dos Santos asked the top Cuban leadership for help in repelling the operations in the south. On the 15th of November 1987, the Cuban government decided to reinforce its troops to deal with the problem.

That was how the operation known as the 31st Anniversary of the FAR Manoeuvre began. Its first mission began on November the 23rd: To transport by sea and air thousands of men, hundreds of tanks and artillery pieces and dozens of airplanes to form a force sufficient to repel any aggression was an enormous logistical challenge for a small country such as Cuba. The number of Cuban forces would eventually total nearly 50 000 in Angola.

An advance force of advisors and technical personnel for artillery, tanks and other material marched towards Cuito Cuanavale under cover of the Mig-21s and Mig-23s. South African and UNITA troops, in what they called Operation Hooper (which began on the 15th of December 1987) continued with their non-stop bombings of Cuito and surroundings.

A notable clash was to follow: On January the 13th, several Migs took off from Menongue, and together with artillery fire, they destroyed Olifant tanks, Eland armoured vehicles and a number of other hard- and soft-skinned vehicles. They dealt another blow on January the 16th, when two Mig-23ML reconnaissance planes discovered a group of tanks and infantry and attacked after being reinforced by six more Mig-23MLs, inflicting heavy damage.

After their initial failure, South African forces took a month to regroup. On February the 14th, the South Africans unleashed a large-scale attack with three SADF battalions and six UNITA battalions using more than 100 armoured vehicles of various sorts, and broke through the defence east of the Cuito River. On February the 20th, a Mirage F-1 SAAF-245 fighter plane was shot down. Numerous other South African aircraft suffered damage while on missions. Given the south-bound anti-air defences of the FAPLA/Cuban forces, South Africans found engagement by air difficult, if not impossible.

Under the orders of General Cintra Frías, the Cuban command reorganised their lines of defence. With great effort it was able to move the majority of its forces toward the western region, while maintaining a heavily fortified redoubt with a brigade east of the river, with a staggered line of defence and tanks available for the rearguard.

The last South African attacks on the Cuito Cuanavale Front occurred on February the 25th, and March the 1st, 21st and 23rd, but their troops were rebuffed. To Pretoria it became clear that continuous destabilisation of Angola would come at immense cost – and if they wanted to take and hold Cuito Cuanavale, which was the talk of the time, that would come at an even higher cost. However, even remaining in the surrounding areas would become untenable to South African forces given flanking movements by Angolan and Cuban forces.

Offensive towards the south-west

On March the 10th, while the South Africans continued to be bogged down in the vicinity of Cuito, the Cuban command, which had 40 000 of its own troops in the south, along with 30 000 Angolans and several thousand SWAPO combatants, started a march from the right flank towards the Namibian border. The Cuban command decided on March the 22nd to turn the Cahama airstrip into an operations base for combat planes and construction was planned to be concluded by June.

By this time South Africa had lost air superiority in Angola, yet there was no time for Angolan and Cuban forces to fall into a false sense of security. In response to intelligence reports that South Africa may be considering the possibility of carrying out a massive air attack and that it possessed several nuclear bombs, it was proposed to divide the forces into tactical groups and maintain maximum alert under cover of all available anti-aircraft resources at all times. Whether it was realistic or not in retrospect, the Cuban leadership at the time was wary of the South Africans considering a nuclear option as the then South African leader and his securocrats seemed unpredictable and potentially volatile.

The first combat in the south-western direction occurred on May the 4th, when a reconnaissance company comprising 61 Cubans and 21 Angolans ambushed the Second Company of the 101st Battalion of the South West Africa Territorial Force (SWATF), inflicting an odd 30 casualties and taking a prisoner as well as destroying five Caspir armoured vehicles and capturing one. The SWATF company fled south, but was intercepted by a Mig-23ML that had taken off from Lubango and which inflicted further damage.

By June the theatre of operations scenario had changed, with Cuban / Angolan troops just 50 km away from the Namibian border. The tactic of the South Africans at the time was to deal a heavy blow to the Angolans so that the latter would make significant concessions in informal talks between the United States and Angola. In July 1987, a meeting with the United States was held in Luanda and in September more discussions followed with fruitless results. A further meeting was set for January 1988. By now the South African forces faced serious obstacles.

The second war in Angola and the second liberation war of the Angolans demonstrated the mettle of people determined to fight for their own home and hearth. Angola needed Cuba's participation as a counter to US support for UNITA. A Cuban delegation, led by Jorge Risquet, together with Angola participated in the negotiations where the United States now became a "mediator", whereas previously it was, through "constructive engagement", supporting the apartheid forces and UNITA. The inclusion of the Cubans in the process was a setback for the USA, Pretoria and their proxy force, UNITA. The latter's choices, however, were limited given the loss of air dominance over the conflicted space, the tactical disposition of South African forces that depended largely on their belief in superior artillery and repetitive attacks along the same lines, and their logistic lines that could not be upheld even if the movement of Angolan/Cuban forces towards the south on the western side did not result in a successful pincer movement.

Tripartite discussions were held from the 9th to the 11th of March and the 17th to the 18th of March 1988 in Luanda. Cuba proposed a comprehensive solution to the problem by implementing the UN resolution on Namibia and pulling back its units stationed south of the 13th Parallel to the north. The South African-UNITA retreat at Cuito Cuanavale and the continuous arrival of Cuban troops in southern Angola forced Washington and Pretoria to realise the need for negotiation. On May the 3rd and 4th, the first quadripartite meeting was held with the interested parties: Angola and Cuba on one side; South Africa on the other, the United States now turned mediator. The Cairo meeting followed. Pretoria's attempts to dominate other people under the banner of the USA's "constructive engagement" were brought to a halt – at great cost to the Angolan and Namibian people.

One day after the Cairo meeting, the South Africans deployed troops towards the west and released artillery fire with their long-range guns over Tchipa, where the Cuban-Angolan troops were located. The order came from Havana to respond forcefully to the enemy attack and to hit South African facilities in Calueque and its surroundings.

On the 17th of June six Mig-23 MLs took off from Lubango. Two more took off from Cahama. The attack destroyed the bridgehead and the sluice gates, engine room and crane at the Calueque dam. In August 1988 the South Africans completely withdrew from Angolan territory. In March 1990, the process of Namibia's decolonisation culminated in SWAPO's electoral victory and the rise of Sam Nujoma to head of the new state. The last Cuban combatants returned to their homeland on 25 March 1991, 36 days before the agreed-upon schedule.

That was the end of Operation Carlota, which began on the 5th of November 1975 and lasted for 15 years and four months. During that long period more than 300 000 Cuban combatants voluntarily served in Angola through personnel rotation and 2 077 lost their lives for diverse reasons such as combat, accidents and illness.

Notes

1. The main sources for this article were *Conflicting Missions, Havana, Washington and Africa 1959–1976*, by Piero Gleijeses (University of North Carolina, 2002) and the prologue by Jorge Risquet Valdés for the Spanish-language edition, *Misiones en Conflicto*, Editorial Ciencias Sociales, published in Havana in 2002. Interviews with veterans of Operation Carlota and the book *My Life* with interviews by Ignacio Ramonet with Fidel Castro were also helpful (London: Allen Lane, 2007). Other sources were books published in Cuba that shared the experiences of veterans, report backs by those who served there or family members and visits to memorial sites where Cuban combatants were buried. Examples of publications include *La Guerra de Angola*, ed. Marina Rey Cabrera (Havana: Editora Politica, 1989); Hedelberto Lopez Blanch, *Historias Secretas de Medicos Cubanos*, 2nd ed. (Havana: La Memoria, 2005). Other sources were articles that appeared in various accredited journals and personal documents shared with the author. Useful background reading was: Gloria M. Leon Rojas, *Jorge Risquet del Solar a la Sierra* (Havana: Ciencias Sociales, 2006) and Jorge Risquet Valdés, *El segunde frente del Che en el Congo: Historia del batallon Patricio Lumumba* (Havana: Casa Editora Abril, 2006), as well as Piero Gleijeses, "Havana's Policy in Africa, 1959–1976: New Evidence from the Cuban Archives," CWIHP accessed 10 May 1999, http://cwhip.si.edu/cwihplib.nsf/16c6b2fc. Also helpful was Deborah Shnookal, *One Hundred Red Hot Years: Big Moments of the 20th Century* (preface by Eduardo Galeano) (Melbourne: Ocean Press, 2003). Discussions with South African, MPLA and Russian veterans were most informative. All the photos related to Cuban forces used in this book were sourced from the Military Archives in Cuba.

Beware, the Reds are upon us
Another View on the Relations between South Africans and Russians[1]

Ian Liebenberg

The Cold War myopia in the USA media and the "total onslaught" paranoia in South Africa under the rule of President Botha, General Malan and associates resulted in a political environment that thrived on stereotypes and the misreading of the reasons for socio-political conflict in southern Africa (or for that matter the continent of Africa). However, in South Africa the fear for the "Red Threat" started even earlier, as will be demonstrated in this chapter. A Cold War mentality in the USA and the simplistic one-sided South African version of "total onslaught" in which every political act was ascribed to communists, if not Moscow itself, was indeed to bedevil both the understanding of the sources of conflict as well as the ways and means to resolve conflict in the region for many years. As much as the Cold War was an ideological tool of magnitude that caused misery in the so-called "Third World", so was the "total onslaught" rhetoric of Pretoria cause of an ever-deepening historic misunderstanding of the real causes of tension in southern Africa, including Namibia, South Africa and Angola.

This was not only the case in South Africa. Social conflict and oppression in Latin-America was frequently blamed on communists and subversives. Ironically Latin-Americans had resisted the colonial impositions by Spain and the United States of America long before the Russian Revolution took place.[2]

The semantic battlefields and real-life trenches of social conflict also influenced the way the Soviet Union and its people were portrayed in post-1948 South Africa. In this chapter we look at it from another angle – one that differs from the stories government propagandists fed their followers during the era of the Border War. Putting on different spectacles can assist us to see afresh what happened in the past, without the then ideological constraints. In this chapter the relationship between South Africa and Russia / the Soviet Union is explored in more detail. To relate to the involvement of the Soviet Union in South and southern Africa only through the cemented mould of a Cold War and a communist onslaught dims our understanding of the Border War/Bush War. People with different experiences, viewpoints and beliefs, yet all part of common humanity, both make and experience history. Galeano may overstate his point, but there is some truth in his argument that "history makes mistakes, it gets distracted, falls asleep, loses its way. We make it, and it looks like us. But like us, it is also unpredictable. It is (perhaps) with human history as with football; its best feature is its ability to surprise. Against all forecasts, all evidence, the little guy sometimes leads the invincible giant on a merry dance."[3]

If this is so, we may choose to understand that it implies being able to see what is unfolding or was unfolding from different angles. For those who are serious about understanding the past, it is also imperative to understand angles, or to see what happened "on the other side of the hill". This chapter addresses another angle on an old topic which was seen for many years from one viewpoint only, namely the relationship between South Africa and Russia / the Soviet Union over a hundred odd years or more.

In writing this chapter various written sources, some archival material as well as insights gained from contact and interviews with Soviet veterans, Russian citizens and South Africans were used. The Russians (and Soviet citizenry for that matter) did not look at South Africa and South Africans through apartheid spectacles only. This was mainly so because interaction with the southern tip of Africa preceded apartheid rule by many years.

Despite apartheid, the average Soviet citizen did not despise white people (Afrikaners). The historian, Irina Filatova, remarks: "No one can claim with assurance that (despite) all these there is [or rather; *was* at the time] a common element in Soviet perceptions of South Africa. Soviet people rejected race discrimination and sympathised with the struggle the majority waged against the apartheid regime. ... (Yet) *they have never harboured hostility towards the white minority as such; they denounce the regime but not the people.*"[4]

One of the most notable differences between the then Soviet Union and South Africa was that from 1948 South Africa tried to impose an *exclusivist* racial and ethnic programme of *social engineering* ("ethnicity from above") – with or without success, depending on one's view. Conversely the Soviet Union, through social engineering, attempted to steer away from racial, sexual, religious, and ethnic differences after the Revolution – again, with or without success depending on the view of the reader. Thus, the Soviet attempt at social engineering was aimed at *inclusion* and consequently the ideal of an equal social and economic structure, rather than apartheid's *inequality* and *exclusivity*.

Contact between Russians and South Africa date from before the Anglo-Boer War. Refugees from the Kamchatka in eastern Siberia rounded the Cape in 1771. Two of the first Russians to visit South Africa were a junior officer Yuri Lisyansky and a musician Gerasim Lebedev who performed in South Africa thanks to the grace of the then governor.[5] The next British-Russo interaction was less cordial. Captain Vasili Golovnin's ship was confiscated and held in Cape Town during the British-French War of 1808–1809 because Russia was an ally of France. In his memoirs Golovnin described the Boers, the Malay people, the Khoikhoi and the slave society at the Cape.[6] Arguably, more lasting grassroots perceptions by Russians about South Africans were formed during the Anglo-Boer War.[7]

Russian military attaches were present in the *Zuid-Afrikaansche Republic* (ZAR). "The Russian Empire sent six official military attaches to the South African War theatre in 1899–1900."[8] The Russian people and their leaders saw the Boers as "the good people" and had sympathy with them in their struggle against British imperialism.[9] Davidson and Filatova remark on the situation in Russia: "Boer mania reached … a pitch and the authors noted that 'Wherever you go these days, you hear the same stories, the Boers, the Boers, the Boers'."[10] Orchestras played the Republican Anthems of the Transvaal and the Free State on request. *Sarie Marais*, a Boer folk song (*volksliedjie*) was translated into Russian and sung in Moscow and St Petersburg (in Soviet times renamed Leningrad). *Transvaal, Transvaal, my own true land* became a popular song at the time. Funds were collected for the Boer wounded.[11] Political groupings such as the Social Democrats felt that the Boers stood for democracy against a system of oppressive monarchism. Amongst others, Vladimir Illiich Ulyanov (Lenin), then a young Social Democrat, spoke favourably of the Boers in their newspaper *Iskra*.[12] So did some Russian Conservatives.[13] Radical factions and the Conservatives were apparently of one mind in their sympathy for the Boers. Olive Schreiner's works were published widely in Russia.[14] Paul Kruger and General De Wet's memoirs were translated into Russian. Much later, works by Uys Krige, Breyten Breytenbach, Ingrid Jonker and Barend Toerien (among others) were translated.

Together with others from Ireland, Germany and France, Russian volunteers embarked on the long voyage to the ZAR and Pretoria, while German and Russian government pleas to negotiate a settlement fell on deaf ears in London.[15] Many of the Russian volunteers had departed without the permission or knowledge of their government. Some resigned their military ranks before their departure in order not to embarrass the Tsarist government or to prevent disciplinary steps against them. According to earlier Afrikaans authors the (majority of the) Boers saw the majority of the volunteers as loyal and admirable friends.[16] *"Die Boere het nie alleen gestaan toe hulle in hul uur van nood hulle toevlug tot 'God en Mauser' geneem het nie. Van heide en ver het vreemdelingvriende hulle na die oorlogstoneel gehaas om die Afrikaners in hul tweede vryheidsstryd met woord en daad behulpsaam te wees."*[17]

Prince Nikolai Georgiivitch Bagration-Mukhransky was fondly nicknamed "Niko the Boer". Lieutenant Colonel Yevgeni Yakovlevich Maximov joined the Boers as an experienced officer. After being wounded near Thaba N'chu in the Free State, he received a hero's welcome in Pretoria and was elected *Veggeneraal* ("Combat General") – the highest rank awarded in Boer military structures. Paul Kruger, while in exile in Switzerland, wrote a personal letter to thank Maximov for his contribution. Only one other foreigner was bestowed this honour: the Frenchman, Colonel De Villebois-Mareuil, who died early in 1900 when his corps was routed near Boshof by General Methuen's superior forces. Mareuil was appointed to the rank of *Veggeneraal* in the field.[18] Not all was well in the state of *Pretoriana*, however. Russian observers commented on the treatment of blacks and they portrayed black people as victims, rather than as participants in history.[19]

By 1910 the land where Boer and Brit fought against each other in one of the first modern resource wars was to become the land of Boer *and* Brit. But resistance was brewing. Earlier, in 1906, the black people in Natal had embarked on the failed Bambatha rebellion. The rebellion started in February 1906 and for more than a month the rebels resisted with a guerrilla campaign in the Nkandla forests.[20] In June the rebellion was crushed, but further resistance broke out in Mapumulo, which was also crushed.[21] Between 3 500 and 4 000 Africans were killed, according to one historian.[22] One of the outcomes of the rebellion was "a cogent factor in promoting the idea of inter-African cooperation throughout South Africa".[23]

The South African Native National Congress (SANNC) – later to become the African National Congress (ANC) – was established in 1912. In the following year the discriminatory Land Laws were passed and thousands of black people lost their land and had to move to "reservations".

South Africa was a country of painful contradictions. Not only did black and white have diametrically opposed visions of the future, but the white community had also been divided since the end of the Anglo-Boer War. In July 1913 a strike occurred on the gold mines. This was followed in January 1914 by another strike by railway workers which was solved through negotiations. In 1914 the Rebellion against the Union government took place and at its end societal divisions were even more visible.[24] This was not the end. The 1922 mineworkers' strike shook the Witwatersrand. One historian summed it up:

> Duisende mense het deur die strate gedrom en 'n ware skrikbewind het losgebars … dit was feitlik die begin van 'n rewolusie wat baie mense herhinner het aan die bloedige Russiese omwenteling van 1917. Die kapitaliste het dit ook werklik so beskou, veral omdat die kommunistiese elemente hulle nou laat geld het. Die rewolusionêre lied die *"Rooi Vlag"* is gehoor en daar is gepraat van die stigting van 'n swart republiek.[25]

The spectre of a Russian-like revolution under the red banner caused extreme concern amongst the white ruling elite, financial bosses and mine magnates (described vividly as capitalists by the armed rebels). Fearing a communist revolution, the Smuts government unleashed the police, the military and the newly established South African Air Force in force against the strikers with devastating effects. The strike was broken with the loss of more than 200 lives. The strike commanders were captured and sentenced to death, while others committed suicide when the strike collapsed.

Meanwhile the whittling down of the rights of native South Africans continued. As the historian Davenport suggested: "South Africa is a country of many baffling contrasts.

There have been few societies in history in which so much dedicated enthusiasm for (one) cause has been manifested by one section of society while another section complained so persistently to be suffering from indignity and pain as result of the policies ostensibly designed for their long-term benefit."[26] The Cape Native Locations Act (1879), the Glen Grey Act (1879), the 1913 Land Act and Hertzog's land bills of 1926 and 1936 are but some examples of discrimination in land affairs before the apartheid government came to power, committed to entrenching and refining these approaches.[27]

But, let us go back to the 1922 mineworkers' strike. D.F. Malan, the Nationalist Afrikaner leader, had sympathy with the actions by the striking miners and in 1929 likened the National Party to the *Bolsjewiste* (Bolsheviks) in one of his orations (talk by Apollon Davidson at the National Research Foundation, Pretoria circa 2001). A decade or two later, the same D.F. Malan regularly referred to the dangers of communism.

The Second World War

On the 1st of September 1939 Nazi Germany invaded Poland, starting one of the most destructive wars of the twentieth century. On the 3rd of September Britain declared war against Germany. On the 4th of September the then South African Prime Minister J.B.M. Hertzog's motion for neutrality was defeated in the South African parliament. The United Party of Smuts argued for entering the war on the Allied side. Consequently the Union of South Africa was on the side of the Allies against the Axis Forces of Adolf Hitler and later Italy's Benito Mussolini. The Labour Party, the Dominium Party, the Natives' Representatives in parliament and some of the Hertzogites supported Smuts. Many South Africans within the National Party and two major right-wing movements, the Ossewa-Brandwag headed by Hans van Rensburg and the New Order Party ("Nuwe Orde") headed by Oswald Pirow, were supportive of the Nazis.[28]

South African politics is riddled with paradoxes. The Second World War brought about quite a few. Nazi Germany was bound by a non-aggression pact with the USSR and it was only in 1941 with the German surprise attack on the Soviet Union, Operation Barbarossa, that South Africa found itself on the side of the Soviet Union, now one of the Allies. Those of socialist orientation in South Africa faced stark choices. To be pro-war meant to be also against the non-aggression pact between Stalin and Hitler. After Operation Barbarossa and Hitler's negation of the earlier pact, choices were no less complicated. For those Marxists who deeply differed from Stalin's policies (the Trotskyites) it meant that an anti-war stance could be seen as pro-Hitler.

Hirson argues: "The war ... had been expected by both Stalinists and Trotskyites. The Stalinists followed the USSR blindly, switching policy in line with changes in Europe ... (and) vacillated when war was declared until the 'line' was made clear from Moscow [in this case meaning the invasion of the Soviet Union] … The Trotskyites were anti-war and were agreed that they would oppose the war. In line with Lenin's (1915 call) they called for the defeat of their own government (in Russia) …" BUT; "At the same time, they supported Trotsky's call for the unconditional defence of the USSR."[29]

Many South Africans were in favour of the war. Many had sympathy with the Soviet Union as one of their allies. The Soviet Union eventually lost around 20 000 000 citizens and soldiers during the Second World War. South Africans were well aware that the "Russians" – in other words the Soviet Union – sacrificed people, material, and their future to defeat Fascism and Nazism.

A South African organisation, Medical Aid for Russia, acted upon a request from the Soviet Red Cross to provide "ten thousand bottles of human blood serum" for the "soldiers of the Red Army". Amongst others, members from Kimberley, Bloemfontein, Port Elizabeth, East London, Pietermaritzburg, Durban, Johannesburg and Pretoria contributed. The mobilising slogan simply read: "Give your blood that they shall not die!"

A letter dated the 16th of October 1942 from the Minister of Posts and Telegraphs and Public Works to the Consul General of the USSR in Pretoria, Nicolai Demianov, stated that a resolution of the United Party in Klerksdorp read: "This meeting of the United Party wishes to express its admiration and gratitude to the heroic Russian Armies who with so much valour fight against the Nazis." It continues: "It is our earnest prayer that the awful struggle will soon be brought to a successful conclusion and that every Nazi will be driven out of Russia".

The South African Medical Aid for Russia, apart from cash donations totalling roughly £800 000 also supplied anti-gas gangrene serum, anti-bacterial dysentery serum, anti-typhus vaccine, 7 452 bottles of human blood serum, 600 000 yards of bandage, 5 000 000 Vitamin B (Complex) tablets and 80 tons of tuna. Correspondence from the Medical Aid for Russia dated January 1945 addressed to the Soviet Consulate proves that deliveries continued until 1945.[30] South African seamen also served on board naval vessels in the operations to relieve Leningrad (now St Petersburg) during 1941/42. In 2005 the Great Patriotic War commemorations in South Africa took place in Cape Town in order to honour some of the seamen who were still alive and who took part in the so-called "Arctic Convoys".

A glimpse of the divisions within the white community at the time is given in a letter from the Afrikaans Reformed Churches to Smuts. The Afrikaans Reformed Churches appeal to his government to be aware of the "dangers of communism" (die gevare van die kommunisme) and "the pressures of communist propaganda" (die druk van kommunistiese propaganda). The letter signed by eight church leaders mentioned the utter unacceptability of "communist principles that are materialist, godless and unchristian".[31] The Trade and Labour Council, the Trade Unions and the Friends of the Soviet Union were mentioned by name. The letter appeals to the government to ban all communication between the Soviet Union and unions.[32] At the time the Dutch Reformed Church members were mostly Afrikaners. The Afrikaans Reformed Churches (the *Nederduits Gereformeerde Kerk*, the *Hervormde Kerk* and the *Gereformeerde Kerk*) were deeply infiltrated by members of the Broederbond. These churches were, with qualification, also sympathetic to the authoritarian National-Socialist movement, the Ossewa-Brandwag, of which many members were interned by the Smuts government.

In 1948 the National Party came to power. It was not a landslide victory, but its consequences were to be enormous. The National Party and its cultural cohort, the Afrikaner Broederbond, now had the final say in South African politics. While the international community accepted the Universal Declaration of Human Rights in 1948, the National Party and its cohorts came to power with the slogan *Apartheid* (Separateness) soon to be transformed under the Premier Hans Strijdom to *Baasskap*.

A small cold war in southern Africa, with compliments from apartheid

During the period 1950 to 1970 the South African elite (and perhaps many white South Africans) viewed the Soviet people with grudging admiration that later turned into fear. It was the beginning of apartheid's social engineering, legalised racialism, the Red Bear syndrome, and paranoid fears of communism. The South African Minister of Justice, C.R. Swart in 1949 referred to "communism as a snake in the backyard which had to be killed before it bites".[33] From the days of D.F. Malan, the first National Party Prime Minister, to those of Verwoerd and Vorster "(A)ll along the Soviet Union was regarded as the source of communist evil."[34]

It has to be mentioned, however, that numerous South African World War II veterans who fought with their countrymen of "other races" (in other words "Coloured people" and "Black people") deeply resented the National Party's discriminatory policies implemented after 1948. These men served side-by-side through Abyssinia, Egypt and later Italy in the war against Fascism and Nazism, and by implication also on the side of the Soviet Union. Members of the Springbok Legion ("the trade union of the ranks"), disillusioned about demobilisation, and even more so after the National Party came to power, fought for social justice. Their ranks held radical and communist members.[35] Another ex-servicemen's group entitled the Torch Commando arose. The organisation mobilised thousands of veterans to support the United Party in an attempt to reverse the outcome of the 1948 elections. They were especially upset about the National Party's plans to scrap so-called Coloured voters from the common voters' roll in the Cape Province.[36] Despite their demonstrations and protestations, the National Party passed wave after wave of racial legislation, and equality for all was whittled away day by day.

Following the Sharpeville shootings on the 21st of March 1960 where 69 people lost their lives, the Unlawful Organisations Act (Act 24 of 1960) was passed. The PAC and ANC were banned. Between 1962 and 1966 the General Law Amendment Act (1962) and the further General Law Amendment Act (Act 37 of 1963) were passed outlawing various organisations. The Affected Organisations Act of 1974 and the Internal Security Amendment Act, No 79 of 1976 were to follow. Between 1960 and 1975 several organisations were banned. Following the Internal Security Amendment Act another eighteen organisations followed. Amongst them were Parents and Teachers Organisations, Youth and Black Journalist Organisations and various Black Consciousness Movement-related organisations. Several publications, *The Rand Daily Mail*, for example, were harassed and the Christian Institute headed by Beyers Naudé and its newsletter *Pro Veritate* were banned.

The Afrikaner political elite provided with, and fully exploiting, Cold War talk, led their followers into the psychosis of a presumed "total onslaught". Internal hard-handed policies were maintained, if not increased. Hard-handed and hard-headedness also impacted on foreign policy, which, after the 1975 invasion of Angola, increasingly reflected a military projection of power. The isolated state's actions increasingly invited a deepening diplomacy of isolation, perceiving all critics as enemies. White society and state became militarised, while citizens of colour increasingly became frustrated with a state from which they felt deeply alienated. South Africa's minority, due to increasing international criticism and later isolation, in the view of their political leaders, stood alone.

The South African regime and its followers felt betrayed by the United States of America that temporarily withdrew its initial support to South Africa and the rebel movement UNITA after the 1975 invasion of Angola by South African battle groups. At least two battalions of infantry from Zaire assisted the FNLA of Holden Roberto, mainly funded by the CIA (with some limited French funding) and the South Africans. A complex love-hate relationship developed between South Africa and Western powers.[37]

Before and after apartheid South Africa cooperated with France on nuclear energy and security issues and imported military transport aircraft via Morocco from Western states. Major oil companies such as Shell and British Petroleum exported oil to South Africa and South Africa continued to work closely with Western-supported states. The latter included Argentina, Chile, Israel and Taiwan. Relationships with US-backed states like Zaire of Mubutu SeSeseko remained warm (Mubutu's air force was French supplied, for example). Outspoken anti-communist statesmen on the continent, like President Hastings Banda of Malawi, were hailed in South Africa as much as the corrupt president of Zaire.

"Jy kan 'n Kommunis vertrou om 'n Kommunis te wees" ("You can trust a communist to be a communist") became the slogan used by National Party/Broederbond leaders from the 1950s onwards in order to mobilise whites and "moderate" black people against internal

and external resistance, which was presumed and portrayed to be orchestrated from the Soviet Union. For many, Moscow became a loathsome word, in contrast to the time of the Anglo-Boer War. The schisms deepened and different sections of the population in South Africa, and presumably the Soviet Union/Russia, viewed each other with feelings that varied from admiration, grudging respect and sheer adulation to scepticism and hate. Needless to say, the political elite and their faithful media on both sides played a major role in influencing opinions.

Closer links and loyalties between the ANC/SACP and Soviets developed. The Afro-Asian Solidarity Committee in Moscow played a major role in this regard. ANC cadres went for training in Russia. Many of them still speak the language. Many students from "Third World" countries went to study in the USSR at the People's Friendship University, amongst them many South Africans. Others went for military training. In South Africa, following the transition to democracy, the newly created South African National Defence Force (SANDF) incorporated, amongst others, MK cadres that had been trained in the Soviet Union in special operations and various other arms of service.

The South African regime also had anti-communist advocates outside the country. In 1988 (the same year that Gorbatsjov's *Perestrojka* – in Dutch – saw its 10th impression in the Netherlands) a Dutch scholar, M. de Haas, wrote *Sovjetbeleid ten aanzien van Zuidelijk Afrika*. He spent much of his work pointing out that the Soviet Union was delivering arms to sub-Saharan Africa. As did South African magazines of the time such as *Die Huisgenoot*, *Scope*, *Paratus* and others, De Haas listed the perceived quantities of equipment delivered to African countries. No mention was made that Western powers also supplied arms to African states, or that perceived communist states such as Angola also imported equipment from Western countries, depending on price or availability. The impetus of De Haas' work was pointing out the Soviet Union's attempt to isolate South Africa and the Soviet propaganda onslaught (*een propagandacampagne*) against South Africa.[38] De Haas, for example, referred at the time, without qualification, to the ANC and South West African People's Organisation (SWAPO) as "terrorist organisations".[39] Incidentally, the USA also classified the ANC as a terrorist movement, not a liberation or nationalist movement.

In 1981, Ronald Reagan said about the South African government and US relations: "Can we abandon a country that stood behind us in every war we fought, a country strategically essential to the free world in its productions of minerals that we must have and so forth?"[40]

Oliver Tambo, President of the ANC, responded: "We stood together with the Soviet Union and the Allies in fighting Nazism in the Second World War ... the Soviet Union and other socialist countries stand with us to this day fighting the apartheid system and its leaders ... of Nazi ideology and practice."[41] Interestingly enough, at this time the People's Republic of China had made a shift in policy, trying to establish closer contact with the

ANC and the SACP. The "Chinese question" was to be discussed with the CPSU during a visit by Moses Mabhida, SACP representative, when he attended Brezhnev's funeral.[42] In 1982, the SACP Secretariat discussed the issue in Maputo and decided "that we should be cautious about the issue but should not reject the overtures [by the Chinese]". Shubin argues that the decision was an example of SACP and CPSU relationships. "The Soviet did not dictate their position to the SACP, nor did they prevent the SACP from developing relations with Beijing."[43]

Conflict escalated after the 1976 Soweto Rebellion, which was not restricted to the (then) Transvaal only. The 1980s brought many contradictions in South African politics. The hate for communism that had been carefully cultivated since the 1940s by organisations such as the Broederbond and South African Bureau of Racial Affairs (SABRA), received a new impetus with the tacit acceptance of a so-called Cold War discourse and the ideology of a "total onslaught" propagated by PW Botha, Adriaan Vlok, Magnus Malan and the securocrats.

Divisions between South Africans were to deepen substantially between 1940 and the 1980s. Children born in 1960 were to hear over South African Broadcasting Services that a revolutionary (the term to equal "terrorist" or "anarchist"), Ché Guevara, had eventually been gunned down in a far-off Latin American country, Bolivia. They would hear that South Africa's northern neighbour Rhodesia was under threat from a communist and terrorist onslaught. That Communist China and the Soviet Union were aiming at total control of Africa and the destruction of Western civilisation with the help of puppet states. These perceptions were strengthened as South Africa became internationally isolated by illegally occupying Namibia (then South West Africa), and became embroiled in the Angolan civil war with initial US support. Starting in 1975, South Africa's involvement in, and destabilisation of, Angola would last for more than twelve years before South African forces were forced to withdraw from Cuito Cuanavale and the surrounding areas due to international political pressure and a controversial stalemate brought about by Cuban military strategic thinking.

During the 1980s, as South Africans regressed increasingly into a society in conflict, the glib mantras of "communism" and "Moscow's agenda" succeeded in mobilising the majority of the white electorate to vote for the National Party (including the implementation of the divisive Tricameral Parliament). The 1980s were marked by a government strategy of (sham) reform and repression, rhetoric of political devolution while power was centralised. Those advocating democracy (even a negotiated settlement) were vilified. Nevertheless, organisations such as the Institute for Democracy in South Africa (IDASA) arranged meetings between South Africans and Soviet academics which played a role in de-demonising the stereotypes of the Soviet Union. Simultaneously international pressure and internal resistance (also from the white community) forced the National Party towards the one reasonable option: a negotiated transition to resolve ongoing conflict rather than a civil war or revolutionary transfer of power.

Conclusion

Twice in South Africa's history, albeit under difference circumstances, the Russian people stood by the South Africans. Firstly during the Anglo-Boer War, which is now thoroughly documented. The second time was during the era of South Africa's struggle for liberation after the 1940s, which fortunately is now also well documented. Ironically, in both cases the Russians/Soviets were in solidarity with the underdogs in their (nationalist) struggle against colonialism.

Given the history of relations between these two countries, to reduce the solidarity between South Africans in their struggle for freedom (and democracy in the second case) to a limited concept such as "the Cold War", substantially limits our understanding of the historical ties and emotional bonds between them.

Notes

1. For a detailed article on the relations between South Africa and Russia from the 1890s to 2010, consult Ian Liebenberg, "Viewing the Other over a Hundred and a Score more Years: South Africa and Russia, 1890–2010," *The Journal for Transdisciplinary Research* 6, no. 2 (December 2010): 428–460. Also consult Gennady Shubin and Vladimir Shubin, "Relations between South Africa and Russia, 1898–2004, in *A Century is a Short Time: New Perspectives on the Anglo-Boer War*, ed. Ina Snyman, Ian Liebenberg, Gert van der Westhuizen & Mariaan Roos (Pretoria: Nexus Publishers, 2005), 334–347.

2. See Deborah Shnookal, *A Hundred Red Hot Years* (Melbourne: Ocean Books, 2003), 7–9, 11–13; Julio de Reverend, *Brief History of Cuba* (Havana: Instituto del Libro,1997), 46ff, 59ff, 92ff; Charles Arnade, *Bolivian History* (La Paz-Cochabamba: Los Amigos del Libro, 1984), 51ff, 65ff, 73ff.

3. Eduardo Galiano in *A Hundred Red Hot Years*, ed. Deborah Shnookal (Melbourne: Ocean Books, 2003), 2.

4. Irina Filatova, "South Africa as seen by the Russian and Soviet People and their Perception of the 'South African Problem'," *IDASA Occasional Paper*, no. 14 (Mowbray: Institute for Democracy, 1988), 7.

5. Ibid., 2.

6. Ibid., 4.

7. Ibid., 3.

8. Gennady Shubin, "Russian Perceptions of Boer and British Armies: An Introduction to Russian Documents," *Scientia Militaria* 30, no. 1 (2000): 13ff.

9. Apollon Davidson, *Cecil Rhodes and his Time* (Pretoria: Protea Book House, 2003); Apollon Davidson and Irina Filatova, *The Russians and the Anglo-Boer War* (Cape Town: Human & Rousseau, 1998), 177ff, 190, 207ff; *Gedenkalbum van die Tweede Vryheidsoorlog*, ed. J. Breytenbach (Kaapstad: Nasionale Pers Beperk, 1949), 338.

10. Davidson and Filatova.

11. Davidson, 27.

12. For more on the thoughts of Lenin of Rhodes as "Millionaire, a king of finance, the man who was mainly responsible for the Anglo-Boer War," see Davidson, 28.

13. Davidson and Filatova, 190.

14. Ibid., 190, 191.

15. A.J. Boëseken, D.W. Kruger & A. Kieser, *Drie Eeue: Die Verhaal van ons Vaderland (Deel 4)* (Kaapstad: Nasionale Boekhandel, 1953a), 255.

16. *Gedenkalbum van die Tweede Vryheidsoorlog*, 279.

17. M. van Niekerk, "Die Vreemdelinge-vrywillegerskorpse in die Stryd," in *Gedenkalbum van die Tweede Vryheidsoorlog*, 279.

18. Roy Macnab, *Die Franse Kolonel* (Kaapstad: Tafelberg, 1977), 77.

19. Irina Filatova, "South Africa as seen by the Russian and Soviet People and their Perception of the 'South African Problem'," *IDASA Occasional Paper*, no. 14 (Mowbray: Institute for Democracy, 1988), 4.

20. André Odendaal. *Vukani Bantu! The Beginnings of Black Protest Politics in South Africa to 1912* (Cape Town: David Philip, 1984), 68.

21. Ibid.

22. Ibid.

23. Ibid.

24. For the perspective of one of the rebel leaders, General Manie Maritz, consult *My Lewe en Strewe* (Johannesburg: The Author, 1938), 65ff.

25. For a historian's perspective at the time, see Eric A. Walker, *A History of South Africa* (Toronto: Longmans Green & Co, 1941 (1928)), 583–586. Compare also A.G. Oberholster, *Die Mynwerkerstaking Witwatersrand, 1922* (Pretoria: RGN, 1982). Translation of passage: "Thousands of people marched through the streets and intimidation took place ... it reminded people about the beginning of a revolution reminiscent of the Russian one of 1917. The capitalist bosses indeed viewed it as such. The revolutionary *Red Flag* was heard and talk about creating a communist republic was rife."

26. T.R.H. Davenport, *South Africa: A Modern History*, 2nd ed. (Johannesburg: Macmillan, 1977), 276.

27. Ibid., 117–119, 219, 336–337, 218–221, 334–335. There is little surprise in this. By 1901, even before the end of the Anglo-Boer War, an author suggests that between Boer and British the land would be controlled. "It is evident that the Boers are and will for many years be the predominant land-owning class ... [the Boers] can still remain the landed aristocrat ..." W. Bleloch, *The New South Africa: Its Value and Development* (London: Heinemann, 1901), 223.

28. On steps taken to deal with organised resistance and covert action by subversives opposed to the war (mostly Afrikaner Nationalists), consult Andries Fokkens, "Afrikaner Unrest within South Africa during the Second World War and Measures taken to Oppress it," *Journal for Contemporary History* 37, no. 2 (2012): 123–142. It has to be mentioned that one "communist", in fact a Trotskyite unionist, Max Gordon, was also interned in 1940/1941 for a year (partly because of being anti-war). See Baruch Hirson, "The Trotskyites and the Trade Unions," in *The Long March: The Story of the Struggle for Liberation in South Africa*, ed. Ian Liebenberg, Gert van der Westhuizen, Fiona Lortan and Frederik Nel (Pretoria: Kagiso-HAUM Publishers, 1994), 67.

29. Ibid., 59.

30. UP Archives, Division of Information, University of South Africa, "Church and Politics", accessed 2005.

31. Ibid., accessed 2005, 2007.

32. Ibid.

33. Deon Geldenhuys, "Official South African Perspectives of the Soviet Union: From Confrontation to Accommodation," *IDASA Occasional Paper*, no. 14 (Mowbray: IDASA, 1988): 8.

34. Ibid., 9.

35.   Neil Roos, *Ordinary Springboks: White Servicemen and Social Justice in South Africa 1939–1961* (Aldershot: Ashgate Publishing, 2005), 5–6, 50, 100ff.

36.   Ibid. Consult especially Chapter 9.

37.   Geldenhuys, 9.

38.   M. De Haas, *Sovjetbeleid ten aanzien van Zuidelijk Afrika* (Utrecht: Uitgeverij De Banier, 1988), 33.

39.   Ibid., 34ff

40.   Vladimir Shubin, *The ANC: A View from Moscow* (Cape Town: Mayibuye Publishers, 1999), 234.

41.   Ibid.

42.   Ibid.

43.   Ibid.

Cold War and Definitions of Cold Wars

The state of the USSR–USA relations played a role in Moscow's decision making on Southern Africa, just as the Russia-British tensions during the Anglo-Boer War did. The Soviets did not look at the assistance to the liberation movements and African Front Line States as "a Cold War". In the language of those days, assistance was regarded as a part of the "anti-imperialist struggle waged by the socialist community, the national liberation movements and the working class (of the capitalist countries)" – not just a Moscow-Washington confrontation. The "Cold War" was not a part of our political vocabulary; rather, the term was used in a strictly negative sense as a creation of "war mongers" and "imperialist propaganda". The global struggle was not a battle of the two "superpowers" assisted by their "satellites" and "proxies". It was seen as a joint fight of the world progressive forces against imperialism. Petr Evysukov, who has been involved for 15 years with the liberation movements of the Portuguese colonies, argues that "assistance to nationalists from socialist countries and, first of all, the Soviet Union was a natural reply to their appeal for such help".

Vladimir Shubin, 2008.

The Soviet Involvement

Vladimir and Gennady Shubin

In what was described by the West as a Cold War, and by the Soviet Union as support for national liberation movements in an anti-colonial struggle, Angola became a notable case.

The Portuguese revolution which opened the prospects for Angola's rapid transition to independence saw Moscow's relations with the MPLA at a low due to a crisis in this movement. It took the USSR leadership some months before eventually deciding to support Agostinho Neto as the MPLA's leader.

A critical moment was the "Congress of MPLA" convened in Zambia in August 1974. The inverted commas are relevant here. The gathering was organised not so much by the Angolans, but by their "host countries": Zambia, Congo-Brazzaville, Zaire and Tanzania, who determined the composition of the delegates.

During the conference Neto and his supporters took a decision against further participation and left the venue on the 22nd of August. A month later, they convened the Inter-Regional Conference of MPLA Militants in Moxico province inside Angola. There, Neto was confirmed as leader and the MPLA's Politbureau was formed.

In December 1974 Moscow hosted an MPLA delegation headed by Henrique (Iko) Carreira, later the first Angolan Minister of Defence. Members of the delegation were regarded as guests of the Communist Party of the Soviet Union (CPSU). They stayed in the well-known (though modest) hotel Oktyabskaya in Plotnikov pereulok (Carpenter's Lane), near Arbat, a famous Moscow street.

At that stage Mobutu Sese Seko, president of Zaire, had moved closer to the West, particularly the USA and France. Mobutu had a warm relationship with the National Front for the Liberation of Angola (FNLA) of Holden Roberto, who was on the CIA's payroll. The FNLA forces, via their leadership based in Zaire, was seen by some Western countries as one avenue of expanding their power into Angola. Meanwhile the debate over the "split in the MPLA" subsided. Tanzania, Zambia and Mozambique, where a Transitional Government headed by FRELIMO had been formed, now supported the MPLA led by Neto.

The three movements (MPLA, FNLA and UNITA) and Portugal signed an agreement in January 1975 in Alvor near Lisbon that decreed joint rule in Angola before independence, which was scheduled for the 11th of November. However, the Alvor Agreement was not rooted in solid ground and tensions soon arose. The planned transitional government in Angola was problematic. The organisations that were to form the transitional government consisted of forces that had been rivals for many years. Foreign interference also played a significant role. Nine days before the inauguration of the Angolan transitional government, on the 22nd of January 1975, a committee of the USA National Security Council approved a grant of $300 000 for Holden Roberto "to compete" with other Angolan movements (Roberto had already been financially supported by the CIA much earlier on). In February 1975 Roberto's well-armed forces moved from Zaire into Angola and began attacking the MPLA in Luanda and northern Angola, thereby dealing a severe blow to any hope for an effective transitional government.

Agostinho Neto was met by enthusiastic crowds when he returned to Luanda on the 4th of February – the fourteenth anniversary of the beginning of the uprisings in the city.

The Soviet Union at the time supported the Alvor agreement. Against the changing background of growing assistance to the MPLA's rivals (Zaire and the FNLA) by South Africa, the USA, a number of other Western countries and, for a brief period, China, the Soviet Union chose to support the MPLA, which by all available observations was not only the most viable and well-organised movement, but seemingly had widespread support from Angolans of all backgrounds.

A month after the Portuguese revolution, on the 29th of May 1974, a group of 112 Chinese military advisors arrived in Zaire to train Roberto's troops. Later, in July 1975, an FNLA delegation was received in Beijing by Deng Xiaoping, then Vice-Premier, and Ho Ying, Chinese Vice-Minister for Foreign Affairs. China published a press release on their arrival.[1] Apparently China expected the FNLA to play a leading role in an independent Angola and wanted to demonstrate its contribution to Roberto's future successes.[2] China's contacts with UNITA intensified as well. In March 1975, Deng Xsiaoping received a UNITA delegation headed by UNITA's General Secretary Samuel Chiwala.[3]

Meanwhile, a number of MPLA members left for training in the USSR. These recruits constituted the core of the future 9th Brigade. (Although named the 9th, it was the first, and at the time the only, regular unit of FAPLA, the MPLA's army). Twenty or thirty commanders underwent a crash course in the famous Higher Officer Courses "Vystrel" in Solnechnogorck near Moscow. Others (about 200) were trained in Perevalnoe, in the Crimea.[4] On their return some remained in the 9th Brigade and some of them were deployed in the south.

At that stage the MPLA consisted of about 6 000 militants. Not all of them were trained. Many were urban activists with virtually no military training or experience. These members were based mostly in Luanda and along the coast. Many were trade unionists or workers with little military training.

John Stockwell, an ex-CIA operator, recalls the words of a CIA desk officer: "The Soviets did not make the first move in Angola. Other people did: The Chinese and the United States."[5] He claims that the Soviet Union began "significant arms shipments" to the MPLA in March 1975 and then "in response to the Chinese and American programs" launched "a massive airlift", using An-12 and giant An-22 transport planes.[6] Despite this claim, by mid-May 1975 hardware was not on its way to Angola. According to Boris Putilin, then an official of the Soviet Embassy in Congo-Brazzaville (and a military intelligence officer), the airlifting of supplies only began later.[7] The Soviet supplies that were delivered later included "a large quantity of small arms, 82 mm mortars, some portable Grad-Ps" (122 mm missile launchers). The portable missile launcher should be clearly distinguished from mobile (wheeled) missile launchers such as the BM-21 that were used in the war only later, after the independence of Angola.[8]

General Monterio "Ngongo" recalls that larger quantities of military supplies found their way to Pointe-Noir around August-September 1975. Inscriptions on the boxes were in Russian (he could at least read them) and he was sent there to find fuses for mortar shells to send to Benguela.[9]

In Washington, July 1975 was a month of decision making on Angola. According to a CIA memorandum, "large supplies of arms to Roberto and [Jonas] Savimbi would not guarantee that they could establish control of all of Angola, but that assistance would permit them to achieve a military balance which would avoid a cheap Neto victory".[10] On the 16th of July the Africa Division of the CIA prepared a covert action plan for the Angola operation. The matter was apparently regarded as urgent because President Gerald Ford approved it on the same day. On the 27th of July $8 million were added to the original sum of $6 million.[11] During the same time, the head of the Bureau of State Security (BOSS) of South Africa visited the US on more than one occasion for consultations.

However, the decision to interfere in Angola on the side of the MPLA's rivals was not universally supported in the US establishment.[12] The CIA station chief in Luanda, Robert W. Hultslander shares Stockwell's assessment: "the MPLA was the best qualified movement to govern Angola.... Although many outwardly embraced Marxism, they were much closer to European radical socialism than to Soviet Marxist-Leninism.... Despite the uncontested communist background of many of the MPLA's leaders, they were more effective, better educated, better trained and motivated. The rank and file also were better motivated, particularly the armed combatants, who fought harder and with more determination ..."

The CIA's association with FNLA and UNITA unfortunately tainted its analysis. As is frequently the case when intelligence collection and analysis are wedded to covert action programmes, objectivity and truth become victims of political expediency.[13]

FNLA troops tried to advance towards Luanda to increase their presence in the capital, but failed. By the end of June, they were concentrated in the two northern provinces. Roberto had to agree to negotiations, which took place in Nakuru, Kenya. According to the agreement reached there, each movement had to reduce its troops in Luanda to 500, and the MPLA, as stated by Carreira who came to Moscow again in August, "took steps to clear the capital from excessive FNLA troops" and succeeded in 3–4 days.[14] In response, the FNLA proclaimed the beginning of war and its column of about 5 000 troops, 11 APCs and Panhard armoured cars, tried to advance towards Luanda, but was successfully halted.[15]

The FNLA still had more troops than the MPLA,[16] but its potential for mobilisation was limited. The main concern of the MPLA leadership was the threat of intervention from Zaire and it tried to come to an agreement with UNITA to jointly resist this. Savimbi refused. Carreira believed that UNITA would agree if it were to feel "the strength of [the] MPLA".[17] This was not to happen.

The MPLA was hoping that the international community would condemn "foreign interference in Angolan affairs". At the same time, the German Democratic Republic shipped valuable medical supplies and ambulances to the MPLA. Ships from Poland and Yugoslavia were also calling at Luanda's port.

All in all, the MPLA's representatives were optimistic. They believed that if provided with more material assistance, their organisation would be in a position to block the routes used by the interventionist forces from Zaire, be able to seize the coastal areas controlled by the FNLA, and then begin the liberation of the northern provinces.[18]

The MPLA's attitude to UNITA was different. MPLA representatives informed the Soviets that it would be "difficult to proclaim independence without UNITA's participation".[19] Talks between the MPLA and UNITA took place in Portugal, but failed. Notwithstanding earlier hostilities, the MPLA did not want to "cut off all ties" with UNITA. They believed that the areas controlled by UNITA did not "constitute a military threat". The MPLA leadership clearly underestimated the threat from South Africa, and this just a month before its massive intervention. At the time the MPLA's attention was still concentrated on the threat from Zaire, even though they referred to "South African Army provocations".[20] South Africa's intervention was soon to go much further than mere "provocation".

South African troops moved from Namibia into Angolan territory on the 8th of August 1975, ostensibly to protect the Calueque dam and waterworks on the Cunene River. By the month's end, they had advanced to Perreira de Eca, capital of the Cunene province.

In September, the South Africans began to supply arms to UNITA and the FNLA and also trained their forces at Rundu in northern Namibia.[21] South African instructors also appeared with UNITA and FNLA units inside Angola.

The date for independence was approaching and the Portuguese authorities faced a political challenge: How is the transfer of power in Angola to be arranged? A witness provided a fascinating story of his meeting with the Portuguese High Commissioner, Lionel Cardoso, who said that a day earlier the Portuguese authorities in Angola had informed the MPLA Politbureau that they could not transfer power to the MPLA alone. They would have to transfer it to "the Angolan people". He reminded a Soviet journalist that the Portuguese troops had earlier helped the MPLA to "chase FNLA and UNITA units away from Luanda". He suggested that if the leaders of these two movements came to Luanda for the ceremonial transfer of power, these organisations could be "beheaded".[22]

At that stage the relations between Havana and Congo-Brazzaville improved. At the request of President Marien Ngouabi, Cuba sent instructors and a combat unit to help protect Congo-Brazzaville against a possible Zairian invasion.[23] According to Putilin, the Cubans knew, even when bringing hardware from Cuba to Angola such as two shiploads of tanks, that they would be replaced by more modern arms from the Soviet Union. Older T-34 tanks also appeared in Angola, sent by the USSR and probably Algeria as well.[24]

Marshall Josip Tito from Yugoslavia also provided twelve T-34s. Soviet-trained personnel with Soviet-supplied arms took part in a decisive battle on the Northern Front on the 10th of November 1975 at Quifangondo, just 30 km from the Luanda city centre. Stockwell writes that 122 mm Cuban rocket launchers fired on Zairean and FNLA troops in salvoes of 20 missiles simultaneously and that the CIA "observers", who were on a ridge to the north of the battlefield, estimated that two thousand rockets poured down like rain on the advancing "small army" of Zairean and FNLA troops with their foreign assistants.[25]

This "army" had heavy guns, albeit a strange combination, some Soviet-designed and supplied to Mobutu by North Korea, and others Western-designed (such as the G-2, 140 mm or 5,5 inch) and brought by a South African ship to the port of Ambriz and manned by SADF personnel. According to Stockwell, however, their range was less than half that of the BM-21 and these Soviet-made rocket launchers were stationed on Ural-375 all-terrain trucks and could be quickly relocated. Moreover, one of the North Korean guns exploded with the first shot, killing its Zairean crew and the second misfired, injuring the crew.[26]

"Fear has big eyes," says a Russian proverb. Apparently this was true for the CIA observers as well, because General Monteiro "Ngongo", who commanded the artillery of the FAPLA 9th Brigade, told quite a different story about Quifangondo as observed from the hill where his command post was situated.

On the previous evening the advancing FNLA/Zairean troops and mercenaries began firing at the Luanda refinery and the area of Grafanil where arms depots were situated. They deployed heavy guns placed on the northern side of the hills. The next morning several French-made armoured vehicles manned by white mercenaries moved towards Quifangondo, while Roberto and Mobutu's infantry concentrated in the palm forest, or rather a grove a bit behind the palm trees. The bridge over river Bengo was blown up by FAPLA and when the APCs approached it, the APCs and accompanying forces were hit by the fire of 76 mm ZIS-3 Soviet-made anti-tank guns with joint Cuban and Angolan crews. Soviet-made recoilless 82 mm B-10 guns were also used. Then the palm grove was targeted by fire from only six portable Grad-P[27] rocket launchers (not mobile BM-21s as reported in Western and South African media) of the 9th Brigade who held their position to the south-east on another hill, near the water reservoir that supplied Luanda. The rocket launchers were behind the top of the hill out of the enemy's sight but the observation post where "Ngongo" and his chief of staff, Enrique, were entrenched was on its northern side.

Initially their task was to silence the enemy's heavy artillery. They fired on enemy positions, but without success. Contrary to Stockwell's story, the range of those portable man-handled rocket launchers (15 km) was far less than that of the South African and Zairean artillery. Then, having received the order from the brigade's commander "Ndozi" (David Moises), the Angolans hit the enemy's infantry in the grove with around 60 (and not two thousand!) rockets. Only six rocket launchers and not 20 simultaneously, were used (according to "Ngongo" the BM-21s, manned by Cubans, were used only later, near Caxito).[28] The 9th Brigade offensive had started, but not with the grandiose mass arms as suggested in media reports at the time.

FAPLA's offensive did not proceed without problems. General "Ngongo" recalls that while the artillery units were well disciplined, infantrymen of the 9th Brigade would sometimes leave the trenches for Luanda. Later, during the advance to Ambriz, his Grad artillerists once found the enemy in a position which was supposed to have been occupied by the brigade's infantry and had to fire at FNLA forces point-blank.[29]

At 11 o'clock on the 11th of November 1975, Soviet representatives attended the inauguration ceremony in the municipal hall followed by a rally in the square. Ambassador Evgeny Afanasenko, who came from Brazzaville, spoke first, conveying a message from the Soviet Union, followed by representatives of Brazil, Nigeria and others.[30]

FNLA and UNITA also proclaimed independence for Angola in a separate ceremony. However, the so-called People's Democratic Republic of Angola[31] proclaimed by the FNLA and UNITA on the 11th of November in Nova Lisboa, was not recognised by a single country. It was dysfunctional from its inception. Moreover, armed clashes between

UNITA and FNLA forces (mostly Chipenda's supporters and former MPLA members) immediately began in that area.[32]

Five days after Angolan independence (16 November) and following recognition by several countries, the first group of Soviet military instructors arrived in Luanda. One of its members was Andrey Tokarev, a 19-year-old student of the Military Institute of Foreign Languages. The group, led by Captain Evgeny Lyashenko, left Moscow on October 31 on a regular Aeroflot flight and arrived in Brazzaville the next day. It had a specific technical and purely defensive mission – to train Angolans in the use of "Strela-2" ("Arrow"), portable anti-aircraft missile launchers. They were informed that Zaire, which supported the FNLA, had obtained Mirages from France[33] and the MPLA leadership anticipated air raids on Luanda. Within a week the group was transferred to Pointe-Noir and on the 16th of November it was joined there by a larger group of instructors headed by Colonel Vassily Trofimenko. On the same day, over 40 Soviet military specialists, including five interpreters, arrived in Luanda on an AN-12 military transport plane with Aeroflot markings.[34] By this time CIA operators and South African "advisors" had already been deeply embroiled in the Angolan conflict for a while.

This second group of advisors and interpreters included specialists in the use of military equipment. Apart from training Angolan personnel on a remote part of the Luanda airport, they often had to go to the front line, especially "Comrade Yury" (Colonel Yury Mitin) who became an advisor to "Ngongo". As a rule Cubans accompanied them on these missions.[35] On the 21st of January 1976 some of these advisors took part in the ceremony transferring the first MIG-17s and MIG-21s fighters to FAPLA.[36]

United States personnel became involved in Angola well before the country became independent. A team of infantry instructors was sent to Zaire allegedly to train selected UNITA cadres, but the CIA station in Kinshasa hurried to redirect them to Ambriz and Silva Porto. CIA "paramilitary officers" were also training UNITA forces in Silva Porto and FNLA troops in Ambriz. A retired US Army colonel was hired on contract and sent to the FNLA Command in Ambriz. Officers acting inside Angola were going around armed.[37]

The Soviet involvement in Angola produced many "unsung heroes". The Deputy Commander of the Air Transport Wing from the town of Ivanovo is one example. On the eve of the Angola's independence, he risked his life and that of his crew to urgently airlift two BM-21 Grad rocket launchers[38] from Brazzaville to Pointe-Noir, where the runway was unfit for the heavy An-22 transport aircraft.

Putilin recalls that these rocket launchers were brought to Brazzaville from the USSR by giant AN-22 ("Antei", that is "Antheus" in Russian). The need to strengthen MPLA troops in Luanda was obvious, and the Soviet Embassy enquired from Moscow how they could be brought there. "We asked the Centre (read: Moscow) to bring them by air directly to

Luanda. But our request was not granted, because until independence nothing for Neto was sent directly to Angola."

Although an AN-22 weighs 130 tons and the runway in Pointe-Noir was fit for only 90 tons, this was the only alternative. Congolese officials rejected the plan. They were afraid of possible damage to the runway. Putilin had to ask German Prevdechnyi, who, as Councillor of the Soviet Embassy, was a liaison with the Congolese ruling party, for help. Only President Ngouabi himself could give the final go ahead, and the Soviets found him at the cemetery: he was praying for his late mother (the 1st of November was Mother's Day in Brazzaville). The landing was then authorised. The only precautionary measure was two tanks stationed near the end of the runway in case the pilot overshot it. Then, on the 2nd or 3rd of November, the rocket launchers were transported in the space of 24 hours by a Cuban ship to Luanda.[39]

The two rocket launchers were placed to the north of Luanda next to the battalion of the elite Special Forces of the Cuban Ministry of Interior who had been sent to Angola.

Fidel Castro, president of the Republic of Cuba, decided to dispatch combat troops there on the 4th of November.[40] The first batch from that battalion left Cuba on the 7th of November in two outdated Britannia aircraft and after a 48-hour flight reached Luanda on the evening of the 9th of November.[41] In Putilin's opinion this unit was hardly fit for regular warfare. The unit was mainly trained to operate as a small group of guerrillas, most probably for deployment in Latin America.[42] Perhaps the Cuban leadership was preparing for the worst: Castro had told the group that, if Luanda fell, they would fight a guerrilla war that would last as long as the one the MPLA had fought.[43]

Later, Moscow provided assistance with the transportation of Cuban combat units to Angola. Soviet Il-62M passenger planes made 120 flights there.

In January 1976, with South African activities in Angola continuing unabated, the first Angolan Minister of Foreign Affairs (and future president), Jose Eduardo dos Santos, visited Moscow twice. The first time he was in transit to Helsinki, where he took part in the session of the highest body of the World Peace Council together with Ambrosio Lukoki, a member of the MPLA Central Committee, and Afonso van Dunem (Mbinda), who headed Neto's Secretariat in the party.

The Angolan leadership regarded the conflict in Angola as a part of the struggle between the forces of imperialism and progress and argued that hostilities there were not a civil war. Rather, they were naked aggression against the new post-colonial government who had struggled long for its independence. "American imperialism is our direct enemy," the MPLA representatives emphasised. In particular they drew Soviet attention to the "strange borders" of Angola, which contributed to the gravity of the situation. There were about 2 200 kilometres of border with Mobutu's Zaire, pro-Savimbi Zambia and Pretoria-occupied Namibia, from which South Africans operated while the northern invasions took place. The only friendly border was with Congo-Brazzaville in Cabinda, isolated from the main part of Angolan territory.

Dos Santos visited the Solidarity Committee's premises. His discussions with the Soviet government officials were intensive. Dos Santos called his mission to Moscow "extraordinary" as it was taking place while "the second liberation war" was waged in Angola against South African and Zairean troops, who had invaded the country under the cover of FNLA and UNITA.[44]

The Angolan Foreign Minister correctly pointed out that apart from the USA and France, South Africa was assisting the invaders. The first aim of the invading forces was to prevent the independence of Angola, but they failed. If they could not achieve this, they were supposed to try to weaken, if not divide, the country. South Africa, whose troops occupied five provincial centres, wanted to establish its control in the south, "to ensure a new border to the north of the Benguela railway".[45] However, according to him, "the Angolan [and Cuban] troops launched a counter-offensive and have already advanced about 60 km towards Nova Lisboa. This offensive was made possible due to material and technical aid of the USSR and assistance of Cuba in training our units and by [their participating] combatants."[46] In the north of the country the situation was good; almost all of the areas had been liberated, though the threat of further interventions via Zaire could not be discounted. Soviet-Angolan cooperation was becoming increasingly an all-around exercise.

Under pressure from the Cubans and FAPLA, South African troops had to withdraw from Angolan territory by the end of March 1976. The Zairean interventionist forces and their allies were defeated as well. This was not the end of the war, as many in Angola and abroad expected. After his visit to Angola in March 1977, Fidel Castro stated: "Things are going well in Angola. They achieved good progress in their first year of independence…. There are no grounds for dissatisfaction there." But at the same time he was concerned about developments in the Angolan Army: "The Defence Ministry is doing hardly anything to fight bandits in the north and south of the country. The bands are particularly active in the centre of the country."[47]

The Soviet Union cooperated with independent Angola in various fields, but because of the complicated situation within the country and in southern Africa, the military aspect became the most important. This cooperation was mutually advantageous. Soviet naval ships could enter the port of Luanda. Moreover, the Angolan capital became the base of the headquarters of the 30th Operational Squadron of the Soviet Navy. In the late 1980s, this squadron consisted of 11 ships, three of which would stay in Luanda with the rest protecting fishing vessels in the Atlantic Ocean. In the opinion of General Valery Belyaev, who served in Angola at that time, "This squadron by its very presence was restraining the South African aggression against Angola…"[48] Soviet surface ships and submarines could refuel and their crews could rest.[49] In addition, Tu-95RTs reconnaissance aircraft of the Soviet Navy were allowed to land in Luanda. Flying from the Soviet North to Havana, then to Luanda and back to the USSR they "were giving a full 'picture' of the situation in the Atlantic".[50]

On the other hand, apart from supplies of military hardware, the Soviet *assessors* (advisors) in Angola carried out their "international duty" under the most difficult conditions, serving on different levels, from General Staff to battalion personnel as well as in training establishments.

The 1980s

The Soviet military mission was headed by a Chief Military Advisor (Glavnyi voennyi sovetnik – GVS in Russian) who usually replaced each other in cycles of two or three years. The most prominent of them was Lieutenant-General (later Colonel-General) Konstantin Kurochkin, who served in Angola from 1982 to 1985. His notebooks contained transcriptions or summaries of his meetings with Angolans and Cubans. The general granted the authors access to his notes to demonstrate that, in spite of overall excellent bilateral relations, differences arose from time to time. For example, one of the "stumbling blocks" was a question of payment for "grey" hardware, such as transport MI-8 helicopters and trucks as well as for the services of the Soviet civilian pilots, though they were risking their lives daily.[51]

It has to be mentioned that, contrary to Cold War propaganda, Angola had continuous economic ties with several Western powers. Many soft-skinned vehicles intended for military purposes were among the goods imported from Western countries and paid for.

Another issue arose when newspapers in Lisbon reported in January 1983 that Angola had requested the help of Portuguese military instructors.[52] When Kurochkin raised this question with "Pedale", the Minister of Defence explained that the instructors would be recruited from among Angolan citizens who used to serve as commandos in the colonial army and "would be helped by progressive former officers".[53]

The Angolans admitted later, though confidentially, that the Portuguese authorities agreed to train up to 40 Angolan commando instructors in Portugal. They tried to convince "General Konstantin" that this "temporary measure" did not mean the replacement of Soviet and Cuban advisors and the training of one or two commando battalions would not prevent the formation of the assault brigades agreed upon earlier.[54]

Several commando battalions were formed. In Kurochkin's view their training was sub-optimal. Individual training was deemed good, but their performance as platoons, companies and battalions was poor and discipline was not up to standard.[55]

High-level cooperation and mutual understanding between the Soviets and Cubans is demonstrated by the fact that in February 1983, at the request of Dos Santos, recommendations on the struggle against UNITA were jointly worked out and presented to the Angolan president.[56] Soviets and Cubans jointly participated in drafting the plan of a major operation, approved by Dos Santos as commander-in-chief. [57]

South African support for UNITA continued. With the support of arms provided by South Africa via occupied Namibia, UNITA concentrated several thousand troops in the region.[58] By the 2nd of August 1983, UNITA had reached the airfield of Cangamba. Ninety-two Cuban servicemen and about 800 Angolan troops were surrounded in the area.[59] They successfully defended the town and on the 9th of August UNITA was forced to withdraw. Then, as it had happened earlier and would happen later, Pretoria came to UNITA's assistance by bombing the town.[60]

The Cuban High Command in Havana subsequently decided to change the plan of operations. They began a new operation on the 8th of August, having sent a battalion of special paratroopers to Angola. The operation was to continue for a month and "Polo" had to inform the Angolan president that this would be the last operation in the area in which the Cubans would participate.[61]

Kurochkin did not oppose the Cuban plan, but expressed a number of reservations. In particular, he thought that the operation should be better planned and should therefore start later; and that the brigades stationed in southern Angola should not be redeployed to the north as the Cubans suggested. Kurochkin also initially objected to the involvement of the SWAPO brigade. "The use of the SWAPO units in fighting UNITA should not be a rule, though in some cases they may be pulled in operations to acquire combat experience....[62] This is the future of the Namibian Army and we have no moral right to use SWAPO in the struggle against UNITA."[63] However later, when the situation further deteriorated, he had to give his consent and members of the SWAPO brigade proved to be exemplary fighters.

One of the issues which "Polo" discussed with Kurochkin was the participation of the Soviet advisors and specialists in the combat actions of FAPLA brigades. Kurochkin explained that while five or six Soviet staff members were available in each brigade, their participation in combat actions was "categorically prohibited", but in any case they would take part in preparing the operation.[64]

However, in practice this "categorical prohibition" was not always observed. "General Konstantin" himself insisted that if Soviet assessors were attached to Angolan units they must take part in raids. Later, in 1987, such an approach was endorsed by Moscow: by the order of the Defence Minister Soviet specialists had to accompany FAPLA battle formations and could not stay behind at the command posts as before.[65]

With the intensification of SAAF flights over Angolan territory, the task of defending Luanda became urgent as well. By the end of 1983 *Pechora* anti-aircraft missiles were brought in. Before this, the air defence of the capital was performed by the "Admiral Nakhimov", a "big anti-submarine ship"[66] or, according to NATO classification, a frigate.

A major operation with the participation of Cuban troops was planned for early October, but it was postponed several times. The operation eventually started on the 15th of October.[67] Fidel Castro insisted on success, a victory.[68] The operation was quite successful, both its first stage and the second, which began on the 1st of November.[69] The Air Force played an important part and performed 1 004 combat sorties and 160 reconnaissance flights.[70] This success made it possible to think about the next major operation intended to destroy "the first strategic front" of UNITA in Moxico and Cuando-Cubango in 1984.[71] Meanwhile another operation, named the "27th Anniversary of MPLA", was to begin on the 10th of December 1983 aimed at destroying "the remnants of the 2nd strategic front of UNITA", but again delays occurred.[72]

Finally, the operation started, but some days earlier on the 6th of December Pretoria launched Operation Askari, intensifying its intervention in southern Angola. Most probably Askari had two aims: to relieve pressure on UNITA and to force more concessions from the Angolan government at the bilateral talks which had resumed with the USA as a "mediator". The bombing of FAPLA positions was followed by ground attacks. According to Kurochkin's report to Dos Santos, Pretoria concentrated up to ten battalions there, including three battalions "from Namibia" (so-called SWATF) and two of UNITA, but the Angolan brigades were (initially) effectively repelling enemy attacks.[73] However, the South Africans managed to occupy Cuvelai and defeated the Angolan 11th Brigade stationed there.[74] These actions vindicated Kurochkin's earlier reluctance to transfer units from southern Angola.

The developments in this region brought about some differences between Kurochkin and "Polo". The Cuban general suggested withdrawing three brigades to the north, where air cover could be provided. However, "General Konstantin" thought that it would be wrong to leave well-equipped positions and that these brigades were powerful enough to rebuff even a numerically stronger enemy.[75]

Undeniably the resistance offered by the Angolan troops in late 1983 and early 1984 to the South African intervention was much stronger than before. Constand Viljoen, then the SADF Chief, called this response "unexpectedly fierce".[76]

"Pedale" supported Kurochkin's approach. Pedale could not understand the strategy of the Cuban Command aimed at bringing all the forces back to the second echelon of defence.[77] However, this very approach was confirmed in Fidel Castro's message to Dos Santos divulged by "Polo" to Kurochkin on the 7th of January 1984. He regarded the withdrawal of the Angolan brigades close to the area of the deployment of the Cuban forces (Jamba-Matala-Lubango) as the only way out. Besides, Fidel claimed that the airplanes, based in Lubango, could not operate over "the area of fighting" due to too long distances and the superiority of the enemy air force.[78] At this stage the South African Air Force (SAAF) still held the upper hand, especially since Cuban forces were not deployed over Cahama, Mulondo and Cuvelai.

The Soviet reply was quite different: "By no means should the brigades of the 5th Military District be withdrawn.... By no means should the territories up to Mocademes-Lubango-Menonge line be given up to South Africans, because it is fraught with political consequences."[79] On the contrary, Moscow recommended the strengthening of these brigades by creating two or three tactical groups, preferably with Cuban tank and motorised infantry battalions for each group. Besides, Moscow was of the opinion that their own air forces could be involved in aerial engagements over Cahama and Mulondo. "Pedale" supported this view.[80]

Kurochkin, referring to the request of the Commander of the Military District and "all the fighters of the 53rd Brigade", suggested changing the order of its retreat. "Pedale" replied that it had already been cancelled, though reserve positions had to be prepared.[81]

The Cuban approach was mostly political: their decision whether to take part in the operation or not depended on the results of talks with "Kitu", the head of the Angolan team at the meetings with Americans and South Africans, who was in Havana at that time.

One of the problems, which constantly worried Kurochkin during his stay in Angola, was the weak intelligence capacity of the allied forces and especially the leakage of information to the enemy. He once plainly stated to Dos Santos: "UNITA knows all operational plans."[82]

Tripartite Soviet-Angolan-Cuban consultations, which became an annual event, were held in Moscow in January 1985. This meeting resulted in the decision to strengthen the defence capacity to uphold the independence and territorial integrity of Angola.

General Kurochkin left Angola in June 1985. He himself recommended his successor, Lieutenant-General L. Kuzmenko, who was his colleague. Before going to Angola, Kuzmenko was Deputy Commander of the Soviet Air Borne Troops (*Vozdusno-Desantnye Voiska – VDV in Russian*) for combat training.[83] But to match "General Konstantin" was not easy for anybody. Two years later, in 1987, a replacement arrived, namely Lieutenant-General Petr Gusev, Deputy Commander of the Carpathian Military District in Western

Ukraine. However, the VDV (Airborne Forces) people were there as well. The most prominent of them being Lieutenant-General Valery Belyaev who in 1988–1991 was the advisor of the Chief of General Staff and for some time the Acting GVS.[84]

A major offensive against UNITA's 1st Strategic Front, so important in Kurochkin's opinion, was launched later in 1985, when he had already left Angola. This operation, named "MPLA Second Congress", was planned in two directions: towards Cazombo in the eastern part of Angola and in the south-east. It resulted in the liberation of Cazombo, but its main goal was a different one; that is Mavinga, and the troops were secretly concentrated in that direction.[85] UNITA, as usual supported by Pretoria, tried to keep Cazombo under its control and offered stiff resistance. Part of the forces, destined for advance to Mavinga, had to be transferred to Cazombo. At the time when FAPLA was already approaching Cazombo, an offensive towards Mavinga began as well. UNITA was pushed back and in September 1985 South Africa had to move its troops there in support of UNITA. In previous years, such as the time after the retreat in 1976, the SADF operated mainly in the Cunene province, not far from the Namibian border. However, in 1985 they penetrated much deeper.[86]

Besides FAPLA's actions being hampered by long routes of supply and sandy terrain; vehicles consumed up to two litres of fuel just to progress one kilometre. Air support was complicated as well. South African forces acquired radar to detect aircraft, especially helicopters at low altitudes. Against these odds, FAPLA's offensive was rebuffed with a major loss of arms and equipment.[87]

1987 and 1988

The next attempt was made two years later, in 1987. Meanwhile, Washington's support for UNITA (and therefore, in practice, for Pretoria's troops) was increasing. In July 1985 the USA Congress repealed the Clark Amendment, which restricted aid to UNITA.[88] If Savimbi's visits to the USA were informal earlier on, in January 1986 Ronald Reagan received UNITA's leader in the White House, saying to him "We want to be very helpful to Dr Savimbi and what he is trying to do."[89] This statement by Reagan was an expression of the US policy of constructive engagement. In fact, constructive engagement was to provide Pretoria and Savimbi with space to step up their adventures, and once again the conflict escalated.

Speaking on the occasion of the thirtieth anniversary of the Cuban Military Mission in Angola, Fidel Castro quite correctly said: "Angola's post-victory [in early 1976] prospects without the political and logistic support of the USSR were non-existent."[90] Castro continued: "This is not the right time to discuss the differing strategic and tactical conceptions of the Cubans and the Soviets."

The Soviets advised the military high command and provided ample supplies of weaponry to the Angolan armed forces. Actions based on the advice given at the top level caused the Russians quite a few headaches. Nonetheless, great respect and strong feelings of solidarity and understanding always prevailed between the Cuban and Soviet military.[91] It remains to be added that just as did the Cubans, the Soviets trained tens of thousands of Angolan soldiers. Soviet personnel acted as advisors, not only for the "high command" but also in the combat operations of Angolan troops.

The hostilities in Angola culminated in the "battle at Cuito Cuanavale" in late 1987 and early 1988. There the South African troops were held back without any ability to advance. Their frontal attacks eventually exhausted, the scales turned against the South Africans. In the words of Castro: "… while in Cuito Cuanavale the South African troops were bled, to the southwest 40 000 Cuban and 30 000 Angolan troops [and SWAPO fighters as well], supported by some 600 tanks,[92] hundreds of pieces of artillery, 1 000 anti-aircraft weapons and the daring MiG-23 units that secured air supremacy, advanced towards the Namibian border, ready to literally sweep up the South African forces deployed along that main route."[93] With air superiority lost and virtually no space to manoeuvre except for the use of artillery barrages, the situation for the SADF was moving beyond stalemate.

The rebuffs at Cuito Cuanavale, especially the advance by the powerful Cuban contingent in south-west Angola, spelled the end of foreign aggression. Choices for the apartheid forces were small and withdrawal was on the cards. The debacle of South Africa and UNITA at Cuito Cuanavale, and the advance towards the Namibian border created favourable conditions for the completion of talks on the so-called Angolan-Namibian settlement on conditions acceptable to Luanda and Havana and for signing the December 1988 New York agreements.

Peace was to arrive only years later in Angola following the death of Jonas Savimbi whose ineffectual movement, UNITA, had been built up through foreign intervention since 1975 to become a major destabilising factor in Angola. What was in Western corridors glibly called a "small war" was by no means a small war for Angola and its people.

Notes

1.   Stockwell, J., *In Search of Enemies. A CIA Story* (London: Andre Deutsch, 1978), 67ff.
2.   The Chinese were soon to withdraw their support from these two movements upon realising that they received support from the CIA (Western intelligence sources and Pretoria).
3.   Ignatyev, O., *Secret Weapon in Africa* (Moscow: Progress Publishers, 1977), 118.
4.   Presentation by Roberto Leal Ramos Monteiro "Ngongo", Angola's Ambassador to the Russian Federation at the meeting with the Soviet veterans at the Angolan Embassy in Moscow on the occasion of the 25th anniversary of independence, 13 November, 2000.
5.   Stockwell, 66.
6.   Ibid., 68.

7. Interview with B. Putilin, Moscow, 22 February 2007. Daniel R. Kempton, in his *Soviet Strategy toward Southern Africa. The National Liberation Connection* (New York, Westport, London: Preager, 1989: 91) claims that "just prior to independence" Moscow offered "to airlift additional arms directly to Angola", but Neto "declined the offer on the grounds that Soviet personnel were to be used to secure the airport". He does not give any reference, but in any case the Soviets, on the contrary, were ready to do it only after independence. Besides, when supplies did go later from Congo-Brazzaville to Luanda, no Soviet personnel were involved.

8. Interview with B. Putilin and A. Tokarev, Moscow, 10 and 17 November 2004.

9. Interview with R. Monteiro "Ngongo", Moscow, 17 July 2002.

10. Stockwell, 52–53.

11. Ibid., 55.

12. Ibid., 63–64. Much earlier a similar assessment was made by the British Consulate in Luanda: "Of the three Angolan nationalist organisations opposing the Portuguese in Angola, the MPLA would seem to be the most effective both in the present terms and in future potential." (National Archives, FCO 25/266. Portuguese colonies. 1968. M.P.L.A. Brit. C-te–Gen. Luanda, 9 July 1968.)

13. Piero Gleijeses's interview with Robert W. Hultslander, former CIA Station Chief in Luanda, Angola, http://www.gwu.edu/~nsarchiv/NSAEBB/NSAEBB67/transcript.html.

14. Apparently an important role in MPLA's success was played by a couple of Soviet-made BTR-152 APCs supplied by Yugoslavia (or, according to other sources, Algeria).

15. Discussion with the MPLA delegation headed by E. Carreira, Moscow, 19 August 1975.

16. According to Stockwell the CIA chart, prepared for Committee of 40 on the contrary indicated that MPLA had about 20 000 soldiers and FNLA roughly 15 000. He writes: "Roberto had repeatedly claimed to have 30 000 troops, but we had arbitrarily halved that figure because none of us believed him." (Stockwell, 91). Nonetheless, from current information it is clear that the CIA grossly overestimated FAPLA strength.

17. Ibid.

18. Ibid.

19. Discussion with the MPLA delegation (G. Bires and M. Neto), Moscow, 25 September 1975.

20. Ibid.

21. Stockwell, 185.

22. Discussion with I. Uvarov, Moscow, 23 October 2003.

23. Ibid. It should be mentioned that France was deeply involved then (as still today) in central African countries. French interests were also bolstered by military support for "friendly states". Zaire had French support; among others, its air force was supplied with French Mirage aircraft.

24. Ibid.

25. Stockwell, 215. Stockwell mistakenly mentioned 11 November as the date of this battle.

26. Ibid., 214–215.

27. According to Monteiro "Ngongo" Grad-P then moved on bicycles, which were used for the first time by the MPLA on the Eastern Front in 1974, after the Portuguese revolution on the eve of cease-fire.

28. Discussion with R. Monteiro "Ngongo" Quifangondo, 21 November 2004. He was trained as a Grad operator in Simferopol in 1972–1973 and then as an artillery commander in Solnechnogorsk near Moscow in March-July1975. Later he served as Deputy Minister of Defence, Ambassador to Russia, and Minister of the Interior.

29. Interview with R. Monteiro "Ngongo", Moscow, 15 December 2004.

30. According to Putilin, it was Jose Eduardo Dos Santos, a Soviet graduate, who translated the ambassador's speech into Portuguese.

31. The name of this "republic" was hardly accidental. It followed the Algerian model.

32. Chipenda broke away from the MPLA at the "Congress of MPLA" convened in Zambia in August 1974 by its host countries. In Lisbon the ruling Portuguese Movement of Armed Forces and the Portuguese Communist Party, then rather influential, refused to recognise Chipenda as the MPLA's leader. Daniel Chipenda joined the FNLA after his attempt to seize the leadership of the MPLA failed.

33. The first five Mirages arrived in Zaire in 1975.

34. A detailed story of this mission was described in: [Colonel] Tokarev, A., *Komandirovka v Angolu* (*Mission to Angola*), *Aziya i Afrika segodnya* (*Asia and Africa Today*), no. 2(2001): 36–41. Willem Steenkamp in *South Africa's Border War. 1966–1989* (Gibraltar: Ashanti Publishing, 1989), 54, claims that in December 1975 South African forces at Cariango "were attacked by jet fighters"; however, this is just one of many inaccuracies in Steenkamp's rather propagandist book. Unfortunately such inaccuracies also appear in other books published on the war in South Africa, some of them referred to in this chapter.

35. *Aziya i Afrika segodnya*, 38–39.

36. Ibid., 41. 10 MIG-17F, 12 MIG-21MF as well as 30 helicopters were supplied to Angola by April 1976 (www.veteanangola.ru/main/obsuzhdenie/KOL%29SU).

37. Stockwell, 177.

38. BM-21 is a later model of the famous "Katyusha" (BM-13), widely used during World War II.

39. Interview with B. Putilin, 10 and 17 November 2004. "Desyatka" in Soviet military slang meant the 10th Main Department of the General Staff; its successor in Russia is "the Main Department of International Military Co-operation".

40. Gleijeses, 305.

41. Ibid., 308.

42. Interview with B. Putilin, Moscow, 10 and 17 November 2004.

43. Gleijeses, 308.

44. Discussion with J.E. dos Santos, Moscow, 23 January 1976.

45. Ibid.

46. Ibid.

47. Cold War International History Project. Woodrow Wilson International Center for Scholars. Fidel Castro's 1977 Southern Africa Tour: A Report to Honecker. *Bulletin* 8–9.

48. *40 let vmeste. 1961–2001. Materialynaucho-prakticheskoi konferentsii.* (40 years together, Materials of scientific-practical conference). Moscow, Lean, 2002. c.62.

49. Published interview with V.N. Belyaev, *Krasnaya zvezda* [Red Star], 9 September 2000. However, all these facilities were not regarded as Soviet military bases, after all Angola's Constitution (Article 16) expressly prohibited "the installation of foreign military bases".

50. Ibid.

51. Ibid., 86–87.

52. Ibid., 3–4.

53. Ibid.

54. Ibid., 9.

55. K. Kurochkin's notebook 3: 78.

56. K. Kurochkin's notebook 2: 15.

57. Ibid., 29.

58. Press conference of Monterio "Ngongo", Deputy Chief of the General Staff, 24 August 1983, *Angola Information Bulletin*, London, 23 September 1983.

59. K. Kurochkin's notebook 2: 50.

60. *Angola Information Bulletin.*

61. K. Kurochkin's notebook 2: 50.

62. Ibid., 18.

63.   Ibid., 50.

64.   Ibid., 51.

65.   Interview of V.N. Belyaev, *Krasnaya zvesda*, 9 September 2000.

66.   Ibid. K. Kurochkin's notebook 2: 61.

67.   K. Kurochkin's notebook 2: 88.

68.   Ibid., 91.

69.   Ibid., 95–96.

70.   K. Kurochkin's notebook 3: 14.

71.   Ibid., 3.

72.   Ibid., 9, 11, 12.

73.   Ibid., 25.

74.   Ibid., 26. It was found that the brigade acting commander gave an order to retreat as soon as communications were cut off; as Kurochkin said to Dos Santos, "the brigade run away not during the combat, but after it. If the brigade has stayed on its positions, South African troops would retreat". (Ibid., 33)

75.   Ibid., 27.

76.   Minter, W., *Apartheid's Contrast. An Inquiry into the Roots of War in Angola and Mozambique* (Witwatersrand University Press. Johannesburg: Zed Books. London and New Jersey, 1994) 44.

77.   K. Kurochkin's notebook 3: 27.

78.   Ibid., 28.

79.   Ibid., 29.

80.   Ibid.

81.   Ibid.

82.   Ibid., 65.

83.   One of the Soviet specialists recalls: "They [Soviet military authorities] understood and began inviting GVSs from the VDV, because the tactics of the airborne troops are more suitable for guerrilla warfare, while officers from Ground Troops were implanting linear tactics. (Interview with Colonel (Ret) Vyacheslav Mityaev, Moscow, 11 April 2005, by G. Shubin.)

84.   After his return from Angola, Belyaev served as the Chief of Staff of the Russian Airborne Troops from 1991 till 1998 and was promoted to the rank of colonel-general. He died in July 2003 (*Moskovsky Komsomolets*, 19 July 2003).

85.   Interview with R. Monteiro "Ngongo", Moscow, 17 July 2002. A South African medic was captured there, which proved that SADF personnel acted in the depths of Angolan territory.

86.   Ibid.

87.   Ibid.

88.   Hanlon, J., *Beggar Your Neighbours. Apartheid Power in Southern Africa* (London: Catholic Institute for International Relations, 1986), 165.

89.   Ibid., 170.

90.   Speech by Dr Fidel Castro Ruz, President of the Republic of Cuba, at the ceremony commemorating the 30th anniversary of the Cuban Military Mission in Angola and the 49th anniversary of the landing of the "Granma", Revolutionary Armed Forces Day, December 2, 2005.

91.   Ibid.

92.   In another statement Fidel mentioned 1 000 tanks (Castro, Fidel, *Vincicación de Cuba* (Cuba's Vindication) (Havana: Editora Política Publishers, 1989), 404.

93.   Colonel Jan Breytenbach, former Commander of 32nd Battalion admits that South African forces in Northern Namibia were "suddenly faced with a major threat.... The SADF's preoccupation with saving Savimbi had left its Ovamboland flank wide open" (Breytenbach J., *The Buffalo Soldiers. The Story of South Africa's 32-Battalion 1975–1993* (Galago), 316–317.

Secret Solidarity
The Military Support provided for the Liberation Movement in Angola by East Germany

Klaus Storkmann and Ulrich van der Heyden

Introduction

There were extremely wild speculations in the Western press about the extent to which East Germany, or, to be more precise, the German Democratic Republic, provided military support for the liberation movement in Angola.

Consider a few examples: In April 1980, the West German news magazine *Der Spiegel* showed a close-up of soldiers from the East German army headlined in large letters "Honecker's Africa Corps". The Hamburg news magazine had some amazing things to report: For four years at the time, the East German army had admitted military personnel from Africa to its officer training schools. Angolans were exercising with the parachute troops in Prora on Rügen Island. The magazine reported that there were 2720 East German military advisors in Africa, 1 000 of them in Angola alone.[1] As early as November 1977, the West German newspaper *Welt am Sonntag* reported the arrival of "a considerable number of coloured soldiers from Angola" for training in the GDR,[2] although they were probably Congolese.

West German press reports repeatedly mentioned that up to 5 000 East German soldiers were fighting alongside the MPLA in Angola. As early as October 1978, the Munich-based *Süddeutche Zeitung* wrote about "3 500 GDR paratroopers" in Angola, with reference to the London-based *Sunday Times*, which in turn cited "Western secret services".[3] In December 1978, the West Berlin-based *Tagesspiegel* printed a report that 5 000 "soldiers from the GDR army", primarily "elite forces such as paratroopers", were in Angola alone.[4] In February 1980, another West Berlin-based daily newspaper, *Die Welt*, stated that the total number of GDR military experts throughout Africa, that is, not only in Angola, was indeed "around 30 000".[5] In the year of German reunification in 1990, the Bonn-based *Bonner Rundschau* published a report that members of the state security service (Staatssicherheit) were still hidden in the African bushes and continued to support the South African liberation movement.[6] In April 1980, the New York-based *Time Magazine* dedicated a special article to the GDR military activities in Angola, significantly entitling it "Here Come Europe's Cubans".[7]

One could go on citing examples of this kind. Reports about thousands of GDR military personnel in Africa are something like the monster of Loch Ness. Even today, former West

German press statements re-appear in publications and live on in recent scientific works, although they are not based on valid sources. Even as late as 2001, Christopher Coker maintained that in 1982, the GDR had planned and coordinated a large-scale military operation together with Cuba, Angola and Mozambique. According to Coker, the plan had been to fly Cuban troops from Angola to Mozambique and to replace them with East German military personnel. Resistance, however, thwarted the plan. In 2001, Coker still based his unproven claims on the strange press reports of the 1970s.[8]

Outlines of the GDR's policy on Africa

Throughout the forty years of the existence of the second German state, Africa by and large played an important role in the GDR's foreign policy. The contents, intensity, objectives and functions of the GDR's relations to the young nation states and national liberation movements on the African continent were, of course, subject to various domestic and international influences.[9]

The distinct characteristics of the GDR's policy on Africa were support of national liberation movements and consistent opposition to any form of colonialism and racism. This is why the liberation movements in southern Africa, which were fighting for their independence, received particular support. The GDR leadership, and not least state and party leader Erich Honecker himself, had a particular eye for southern Africa. The GDR largely agreed with the representatives of the liberation organisations and the leaders of the young nation states on many international issues and acted – as long-term GDR diplomat Hans-Georg Schleicher emphasised – "pronouncedly as their political partner and ally".[10] According to the foreign intelligence service of the East German secret service, the Western states verbally disapproved of the racist regimes in South Africa and Southern Rhodesia, but were not prepared to support the fight of the African peoples for their liberation.[11] This assessment reflects the view of East Berlin at that time. The GDR's policy on Africa was also an interaction with the West German side, which was regarded as a supporter of the colonial regime in Portugal and the regime in the Republic of South Africa.[12]

Due to its weak and ineffective economy, the GDR was limited in its ability to provide material goods and therefore focused on providing education and training for teachers, engineers and specialists, diplomatic and political assistance, care for the sick and wounded[13] and military assistance. The military support provided by the GDR cannot be seen in isolation, but ultimately in the context of other solidarity efforts.

According to statistic data from GDR files, in the period from 1975 to 1989 the GDR provided some 52 million GDR marks for the ANC, almost 110 million marks for SWAPO, 238 million marks for Angola and 277 million marks for Mozambique.[14]

First requests from MPLA to East Germany

Up until the 1990s, Angola had been a theatre of wars and civil wars for almost four decades. The GDR began to provide military support for one of the liberation movements, the Movimento Popular de Libertação de Angola (MPLA) in 1967, as a result of a decision made by the Politburo of the state party SED. Earlier requests from the MPLA, which the GDR had received via its Afro-Asian Solidarity Committee, had always been denied. The records of the Solidarity Committee contain relevant documents from November 1964, in which reference is made to such requests from groups such as the MPLA, the South African ANC, Mozambique's Frente da Libertação de Moçambique (FRELIMO), the Partido Africano da Independência da Guiné e Cabo Verde (PAIGC) from Portuguese Guinea and the Zimbabwean Zimbabwe African People's Union (ZAPU). A "strictly confidential" internal memorandum from November 1964 about the talks with representatives of these organisations in Lusaka and Cairo read: "During the past months, the following liberation movements have requested weapons or military equipment from us or, since they knew that we had denied such deliveries as a matter of principle, have put out a few feelers to see whether our position has changed." The denial was clear. "In all cases we had pursued our previous course that we were unable to deliver weapons."[15] In an archived translation of an undated letter from the MPLA to the state party SED, the Angolans asked not only for equipment for 3 000 fighters, 90 guns, 90 mortars, 30 heavy machine guns, 300 light anti-tank weapons and 1 500 submachine guns, sufficient ammunition for six months for all the weapons that would be delivered and uniforms, but also mess kits, typewriters, 6 000 basketball shoes, drugs and school material such as writing books, chalk and pens.[16] This request was by far not the only one of this kind to reach the rulers in East Berlin from Africa. There was an obvious need for a policy on this issue.

Arms for the independence struggle

On 10 January 1967, the leadership of the state party SED for the first time decided in favour of "delivering non-civilian goods to national liberation movements in Africa."[17] The decision stated that in addition to the secret service and the police supplies, the armed forces were also to provide military equipment and weapons from their stocks. Initially, the liberation movements in Zimbabwe, Mozambique and Portuguese Guinea were to be the recipients of military deliveries in addition to the MPLA in Angola. As indicated in the table, deliveries consisted mainly of older models of small arms and the associated ammunition.

Table listing the weapons and ammunition to be delivered to the African liberation movements in accordance with the Politburo decision of 10 January 1967 (Excerpt).[18]

Item	Designation	FRELIMO	ZAPU	MPLA
1	98 K 7.9 mm carbine	4 800	3 200	1 600
2	Type 34 … 7.9 mm light machine gun	110	75	40
3	7.9 mm cartridges for items 1 and 2	900 000	470 000	240 000
5	7.62 mm sniper rifle	60	40	20
8	Type K. 7.62 mm submachine gun	80	60	30
9	7.62 mm cartridges for item 8	76 000	57 000	28 500
10	Type 43/44 … 7.9 mm submachine gun	80	50	30
13	Anti-personnel mines	2 000	1 000	500

Most of the weapons delivered were old Second World War stocks of the German Wehrmacht that had been kept at GDR depots, but some of them were still in active use. Modern weapons, like the Kalashnikov submachine gun (item 8), were delivered in small numbers only. The anti-personnel mines (item 13) are worthy of note since the mines that were used in large numbers by all the warring factions in the Cold War conflicts in Southern Africa continue to claim victims from the civilian population to this day.

In a detailed four-page statement on the decision, the GDR Ministry of Foreign Affairs provided assessments and evaluations of the situations in the respective countries as well as of the positions of the liberation organisations there. The document argues that the ZAPU, FRELIMO, PAIGC and MPLA were the "most important", "most successful" and "most progressive" liberation movements in their regions, which were characterised by "anti-imperialist attitudes".

What looks like an isolated decision in the wording of the Politburo was *de facto* a precedent-setting fundamental decision. The order derived from that decision for the Minister of National Defence and the Minister of the Interior is indicative of that. They were to retain reserves from their stocks for future requests. The decision of 10 January 1967 thus marked a change in the position of the GDR on weapons deliveries to African liberation movements. Hitherto, general restraint had been exercised; henceforth such deliveries were not simply allowed, but indeed endorsed as acts of "active solidarity" with the fight of the African peoples.

Portugal's membership of NATO contributed to the conviction to support the struggle of the MPLA, FRELIMO and PAIGC against the Portuguese. By 1967, the oldest dictatorship in Western Europe still ruled in Portugal. The power of Antonio de Oliveira Salazar had remained untouched by the allies in 1945. As both a NATO state and a dictatorship, which for East Germans was much like fascism, Portugal provided a double enemy stereotype for the GDR. From the viewpoint of the GDR, the support of independence fighters in

Angola, Mozambique and Guinea-Bissau could be connected to the bloc confrontation between NATO and the Eastern bloc in Europe. The memories of fascism and the type of regime in Portugal certainly also played a role.

Military assistance and the civil war

The attainment of independence from the Portuguese colonial power in 1975 did not bring peace to Angola. Instead, wars and civil wars raged for more than two decades. The MPLA, the União Nacional para a Independência Total de Angola (UNITA), and the Frente Nacional da Libertação de Angola (FNLA) fought for power in the new state. While the MPLA held the capital of Luanda and thus formal government power, the opposition groups that were actively supported by South Africa, Zaire and at least indirectly the United States and West European governments ruled over the provinces in the north and the south. With respect to their actions in the Cold War on the side of the West, the government, military and secret service of South Africa saw themselves as a "bulwark against the Communist aggression" in a "proxy war".[19] Angola and the other direct or indirect neighbours of South Africa, who called themselves "front line countries", were on the other side of this war – and thus, whether intentionally or unintentionally – on the side of the Eastern bloc and the Soviet Union. Consequently, the Soviet Union, the GDR, Cuba and other states provided military and other aid.

Luanda never stopped submitting requests for military assistance from the GDR. In 1975 and 1976, the SED Politburo dealt with "non-civilian" aid for the MPLA on a monthly basis, sometimes even several times a month. "Non-civilian" was the term used by the GDR government for military assistance. The delivery for which the decision was made on 5 December 1975, for instance, was worth 6,3 million GDR marks, while the delivery for which the decision was made on 3 February 1976 was worth 6,5 million GDR marks.[20] SED Secretary General Erich Honecker often saw to the details of the military deliveries himself. Honecker's affinity with the Third World was well known among the Africans, who often used their personal contacts with him to secure new or additional military assistance from the GDR.

The leader of the MPLA, Agostino Neto, also expected such assistance. During the fierce struggle for power in Angola preceding the declaration of independence planned for November 1975, Neto personally addressed Honecker in a letter. The letter was handed over by the military leader of the MPLA, Iko Carreira, during his visit to East Berlin in August 1975. The same day, Honecker confirmed the proposals for military support submitted by Carreira's negotiating partner, Horst Dohlus. The GDR's immediate military assistance for MPLA included 10 000 submachine guns and ten million cartridges,

10 000 hand grenades, 4 000 fragmentation and hollow grenades, 40 pistols, steel helmets and uniforms.[21]

In urgent cases, the Secretary General made decisions quickly and on his own. A "formal" Politburo decision was submitted later, if necessary, as was the case in this instance. The Politburo approved Neto's "request" for immediate military assistance at the next meeting on 9 September 1975. The cost of six million GDR marks was to be covered by the Solidarity Committee.[22] In November of the same year, Honecker responded in the same unconventional manner to a new appeal by Neto to the SED Central Committee on 31 October 1975. Neto's list included 15 82 mm guns, eight 120 mm mortars, several thousand grenades and 1,4 million rounds of ammunition for the Kalashnikov submachine guns.[23]

Between October 1975 and April 1977, the GDR delivered military equipment worth 17,5 million GDR marks to the MPLA.[24] The delivery lists, which are accessible today in the archives, clearly show the ratio between military and purely civilian assistance. In 1975, the ratio between civilian and military assitance was twelve to six million GDR marks.[25]

Angola expressed its thanks in manifold ways. In June 1977, President Agostino Neto wrote to Erich Honecker to thank the SED and the GDR for the "extensive political, diplomatic and other assistance" that had been granted to his country "in an extremely brotherly and selfless manner". He would continue to count on the solidarity of the socialist states.[26]

The GDR Minister of National Defence's visit to Angola in 1978

The report of the former GDR Minister of National Defence, Army General Heinz Hoffmann, about his visit to Angola, Guinea and the People's Republic of the Congo in May 1978 contains remarkable references to far-reaching promises and assurances Honecker had made to the African partners. The stipulations issued by the party and state leader hardly left any room for the National People's Army's leadership to make any decisions of its own in its talks and negotiations, since the GDR military personnel were bound by Honecker's word. The military deliveries that were agreed in the course of Hoffmann's visit on the basis of the promises made by the SED leader were worth a total of 18,45 million GDR marks. It is no wonder that – according to Hoffmann's report – on several occasions the African partners expressed their sincere appreciation for the policy and solidarity of the GDR and in particular for the "exemplary work of Comrade Erich Honecker" and their "very high appreciation and esteem" for the solidarity of the GDR.[27]

During the talks, the Angolans issued further requests for military deliveries. According to Hoffmann, requests for warships, combat aircraft and communications equipment were immediately denied, as they were considered impossible to meet. Assurance was given, however, that the requests of the Angolan army leadership for engineering and automotive equipment would be examined. Requests for field kitchens, tents and medical equipment were immediately approved by the NVA. Furthermore, the East German defence minister offered to provide training for Angolan military personnel in the GDR, to enable wounded Angolan military personnel to receive treatment in the GDR and even to deploy NVA military physicians in Angola.[28]

Irrespective of the extensive solidarity aid, Hoffmann argued in his report in favour of long-term commercial supply relationships being established with Angola. This is how he wanted to compensate for the negative trade balance with Angola. In return, Hoffmann thought that Angola could specifically deliver coffee to the GDR.[29]

By the way: Contrary to what was written in the West German press reports mentioned at the beginning, the GDR did not train military personnel from Angola, that is, from the MPLA. This is the astonishing conclusion that can be drawn after years of research in the files.[30]

Conclusion

It is a well-known fact that the conflict between the superpowers was also fought in the Third World. Both the East and West were aware of the significance of the countries of the South. The East-West conflict of the "North" thus fueled the wars of the "South", the one in Angola in particular. The GDR military assistance for the MPLA and other liberation movements was not a singular occurrence. It was, for one, embedded in the foreign policy of East Berlin in its entirety and for another closely coordinated with Moscow.

The military assistance provided by the GDR cannot therefore be seen in isolation, but must be considered as being embedded in the other solidarity efforts and in deliberate interaction with the actions of the West German side, which the East German government regarded as a supporter of the colonial regime in Portugal and the regime in South Africa. Portugal's membership of NATO might also have contributed towards motivating East Germany to support the struggle of the MPLA against the Portuguese. As a NATO state and a dictatorship akin to fascism, Portugal provided a double enemy stereotype for the GDR.

The GDR leadership was sceptical about deploying military personnel to Africa. The "state and party leadership" and in particular the military top brass saw – and not without reason – the danger of the GDR being drawn into the conflicts and wars there with its soldiers. The GDR and its armed forces did not take this risk – apart from making minor exceptions and sending personnel as members, say, of advisory groups.

The concept of solidarity was an important motivation for the GDR leadership. From 1990 to this day, there has always been talk of the state party engaging in "decreed solidarity" for the peoples of Africa. The sense of solidarity among the people of the GDR, however, was far more widespread and genuine, as relevant research confirms.[31] The commitment to solidarity was born and kept alive by political convictions and the ruling ideology. As former top-level GDR military personnel still recall, the prevailing attitude was that "We have to help", "We have to do something". The GDR leadership regarded the African liberation movements as "natural allies". In this ideology, foreign policy and strategic considerations all merged.

Notes

1. Wir haben euch Waffen und Brot geschickt, in: *Der Spiegel*, No. 10, 1980, 42–61 and front page.

2. Farbige Soldaten in der „DDR", *Welt am Sonntag*, 27 November 1977.

3. Geheimdienste bestätigen: DDR-Ausbilder bei der SWAPO, in: *Süddeutsche Zeitung*, 23 October 1978.

4. Strauß berichtet von 5.000 DDR-Soldaten in Angola, in: *Der Tagesspiegel*, 02 December 1978.

5. Vielain, Heinz: Honeckers Afrika-Korps ist 30.000 Mann stark, in: *Die Welt*, 12 February 1980.

6. Wysacki, Cordula: Stasi-Mitarbeiter im afrikanischen Busch versteckt; in: *Bonner Rundschau*, 19 March 1991.

7. Here Come Europe's Cubans, in: *Time*, 21 April 1980, 14.

8. Coker, Christopher: NATO and Africa 1949–89. An Overview, in: *A History of NATO. The First Fifty Years*, Vol. 1, ed. by. Gustav Schmidt, Houndmills/New York 2001, 153–171, here 167–169.

9. The authors published the results of their research in a piece for the French journal *Outre-Mers Revue d'Histoire* entitled «l'aide militaire accordée par la République Démocratique Allemande aux mouvements de libération dans le sud de l'Afrique» as early as in 2011 (*Outre-Mers Revue d'Histoire*, 2/2011, 107–139). The research findings on military issues are based on the dissertation of Klaus Storkmann entitled "Geheime Solidarität", which was published in 2012 (*Geheime Solidarität. Militärbeziehungen und Militärhilfen der DDR in die Dritte Welt*, Berlin, 2012).

10. Schleicher, Hans-Georg: Spurensuche im Süden Afrikas. Die Zusammenarbeit mit den Befreiungsbewegungen wirkt nach, in: Kunze, Thomas/Vogel, Thomas (eds.): *Ostalgie international. Erinnerungen an die DDR von Nicaragua bis Vietnam*, Berlin 2010, 48.

11. Bundesbeauftragte für die Unterlagen des Staatssicherheitsdienstes der ehemaligen DDR (Federal Commissioner for the Files of the State Security Service of the former German Democratic Republic – BStU), in the following cited as BStU: MfS-Zentralarchiv: HVA, No. 65, 188.

12. Engel, Ulf/Schleicher, Hans-Georg: *Die beiden deutschen Staaten in Afrika. Zwischen Konkurrenz und Koexistenz 1949–1990*, Hamburg 1998.

13. For information on this: Reichardt, *Achim: Nie vergessen. Solidarität üben!*, Berlin 2006, in particular 77.

14. The expenses indicated for the year 1989 are only mentioned in the statistics as planned payments. Extensive statistic data can be found in: Schleicher, Ilona: Statistische Angaben zur Solidarität mit Befreiungsbewegungen und Staaten im südlichen Afrika, in: van der Heyden, Ulrich/Schleicher, Ilona/Schleicher, Hans-Georg (eds.): *Engagiert für Afrika. Die DDR und Afrika* II, Münster/Hamburg 1994, 152.

15. Federal Archives (BArch), quoted in the following as BArch: DZ 8/31 (no pagination): Memorandum of 6 November 1964.

16. BArch: DZ 8/7301–662 (no pagination): Translation of letter from MPLA, undated.

17. Stiftung Parteien und Massenorganisationen der DDR im Bundesarchiv (Foundation of Parties and Mass Organizations of the GDR in the Federal Archives – SAPMO-BArch), in the following quoted as SAPMO-BArch: DY 30/J IV 2/2/1093: Politburo meeting on 10 January 1967, agenda item 15 and annex 5.

18. SAPMO-BArch: DY 30/J IV 2/2/1093: Politburo meeting on 10 January 1967, Annex 5.

19. "In so doing, the [South African] military acted in the Cold War framework, seeing and presenting 'its role within the international system as the Southern African bulwark against Communist aggression and on the side of the West in a war of proxy'. Quoted from: Pfister, Roger: Trying to Safeguard the Impossible: South Africa's Apartheid Intelligence in Africa, 1961–1994 (*The Journal of Intelligence History*, No. 2, Münster 2007/2006, 25).

20. BArch: DC 20/12853, 47 et seq.

21. SAPMO-BArch, DY 30/ IV 2/12/55, 141 et seq.

22. SAPMO-BArch: DY 30/J IV 2/2/1093: Politburo meeting on 9 September 1975, agenda item 8 and Annex 5.

23. BArch: DC 20/12853, 82 et seq.

24. BArch: DC 20/12853, 5–7.

25. BArch: DC 20/12853, 40–44.

26. SAPMO-BArch: DY 30/IV 2/2.033/85, 1 et seq.

27. SAPMO-BArch: DY 30/J IV 2/2A/2155: Politburo meeting on 30 May 1978, agenda item 2 and Annex 1.

28. Ibid.

29. Ibid.

30. For more details, see Storkmann: Geheime Solidarität, 389–500.

31. Schleicher, Ilona: *DDR-Solidarität im südlichen Afrika. Auseinandersetzungen mit einem ambivalenten Erbe*, Berlin 1999.

National Service and Resistance to Conscription in South Africa, 1968–1989[1]

Gert van der Westhuizen, Ian Liebenberg and Tienie du Plessis

OK people get up off your feet
It's time to move to a different beat
We don't like the way they're running our days and nights
Our lives are out of phase
We're Black White separated
Right from birth indoctrinated
Years and years developed apart
Brainwashed each in the name of God
Let's de-educate ourselves
Let's re-educate ourselves
Hey white boy get your feet off the floor
The Lord gave you legs to march to war
Your leaders want you in a sporting affair
So put on your boots and cut your hair
Don't talk back or stop to think
When you're in Angola you can have a drink
Obey Obey they know the way
From here you go to SWA
Where they don't dance when facing such hostility
They don't dance
Cos the SADF's there to see that we all enjoy democracy
Cos the SAP are there to see that we all enjoy democracy.[2]

Introduction

While volumes have been written on the Bush War/Border War, very few people then (and perhaps now) had insight into why young men refused to serve in the apartheid army, or, for that matter, why others served at first and then later objected to further service. Few people know that increasing numbers of soldiers called up for "further duties" chose not to report for camps or border (later township) duty. The number of conscript veterans who "voted with their feet" by not reporting for further "camps" or border stints is unknown, while the SADF admitted that the number of people who refused to heed call-ups were becoming a problem.

111

South African soldiers who had distinguished themselves on the battlefields of Africa and Europe during two world wars (or even in military clashes as late as 2013 in the Central African Republic) were neither conscripted nor forced into military service. After the Second World War the South African government relied mainly on the Active Citizen Force. The Citizen Force functioned on a voluntary basis as a supplement to the manpower needs of the country's armed forces. The National Party government came to power in 1948 on the strength of its policy of apartheid. The barrage of laws that followed legalised and entrenched racial discrimination in an era of decolonisation and increasing concern for human rights after the horrors of Nazism. To maintain apartheid against opposition from what the regime considered a hostile world, it soon required increased manpower.[3] Eventually, more than half a million young white men[4] were conscripted in a doomed attempt to maintain apartheid at home and sustain Pretoria's military adventures in southern Africa. Of these, roughly 320 000 served on the border between South West Africa (Namibia) and Angola in some capacity, although not all of them took part in cross-border operations into countries such as Zambia, Rhodesia (Zimbabwe) and Angola. Significant numbers of these men saw deployment in northern Namibia and some in Angola.

Conscription and military service influenced the lives of white men in South Africa during the 1970s and 1980s. "It seemed as if my whole life had been shaped by the army," one author, who emigrated to avoid serving in the South African Defence Force (SADF), remarked.[5] But in the 1980s growing numbers grew tired of this continued intervention in their lives, while others opposed conscription on moral grounds. It was not an easy thing to do – to declare publicly in a militarised society that conscription was immoral because the SADF was waging an unjust war. White society was ideologically socialised, limited to top-down "freedoms" and "responsibilities" and sanctions for dissent were harsh. Consequently, the anti-conscription movement never became a mass movement, but its influence was felt widely in an era when South Africa was, to all intents and purposes, an ideological battleground during the dying days of the Cold War.

The existence of this movement was disconcerting to the government as it pointed to resistance from within white ranks and government acted overtly and covertly against it. Yet, the ideas propagated by the anti-conscription movement led to the establishment of a vibrant sub-culture that attracted more and more young white people to its fold. Even, and from the government's point of view this was all the more disturbing, (young) Afrikaner men and women increasingly embraced the philosophies expounded by the anti-war movement in the country.

This chapter points out how the government and the SADF needed more and more conscripts as its wars outside, and conflict inside, the country escalated. We point out how the need for more and more "willing" conscripts was underpinned by an intense process of socialisation which started at primary school and intensified at secondary school. In the third part of this essay, we will deal with the resistance to what was considered to be an unjust war and the counter measures the government undertook in an attempt to nip this rebellion in the bud. When one thinks of resistance to conscription, the End Conscription Campaign (ECC) stands out because it was very vocal as well as the focal point of public and government attention. But resistance, which was not always as public or visible as that of the ECC, was ever present. As the article deals only with white conscripts, it will not refer to volunteers or to Namibian conscripts and soldiers of other races. The scope will be limited to the white South African community's experience of militarisation.

Conscription under apartheid

According to the 1957 Defence Act, white men were eligible for military service for a period of nine months. Recruits were called up by means of a lottery formula or ballot system; hence the name *lotelinge* for those who served. The first intake numbered 7 000 men and the initial training period lasted three months. This system was done away with in 1967 when the Defence Act was amended and from January 1968 there were two yearly intakes of national servicemen; in January and June. Some of these recruits were trained as supplementary instructors due to a shortage of manpower in the permanent force. Now approximately 25 000 white men between the ages of 17 and 20 were called up for national service each year, considerably more than the approximately 10 000 men who did annual national service before the amendment. By the late 1970s initial national service was a full two years and servicemen still had to report for regular post-national service commitments.[6]

In 1972 the period of initial service was extended to twelve months. This was to be followed by a further nineteen days of annual service over a period of five years as members of the Citizen Force. By 1975 this service could include border stints or operational duty, ostensibly for three months at a time. But the South African Defence Force and politicians always needed more manpower, especially after military excursions into neighbouring countries became an intrinsic component of South Africa's foreign policy. In 1977, one year after the first invasion of Angola by South African forces, national service was increased to two years plus annual 30-day camps for a period of eight years.[7] A short service system was implemented. Trained members of the Citizen Force, Commandos, Permanent Force reserves and national servicemen had the option of applying for enlistment for a period of three years. A once-off fee of R500 was paid to everyone who agreed to short service and they all received the allowances of normal Permanent Force soldiers.[8] By January 1978 approximately one thousand additional soldiers had taken this option, and after 1978 short service became a useful force multiplier for the SADF as more men joined, some for a second term, and some eventually enlisted in the Permanent Force.[9]

The Defence Amendment Acts making these changes were enacted with the support of the liberal opposition in the white parliament. Ironically few, if any, of the white Afrikaner Nationalist leaders who enforced military service on the children of their white compatriots ever experienced war themselves.[10] The militarisation of South African society, subtly done at first, increased as internal and external opposition to apartheid became widespread during the 1970s and 1980s. The independence of the Portuguese colonies of Angola and Mozambique in the middle of the 1970s and Zimbabwe in 1980 increased the perceived fears of the white population and their siege mentality was further entrenched by the government's "total strategy". By 1972 a State Security Council (SSC) was instituted; a clear indication that hawkish security thinking was on the rise. South Africa became a security state in the making.[11] The securocrats became entrenched in government when P.W. Botha, a former Minister of Defence, took over the leadership of the National Party in 1978. A year later the government came to the conclusion that South Africa faced a "total onslaught" that could only be withstood by implementing a "total strategy". This strategy obviously necessitated the "total" mobilisation of the white community; something that was reflected in the increasing number of conscripts. The Cold War discourse that emanated from the USA became a large-scale window of opportunity for ideologues in Pretoria and the white parliament to bombard (even tacitly intimidate) their followers with the notion of Soviet imperialism and the dangers of terrorism.[12]

Although observers never quite agreed on the exact numbers, it was evident that the state was increasing its military might. According to a 1970 report the army's reserve numbered 60 000 men, with 22 000 soldiers under training at any given time. Four years later the International Institute for Strategic Studies (IISS) reported that the Permanent Force consisted of 18 000 members supplemented by 92 000 in the Citizen Force.[13] Eight months after South African forces withdrew from their first Angolan invasion, dubbed Operation Savannah, a weekly magazine with close governmental ties stated that the Permanent Force numbered 16 000 members, and perhaps even more. It hastened to add that two call-ups per year would bring another 30 000 trainees per annum into the equation, while Commandos (territorial defence units) had a minimum manpower of 75 000. It concluded that the Republic of South Africa could mobilise up to 400 000 soldiers in times of war.[14]

Ten years later figures pointed to a significant increase. During the mid-eighties, the number of men in the total reserves had risen to 455 000, those for the active reserve (Citizen Force) to 175 000, and those for Commandos to 130 000. In 1981 a full deployment of the South African Defence Force (SADF) could muster an estimated 168 000 soldiers, only 7,5 per cent of who were Permanent Force members. After the period of service had been extended to two years, it was estimated at the beginning of the 1980s that approximately 60 000 conscripts underwent training every year.[15] The extent to which conscripts provided the backbone of the SADF became evident: "The SADF believed the first demand of a military was manpower. This translated into two avenues: expanding the standing contingent and increasing the cohort and length of national service."[16] At any given time after 1975, the number of conscripts and those on call-up from the Active Citizen Force on an annual basis far superseded the number of Permanent Force members. By 1984–1985, when large-scale incursions into Angola and the first deployment of the military in black townships in South Africa became routine during the first state of emergency, the IISS reported that the armed forces numbered 83 400 of whom 53 000 were conscripts, while the total mobilised strength was 404 500. The Army boasted 67 400 staff members with 10 000 white, 5 400 black and coloured regulars, 2 000 women, and 50 000 conscripts organised into nine territorial commands.[17] At the height of the Angolan War in 1988, the IISS put the number of the South African soldiers at 103 500 which included 67 900 white conscripts. The staff of the Army increased from 67 400 to 75 000.[18]

The load that a member of the Citizen Force had to bear became more burdensome. The issue became even more acute after 1984 when the SADF was increasingly deployed domestically to combat internal unrest. Towards the end of 1984 the SSC ordered 7 000 soldiers to assist the South African Police in controlling spiralling violence in townships. Two years later, soldiers were deployed in some 96 townships countrywide. More than 10 000 troops,[19] mostly conscripts and members of the Citizen Force, were thus kept busy with what a large percentage of them considered to be the duty of the police. "The Border" was no longer a distant place somewhere between northern Namibia and Angola – it now encompassed "home" as well.

The thousands of young white men who went through the mill of national service did so for various reasons, many simply because they saw no other option and just wanted to get it over and done with in order to get on with their lives. Many conscripts thus served stoically or without question. Many others did so enthusiastically, many even with pride.[20] Although the reasons for their willingness to serve in the armed forces varied, the socialisation process they had been subjected to from early, impressionable ages was one of the most important factors in helping to provide the SADF with the manpower it needed.

The willing

Socialisation is a process in which socialisation agents such as parental care and the family, cultural institutions, schools, universities, churches, peer groups, political leaders (as role models), youth movements/organisations, the place of work and sports organisations play a role. It is also a process that from cradle to grave constructs "social realities" and "optic angles" that may differ from others in other societies, or even within the same society. H.M. Johnson argues that most people in isolated societies do not think through the underlying assumptions of their world view or the implications of the customs and habits that they follow. A tendency to accept orders or commands "unquestioningly" characterises especially hierarchical societies. In such cases, non-reflected action is both prevalent and pervasive.[21]

The extensive legislation regulating racial segregation contributed to relatively isolated communities in white apartheid society. South African society, and especially Afrikaner society, was built on a hierarchical approach, even more so within the military. Add to this bureaucracies that "manifest a tendency to routine, a resistance to new ways of doing things" (and thinking anew, one may add) and the picture becomes stark.[22] Military bureaucracies and military life in general result in an acute and "deeply" penetrating socialisation process. This happened to a large degree with potential conscripts and those who served in the military and frequently such socialisation remained with them afterwards. Socialisation for the defence of apartheid started early. Socialisation in an ideologically laden society plays an important part in mobilising the whole population against internal or foreign enemies. This was, and is, not exceptional, and definitely not limited to apartheid society, as examples from ideologically diverse societies such as Nazi Germany, the Soviet Union, Cambodia, Israel, Imperial Japan and the United States of America prove. Garrison-minded societies tend to mobilise people on the homeland principle – against some "other" (the enemy). South Africa was no exception. Early socialisation in an apartheid society, together with further socialisation through selective ideological filters, created the potential for an obedient military labour force. Media censorship and disinformation worsened the situation. The author of the play *Somewhere on the Border* remarked that he did not realise that by doing national service he would defend an ideology rather than a sovereign state. He ascribed his ignorance of the major ideological confrontation in South Africa to censorship and the banning of opposition political movements.[23] This play, it should be added, was promptly banned in 1983 by the censors. One of the reasons given was that its portrayal of the armed forces was "prejudicial to the safety of the state".[24]

The socialisation process of white South African schoolchildren was particularly effective. It was succinctly summed up by an ex-conscript in his memoirs: "I always knew that one day I would be a soldier; every white South African boy knew that. It was what you did when you finished school."[25] The inculcation of such ideas started in the classroom. School curricula made provision for a subject called "Youth Preparedness" (*Jeugweerbaarheid*) that was compulsory in all white secondary schools in the then provinces of the Cape, the Orange Free State and Transvaal. It consisted of six components: "spiritual preparedness, physical preparedness, first aid, fire fighting, an emergency plan for schools, and general affairs".[26] A textbook used in some Transvaal schools stated bluntly that the country was not only threatened on its borders by "anti-Christian forces", but that the *volk* had to battle the "forces of evil".[27] Attempts at indoctrination were taken further in the Transvaal and the Orange Free State where compulsory veld schools (*veldskole*) were instituted for learners in their last year of primary school and in Grade 10 (Standard 8). Learners, boys and girls, were taken to military style camps in isolated rural areas such as Schoemansdal, Hobhouse, Zastron and Glenmore, where they were subjected to a continued stream of propaganda and physical exercise. Lecturers attempted to hammer home the idea of a "total onslaught" orchestrated by "communists". Attendees were told that South Africa's enemies would use every means at their disposal in this onslaught. "In veld school, we did communism, we did the South African flag, we did terrorism, and one whole lecture was about how sex, communism and drugs all go into the music we listen to," one interviewee told an author.[28] Veld schools also served to give boys a foretaste of what they could expect when they eventually had to take up weapons in the SADF to keep these enemies at bay. Similar to cadet camps, some enjoyed it and uncritically saw it as an adventure without consequences.

It was difficult, if not well-nigh impossible, at secondary schools to escape from the militarism that was increasingly becoming the norm.[29] The cadet system at schools also served as a means whereby boys were prepared for military service. From the middle of the 1970s it was put on a firmer footing.[30] By 1974 it was reckoned that the country had approximately 58 000 cadets and 2 000 teachers who acted as officers.[31] Little more than a decade later it was estimated that 658 cadet divisions existed throughout the country with 193 254 cadets and 2 942 officers. The more populous Transvaal had 262 divisions and 105 136 cadets. Only about 20 private schools and 10 government schools had, by this time, not implemented the system.[32] The cadet system was administered and financed by the South African Army and teachers who were officers in the Commandos or had already undergone national service took charge of training. The SADF initially denied that this system was instituted to train the youth as soldiers. It was supposedly rather meant to instil a sense of "national pride, responsible citizenship and preparedness" by teaching learners the basics of drilling, field craft and musketry.[33] Ten years later there was no longer any pretence. Cadets, the official magazine of the SADF told its readers, formed a bulwark against communism and it no longer made a secret of the fact that cadet training served to prepare boys to become better soldiers.[34] In 1987 a columnist in an Afrikaans newspaper sang the praises of the cadet system by pointing out that through it "boys" become better soldiers.[35]

Cadet training and cadet camps were handy propaganda tools for the apartheid government and as the historian of one school wrote, it "is perhaps the least 'neutral' activity in which a school can engage during a time of political conflict".[36] Cadet training was definitely not popular amongst the majority of schoolboys. But there was little, if indeed anything,

Image in a booklet of the South African Chaplain's Services of the SADF, 1974. This booklet provided advice to young men leaving school about to enter military service. SOURCE: Author's archive.

they could do to avoid it. The one avenue of resistance open to boys who despised cadet training was to make a mockery of it:

> The average College boy's attitude to this activity had not changed – just as in the 1920s most of them would have sold their mothers into the harem of a one-eyed sultan to escape this particular brand of martyrdom, but the difference was that most of them now performed as if they had succeeded in carrying out this transaction. In some years, the annual cadet inspections were a source of acute embarrassment, with the detachment resembling a giant octopus with Parkinson's disease.[37]

Many schools, certainly not all of them Afrikaans, prided themselves on their cadet detachments and bands and took regional and countrywide competitions very seriously. A school's prestige was also enhanced if its detachments and bands could perform during public occasions such as the visits of high-ranking government officials, ministers and even the state president to a town or city. In these circumstances, active opposition to cadet training within government schools was nearly impossible. The End Conscription Campaign (ECC) did launch a "Cadets Out" campaign, but its impact was mainly restricted to private schools where some teachers sympathised with the ECC's aims and alternatives to cadet training already existed.[38]

Learners took the ideologically slanted ideas taught at schools with them to university.[39] A study conducted at traditional white universities in 1989 found that 46,6 per cent of students at Afrikaans universities felt "very sympathetic towards the security establishment and 38 per cent sympathetic". Thus only 15 per cent of white Afrikaans-speaking students were apathetic or unsympathetic towards the security forces.[40]

A similar pattern can be observed in attitudes towards conscription and the refusal to do military service as a form of political protest. Among Afrikaner male students 86,3 per cent said that they would never refuse to do military service as a form of protest, while 55,7 per cent of English speaking males said so ... Among Afrikaners only 2,7 per cent said that they would do so (refuse military service) and a further 7 per cent that they would consider it ... among the Afrikaners the ECC (End Conscription Campaign), an organisation that has denounced the political role of the SADF and which actively discourages military service, has had very little impact whereas it has a strong support among English speaking students.[41]

Repression potential (agreement with hard-handed action towards protest, even if peaceful) was high. Nearly 90 per cent of Afrikaans-speaking students said that protest meetings should be broken up by security/police forces. Sixty one per cent of National Party supporting students felt that it was justified to break up protest meetings and 74 per cent of Conservative Party members agreed.[42]

Nationhood, civil strife and moral objections: The not so willing ...

By the beginning of the 1980s, it could have appeared to the casual observer that the socialisation and militarisation of white apartheid society were strengthening the hands of the government in its military endeavours. But it was not a monolithic society. It was a deeply divided one; and cracks were starting to appear. Opposition took many forms, of which resistance to conscription was one. More and more conscripts moved on the spectrum from enthusiastic to willing and then unwilling, while a small minority embraced total resistance through peaceful and violent means. Conscripts and members of the Citizen Force were becoming increasingly frustrated with the continued intervention in their lives and compulsory military service was becoming more and more unpopular. There were several reasons for this. Conscripts had to face the real threat of social and economic disruption, and there were even complaints that employers were prejudiced against members of their workforce who were called up for annual camps.[43]

As political objection to conscription was punishable by law, other avenues of avoidance were explored. Some, like 4 622 men in 1980, simply decided not to report for military service, and others tried to avoid conscription by not notifying the authorities of changes of address.[44] Incidences of courts martial grew exponentially with the SADF's increased involvement in active combat in the operational area. Magnus Malan, the Minister of Defence, admitted that more than half (263) of the 484 conscripts in detention barracks at the beginning of 1982 were detained for refusing to do duty. And the Prime Minister, P.W. Botha, reckoned that only 20–30 per cent of national servicemen were highly motivated.[45]

Some people were also starting to doubt the morality of joining the escalating war. South Africa experienced a low level insurgency war inside the country, and in its efforts to maintain control over Namibian politics, the government and its generals contributed to the civil war in Angola with dire effects on the infrastructure of the country and the resultant large-scale dislocation of people in southern Angola. Other countries, apart from occupied Namibia, also bore the brunt of South Africa's total strategy. Attacks by air, special force operations and even assassinations were all part of South Africa's attempts to coerce the Frontline States to toe its line. South Africa supported the renegade Renamo movement in Mozambique, for example, and was not averse to launching attacks in countries such as Zambia, Zimbabwe, Lesotho, Swaziland and Botswana. Economic pressures were frequently used to augment these security operations in an attempt to maintain a grip on the region. But the regional war was also increasingly coming home: the apartheid government simultaneously waged a low-key civil war against its own citizens inside the country.[46] The government tried to justify its strategy as a battle on behalf of Christian civilisation against godless communists, terrorists, and agitators under the control of Moscow who masterminded a strategy to engulf South Africa and its strategic resources.[47] It should have been easy to justify such a strategy in a country where approximately 70 per cent of the population professed to be Christian. However, the socio-political dynamics in South Africa were understandably more complex given the composition of South African society.

Religiousness/spirituality and objection to apartheid at war

Through the ages Christians have a long and proud tradition of opposing what they regard as unjustified war. South Africa itself did not have a strong tradition of Christian Pacifism. John de Gruchy argued: "First of all, it should be understood that there is virtually no pacifist tradition in South Africa."[48] Some, by conviction, resisted any form of violence under any circumstances including serving under the arms of the state. Others believed in just resistance – even if violent – but they were opposed to serving an unjust cause on behalf of an iron-fisted state that upheld injustice.[49] It should have come as no surprise then that the war was viewed with suspicion by many Christians, even if the apartheid state claimed to fight on behalf of Christianity and many in uniform, including the chaplain services, declared the apartheid state a bastion and homeland of Christianity.[50] Increasing social tensions and violence led to moral concerns which eventually resulted in resistance. Christian pacifists initially resisted the notion of joining the SADF as *lotelinge* or conscripts.

The majority of these objectors were Jehovah's Witnesses who were widely discredited by the Afrikaans churches and the media. Despite anti-conscription activities having been criminalised by the Defence Amendment Act of 1974, this type of resistance increased. More objectors joined the fray, many of them members of the mainstream churches. A Board for Religious Objection (Act 34 of 1983) was eventually created to allow such persons to object to military service on the grounds of religion. The state decided that objectors could apply for alternative service on the grounds of religious conscience, not secular or political beliefs.[51] Thus, a Christian conscience that dictated that the defence and upholding of apartheid was tantamount to an unjust war, while Christian support for the struggle of the oppressed was just, would not have impressed the authorities.[52] To argue that one was an atheist, yet a pacifist or a non-Christian agnostic who was opposed to wielding the sword on behalf of the state, would have been just as problematic. Needless to say, the argument that one was an atheist who morally disagreed/agreed with violent resistance against the dehumanising structural violence of apartheid was even less likely to be tolerated or entertained by the board. Yet the number of men who chose to walk the gauntlet of alternative service, despite public vilification and slandering, rose. Between February 1984 and September 1989 some 1 890 potential conscripts applied for alternative service. In 1989 alone 286 conscripts applied for alternative service.[53]

South Africa's ruling regime, driven by an ideology of (white) Christian Nationalism, did not lend a sympathetic ear to non-religious objectors to the war in defence of "Christian civilisation". Even judges seemed too scared or chose not to object to the limited range of what the legislation at the time allowed in terms of objection to war. In short, the security minded mentality of the state and white society was increasingly undermining the moral and social fabric of South African society.[54] Jurists and legal practitioners offered critical perspectives. They broadly argued that the destruction of the rule of law by security legislation was to have negative consequences for democracy in a future South Africa.[55] Security legislation limited the rights of white South Africans as well as those rights supposedly available to blacks. So did the amendments to the Defence Act.[56] In South Africa then, even in law, conflict resolution was based on domination or coercion. As a result, control by the civil authorities within the apartheid state (including the "reformist" version) was precariously weakened.[57]

The objection of universal pacifists, those who through convictions other than Christian beliefs resisted war, was initially not accepted as "legal" despite many appeals to government. One needed to be a universal pacifist on grounds of the Christian faith to be considered a conscientious objector. Objectors fell into two categories: (1) Those who objected to apartheid's war against other South Africans because they saw the minority government's war as unjust, but not necessarily to all wars; (2) those who were convinced that violence in any or all circumstances was against their beliefs, including serving in the military forces of any state anywhere in the world. Add to this that moral repulse against violence and oppression is not the domain of Christians only, and the issue becomes more complex.[58]

Voices critical of church involvement in the military were heard. A Dutch Reformed Church (DRC) (*Nederduits Gereformeerde Kerk,* NGK) group representing the *Aksie Sosiale Geregtigheid* (Action for Social Justice) and the *Leer en Aktuele Sake Kommissie, NGK Kerkjeugaksie* (Dutch Reformed Church Youth movement) in Stellenbosch, for example, proposed a motion to the Western Cape Synod of chaplain services in 1985. They argued that the role of chaplains in the SADF was problematic because they wore the uniform of a biased and discriminatory state. The proposal was submitted to the conservative Dutch Reformed Church leadership at the Western Cape Synod and called for the structure of the chaplain services to be changed in order to allow people to conduct pastoral care without uniform and without being forced to get security clearances. The submission argued that a pastoral counsellor had to be neutral and not a representative of the state, or at least free to provide human care. A "chaplain" was supposed to affirm the support of a religious person to another in need as implied in the Christian scriptures.[59] The Action for Social Justice followed the example of the *Belydende Kring* (Witnessing Circle) and the Student Union for Christian Action (SUCA) in arguing that racial segregation and the policies of the government contradicted the unity of being that the New Testament preached. For these objectors the issue was one of a moral nature and deep conviction, although opponents labelled it as "black theology", "subversive" and even "un-Christian". Those opposing the state and its loyal church bodies soon found themselves isolated in a *verligte* (enlightened) Stellenbosch, which at heart tended to be either cautious or conservative despite the progressive liberal utterances and lip service to "reform".[60]

Some of those who voiced protest and resistance from within the ranks of the Dutch Reformed Church eventually defected to other churches or left the church altogether. The *Belhar Belydenis* or Belhar Confession within the "non-white" Dutch Reformed Mission Church (*NG Sendingkerk*), Dutch Reformed Church in Africa (*NGK in Afrika*) and Indian Reformed Church (IRC) played an important role in mobilising against what was seen as the heresy of apartheid and the ways in which it was upheld.[61] (Until today, the DRC has not seen its way open to signing the Belhar Confession unreservedly.) The Kairos Declaration followed and referred to the use of religion, specifically Christianity, as a state theology. After the Cottesloe meeting and Hammanskraal resolutions taken earlier on by church leadership critical of apartheid and the structural and physical violence with which it was upheld, the gulf between the militarised apartheid state and the churches widened considerably. The South African Council of Churches (SACC) expressed solidarity with resisters despite minority objections. Several people of various denominations openly spoke out against compulsory military service. The Anglican Church was confronted with a debate on the issue of conscription and some individuals in the Presbyterian Church followed suit. The Catholic Church had always had its reservations about segregation and hence also with the way in which the state deployed its security forces. The South African Council of Churches and the South African Catholic Bishops' Conference (SACBC) at first declared empathy and later solidarity with war resisters.[62]

Stark choices: Exile or internal resistance?

One of the few options available to objectors during the 1970s was exile. It was estimated that approximately 1 000 South African objectors were granted exile in Britain alone between 1977 and 1981.[63] They were assisted by organisations such as the Committee on South African War Resistance (COSWAR), the South African Military Refugee Aid Fund in New York and the Stichting Werkgroep Kairos in the Netherlands. Apart from providing help to war resisters in exile, COSWAR clandestinely spread pamphlets to would-be conscripts, lobbied liberal bodies, political parties, churches and religious organisations and individuals. These organisations laid the groundwork for more organised and vocal resistance to conscription in South Africa where the Conscientious Objector Support Group had already been established in 1980. As early as 1982, student organisations, including the National Union of South African Students (NUSAS), distributed booklets such as *Know your Rights* to prospective conscripts. At the University of Cape Town a Conscription Action Group and support groups were established. The Black Sash openly expressed itself against conscription at its 1983 conference and in the same year the End Conscription Campaign (ECC) was established.[64] The ECC comprised people of pacifist conviction as well as people who were against the unjust war of apartheid, not necessarily all wars. Some in the ECC accepted the notion of a just war for a just cause, even in the case of apartheid's non-democratic rule.

The ECC was to become one of the organisations that verbalised resistance to military service eloquently and visually. It also pointed out successfully the extent that government was militarising politics without considering other ways to bring about an end to civil strife. The ECC's first public attempt at objecting to military service drew the support of eleven people who refused to serve in the SADF. This grew to more than twenty and later to more than a hundred objectors.[65] This figure eventually increased to more than 700 in 1989 and included ex-servicemen and commissioned officers. Others, some who had even belonged to elite units such as the Parabats (paratroopers), also "objected" by ignoring their call-up papers. In the Afrikaans-speaking community, which was more militarised and where tighter social sanctions applied, "objectors" rather voted with their feet by not reporting for further camps.

State reaction

The ECC, though never a mass organisation in the true sense of the word, was vocal enough to disturb the authorities. Its meetings were increasingly monitored by security police, especially after the SADF was deployed in townships. Before it was eventually banned in 1989 under emergency regulations, its members were verbally abused, lambasted in public, monitored, ridiculed, harassed, detained, restricted and banned, while several were also sent to prison for refusing to don the uniform of the SADF.[66] Counter-intelligence operators spent a significant amount of time and money on isolating and vilifying the ECC; ironically claiming at the same time that the ECC and its supporters were a minority, a lunatic fringe, isolated and misled. South African Military Intelligence was deeply involved in attempts to minimise the effect of the ECC. Government officials spoke out against the ECC whenever possible and the media joined the fray.[67] A favourite ploy of detractors was to question the manhood and patriotism of members of the ECC; two qualities on which the masculine, militarised society that was South Africa thrived and put a very high premium. The ECC was dubbed Every Coward's Choice and its members and sympathisers were castigated as traitors, liberals, communists, useful idiots for Marxism-Leninism, anarchists, losers, and mad. They were also called *moffies* (gays), *holnaaiers* (faggots), and *banggatte* (fearful ones). One euphemism used for ECC supporters was *die agtermekaar-kêrels*, a clear reference to conscientious objectors being regarded as gay (homosexual) and by pejorative implication, fearful in nature.[68]

The nefarious activities of the state's counter-intelligence activities against the ECC were augmented by the establishment of various student and other bodies which were funded by the government. These included Veterans for Victory and the short-lived *Jeugkrag Suid-Afrika* (Youth for South Africa)[69] with the National Students Federation (NSF) being the most vocal and active. The NSF sprang up in the middle of the 1980s and soon established several affiliates on the campuses of Afrikaans and English universities.[70] Danie Kriel, Chairman of the NSF-affiliated Populêre Studente-alliansie at the University of Stellenbosch and later the organisation's national president, described the NSF as the "only classical liberal" student movement in the country. The NSF tried to gain credibility by opposing some of the more hard-line apartheid laws such as the Group Areas Act, but it soon became clear on whose behalf it acted. The NSF distributed glossy, expensive brochures and pamphlets, such as one in which it pledged its support for UNITA, the SADF's ally in the battle for Angola.[71] The NSF also joined in the smear campaign against the ECC, accusing it of being "linked to the Kremlin" and "attempting to undermine the integrity of the SADF".[72] What many people had always expected eventually transpired in 1991 when the South African Police admitted to funding the NSF. It was done, the SAP said, in an attempt to establish "stability and law and order" on university campuses that were "plagued with unrest, class boycotts and intimidation of students" during the middle

The streets of our country are in turmoil. The universities are filled with students rioting and rebelling. Communists seek to destroy our country. Russia is threatening us with her might and the Republic is in danger from within and without.

We need Law and Order! Without it our Nation cannot survive.

Adolf Hitler 1932

MAKES YOU THINK DOESN'T IT?

A National NUSAS Campaign

National Union of South African Students and End Conscription Campaign posters against militarisation. SOURCE: Author's archive and exhibition at University of the Western Cape.

of the 1980s.[73] Security police involvement with the NSF apparently had more sinister undertones than mere funding. Allegations based on an official police document stated that the NSF was a front for covert state operations on campuses and that some NSF officials even had police code names.[74]

The concerted attempts by the state to discredit, harass, threaten and detain those who opposed apartheid through moral conviction, apparently had the opposite effect. Resistance against the apartheid war, its politicians, spies and generals persisted. Resistance against war in the white community was far more widespread than just the activities of the ECC, or, as it was known in Afrikaans, the *Be-eindig Diensplig Kampanje* (BDK) or *Eindig Diensplig Veldtog* (EDV). At Pretoria University the *Studente vir 'n Demokratiese Samelewing* (SDS) advocated resistance to apartheid and the tricameral system that excluded black South Africans from political participation. They openly organised activities to enhance non-racialism and non-sexism despite being vilified and harassed. At the Randse Afrikaanse Universiteit *Afrikane teen Apartheid* (ATA) criticised the use of the military while it advocated non-racial democracy, and at Stellenbosch the *Verenigde Stellenbosche Front* (VSF) continued their activities. All these groups expressed sympathy, if not solidarity, with the ECC. A debate on alternative national service (i.e. non-military service) sprung up.

The Centre for Intergroup Studies based in Rondebosch, earlier known as the Abe Bailey Institute, headed by H.W. van der Merwe, attempted to arrange meetings between the government and people trying to express their discontent with the militarisation of white society. The centre for some years also attempted to facilitate meetings around forms of non-discriminatory alternative service for conscientious objectors, be they Christian or non-Christian.[75] The success of these initiatives varied, but mostly ended with pro-government spokespeople suggesting that the government was doing its level best to "accommodate *these* people" who may have "had good intentions, but were naïve".[76]

Waar gaan dit eindig? (Where will it end?) Objection grows within the Afrikaner community

It was clear that the debate on compulsory military service and the immorality of apartheid was slowly but surely permeating the Afrikaans community, where different forms of resistance manifested in a vibrant, if somewhat hedonistic, "alternative" sub-culture towards the end of the 1980s while the country was inexorably on the march to a new political dispensation.

Towards a military dictatorship

Cartoon in Christian newsletter, University of Cape Town, circa 1985. SOURCE: Author's archive.

ECC poster circa 1985. SOURCE: Author's archive.

Afrikaans musicians and groups such as the Kalahari Surfers, Cherry Faced Lurchers, Johannes Kerkorrel and the Gereformeerde Blues Band, Bernoldus Niemand, and André Letoit (Koos Kombuis) criticised the white state and its authoritarian leaders. Their songs were played by radio stations on Afrikaans campuses and their popularity steadily increased until it reached a crescendo with the Voëlvry tour of 1989 in which several of these artists participated. "The Total Onslaught's name is Voëlvry," proclaimed *Vrye Weekblad*, and the *Cape Times* described it as "an unprecedented orgy of Afrikaner anarchy".[77] The revolt was not limited to the musical arena. Small Afrikaans struggle publishers such as Taurus Publishers joined in with books such as *Forces Favourites, Stanley en die Boikot* and an alternative journal called *STET*. *Die Suid-Afrikaan* and later *Vrye Weekblad* painted a picture of a South Africa very different from that portrayed in the mainstream media and by *verligte* academics. All these small but by no means insignificant initiatives not only strengthened the case against conscription, but also gave impetus to resistance.[78]

The alternative publications subverted the heroic image of Afrikaner Nationalist authoritarianism and painted a picture of a socio-political regime increasingly caught up in sad absurdities and glaring discrepancies.[79] Within Afrikaans literary circles a whole genre of literature critical of apartheid militarisation that became known as *grensliteratuur* (border literature) appeared in the 1980s. It was disconcerting to the authorities that some of the authors were men who had already served in the military and experienced contacts on the border. They could not simply be written off as *misleides* (the misled) or *sissies* (feminine or "girly" types).

The Institute for Democracy in South Africa (IDASA) also played its role in disseminating anti-apartheid ideas across South Africa. Its activities drew the ire of the authorities, especially after it sponsored a delegation that engaged in talks with the banned African National Congress (ANC) in Dakar, Senegal, in 1987. The backlash from the government and the Afrikaans media did not deter Idasa. It even managed to organise a debate on the ANC's Freedom Charter at the University of the Orange Free State in Bloemfontein that elicited a vehement right-wing response from organisations that included the NSF.[80] But the tide of history was turning against those opposed to democratisation. The Border War ended in 1989 and Namibia became independent in 1990, the same year in which the "new" South Africa was born when the ANC and other liberation organisations were unbanned. The NSF disbanded in shame in 1991 when its links to the Security Police became known and two years later there was no longer any need for the ECC when conscription was abolished. The ECC reckoned that only approximately 60 per cent of conscripts who were called up in 1993 reported for duty. The SADF refused to comment on this, only saying that the total intake was 16 per cent more than expected.[81]

Conclusion

The history of warfare in South Africa over the past centuries was also one of division and clashing perspectives. South African people were divided by economic, ideological, racial, religious and other factors during the Anglo-Boer War, the stormy twenties and both world wars. The era of the Border War that spilled over/was exported to Angola and the insurrection in black townships were no exception, although the ideological battle was perhaps fiercer and carried on far longer than previously.

Most white males were confronted with call-up papers during this era. The majority of them did eventually serve in the SADF; some enthusiastically, proudly, blindly, stoically and perhaps grumbling softly to themselves. Some recalled their experiences with pride and joy, others with reservation. Some later questioned the way in which they were selectively informed and one-sidedly press-ganged to uphold a regime that abused even its own citizens. Very much the same applies to their loved ones and families (past or present). Some stated boldly afterwards that they would do it again; others said "never again". Some fondly recalled moments of humour and comradeship in somewhat challenging circumstances and adverse conditions. Others remembered friends (and enemies) who had passed away or are living with nightmares. Some speak about their experiences, while others prefer to keep quiet. Each one of them has dealt in a different way with their bag of memories/experiences, some more successfully than others. Fortunately, some of them decided to speak up for themselves rather than allow the ideologues or generals to do so.[82] Their reflections on the history of the war and the social nature of South African society, then and now, has added value to an ongoing dialogue.

It is said that it takes a brave man (or woman) to go to war. Resistance to conscription during the apartheid era showed that it takes an even braver man (or woman) to resist war; that it requires moral fibre of a different kind. Resisters had to face dire consequences as we have shown. Even today, two decades after the end of the Border War, resisters are still referred to as cowards by some die-hards.[83] But the "resisters" and others who decided to "de-educate" and "re-educate" themselves in the heady days of the 1980s, played no small part in hastening the end of apartheid. The first president of a democratic South Africa, Nelson Mandela, lauded these uncompromising South Africans for turning their backs on the privileges of minority rule and making a lived-out commitment to peace. "Your campaign against conscription put you firmly on the side of the democratic forces and contributed considerably to the overall efforts of the people of South Africa to overthrow racial oppression."[84] Richard Steele, one of the jailed objectors, reckoned the ECC was a major threat to the government because its resistance came from within.[85] This sentiment was echoed by an academic who felt that resistance to conscription "opened a crack in the presumption of universal obedience to the state by the enfranchised ... As such it alarmed military authorities."[86]

War resisters here, like elsewhere, left South Africa and the world, a lasting legacy. A religious columnist stated in 1997 in an Afrikaans newspaper that one can find more Christian pacifists in "our churches" than was the case in the 1980s. "It has become quite respectable to be opposed to war."[87] Some erstwhile resisters have turned their attention to other wars such as the conflict in the Middle East.[88] Some returned to rebuild a society disorientated by apartheid; others entered careers contributing to a post-apartheid society without considering emigration. In the end, by their courage and persistence under immense pressure, war resisters in South Africa set a commendable example to people throughout the world; an example anyone who is confronted with moral choices in unjust wars of the future should be thankful for.

Notes

1.   An earlier, shorter version of this chapter by the same authors appeared as an article entitled "The Willing and the not so Willing: Conscription and Resistance to Compulsory Military service in South Africa, 1968–1989" in a special edition commemorating the centenary of the UDF/SADF/SANDF of the *Journal for Contemporary History* (Military History 1912–2012), 37, no. 2 (2012): 143–164.

2.   Lyrics of the song *Don't Dance* by the Kalahari Surfers that appeared on the *Forces Favourite: 12 Songs by South Africans supporting the End Conscription Campaign,* a record originally released in 1986 by Shifty Records. See the sleeve notes on the undated re-issued CD by Shifty Records.

3.   On the rise of an authoritarian state in South Africa, consult Ian Liebenberg, "From Racialism to Authoritarianism: South Africa, Militarised Politics and the Implosion of State Legitimacy under Apartheid," ISPAIM Occasional Paper 10 no. 16 entitled *Changing Security Paradigms in Romania and South Africa after the Cold War* (Bucharest, 2011): 64ff.

4.   According to one source 600 000 white males were conscripted. See D. Williams, *On the Border: The White South African Military Experience, 1965–1990* (Cape Town: Tafelberg, 2008), 21. Magnus Malan, former chief of the Defence Force and Minister of Defence, put the figure at more than 500 000: M. Malan, *My Lewe saam met die SA Weermag* (Pretoria: Protea Boekhuis, 2006), 89. The Truth and Reconciliation Commission reckoned nearly 428 774 men were conscripted between 1960 and 1992: Truth and Reconciliation Commission of South Africa, *Truth and Reconciliation Commission of South Africa Report, Volume 4* (Cape Town: 1998), 224. Hereafter *TRC Report.*

5.   D. McRae, *Under our Skin: A White Family's Journey through South Africa's Darkest Years* (London: Simon & Schuster, 2012), 404.

6.   Compare among others, *South African Defence Force Review* (Durban: 1988), 17–21; H-R. Heitman, *Die Suid-Afrikaanse Krygsmag* (Johannesburg: Central News Agency/Bison Books, 1985), 27; Williams, 23ff.

7.   A. Seegers, *The Military in the Making of Modern South Africa* (London: IB Taurus, 1996), 147. Also see M. Alexander, "The Militarisation of White South African Society, 1948–1994," *Scientia Militaria* 30 (2000): 267–289, and G. Callister, *Compliance, Compulsion and Contest: Aspects of Military Conscription in South Africa, 1952–1992* (MA, University of Stellenbosch, 2007).

8.   T. du Plessis, *Diensplig.* Written contribution for a television documentary series entitled *Grensoorlog* (*Border War*) produced for M-Net/Kyknet, Pretoria, 2005 (Liebenberg Collection, Saldanha).

9.   Short service contracts were offered to national serviceme who could join the South African Defence Force (SADF) for a further year on a contract that could be extended. After completing their short service contract, some men chose to join the permanent force as career soldiers/non-commissioned/ commissioned officers. http://www.sadf.info/Title%20Army.html, *accessed 19 September 2012.*

10.   See in this regard the bitter remarks by a disgruntled ex-serviceman in C. Louw, *Boetman en die Swanesang van die Verligtes* (Cape Town: Human & Rousseau, 2001), 10.

11.   C. van der Westhuizen, *White Power & the Rise and Fall of the National Party* (Cape Town: Struik, 2008), 121–123; K.W. Grundy, *The Militarization of South African Politics* (Oxford: Oxford University Press, 1988), 34ff and 58ff; H. Giliomee & H. Adam, *Afrikanermag: Opkoms en Toekoms* (Stellenbosch: Universiteitsuitgewers, 1981), 198–197.

12.   Indeed the ANC (as was SWAPO) was viewed as a "terrorist movement" dictated to by Moscow. For an example of this type of stereotyping, see Ray S. Cline and Yonah Alexander, *Terrorism: The Soviet Connection* (New York: Crane Russak & Company, 1986), 61. For an example of the same thinking in South Africa, compare Henry. R. Pike, *A History of Communism in South Africa*, 2nd ed. (Pretoria: Christian Mission International of South Africa, 1988). Pike misread the fundamental reasons for conflict in South Africa and in a simplistic way consistently equated the liberation struggle with "terrorism". South Africa's "War on Terror" eventually had to subside, not only because of the rising costs, but also when the realisation dawned that the opponents of apartheid were not terrorists, but South Africans and Namibians intent on gaining equal status and not willing to be dictated to by a government in which they had no say. In the case of Namibia it was even more ironic as South Africa projected military power over thousands of kilometres while insisting that they knew what was best for the Namibian people. (History may not repeat itself but some tendencies later begot mirror images. In this sense there is ample opportunity to undertake comparative studies between apartheid's War on Terror, the Total Counter Strategy, and those currently waged by the United States of America, the United Kingdom, France and Israel against "global terrorism".)

13.   The figures provided by Seegers differ from those of the IISS. According to her, the permanent force already consisted of 17 951 members in 1960 and that number increased to 30 749 in 1970. Seegers, 146–147. Published literature here presents some inconsistencies. David Williams in his work entitled *On the Border, 1965–1990* claims that towards the end of the 1970s, "there were about 60 000 [conscripts] in training or trained at any given time". Williams, 24.

14.   "What will happen if South Africa is attacked", *To the Point* 5, no. 50 (10 December 1976): 7.

15.   Williams, 24.

16.   Seegers, 147.

17.   International Institute for Strategic Studies, *The Military Balance, 1984–1985* (London: IISS, 1985), 82.

18.   International Institute for Strategic Studies, *The Military Balance, 1988–1989* (London: IISS, 1989), 139–140.

19.   K. O'Brien, *The South African Intelligence Services: From Apartheid to Democracy, 1948–2005* (London/New York: Taylor & Francis, 2010), 100.

20.   For examples see *Positiewe Ervarings en Boodskappe van sommige Voormalige Dienspligtiges en ander Ondersteuners, SAW Simposium: 30 Aug 1997*. Another example is to be found in I. van Niekerk, "Laaitie tot 'n Man – Hoe die Weermag my van die Lewe geleer het." *Grensoorlog/Border War 1966–1989*. Special edition of the *Journal for Contemporary History* 31 no.3 (2006): 349–369.

21.   H.M. Johnson, *Sociology: A Systematic introduction* (London: Allied Publishers, 1971), 8–9.

22.   Johnson, 310.

23.   A. Akerman, *Somewhere on the Border* (Johannesburg: Wits University Press, 2012), ix. Media censorship, closed communities, group think and international isolation all contributed to an element of collective ignorance within the white South African community. The militarisation of white society and the result of the military occupation in Namibia and aggression in Angola were internationally well known, but, due to strict censorship, sadly not among the great majority of white citizens in South Africa. See for example, Catholic Institute of International Relations, *South Africa in the 1980s: State of Emergency* (London, 1980) on "National Security Ideology" and "State Violence" as well as military involvement in Namibia and Angola. Also compare Kairos Werkgroep,

Kerk en bevrijdings-bewegingen (Utrecht, 1981). But white South African readers had no access to such materials.

24. Akerman, xviii.

25. J. Delaney & J. Greenough, *Staying Alive: The Paratrooper's Story* (Oxford/Grand Rapids: Monarch Books, 2004), 10.

26. J. Frederickse, *South Africa, Different Kind of War: From Soweto to Pretoria* (Johannesburg Ravan Press, 1986), 8 and 186.

27. *Ons vir jou Suid-Afrika*, ed. F.J.N. Harman (Pretoria/Cape Town: HAUM, 1979), 1.

28. Frederickse, 9. Also see 8–11 and 186 for more on veld schools.

29. It is surprising that an Afrikaans historian such as Herman Giliomee denies that white South African society was militarised. In some inexplicable way, the author did not take into account an observable historical development between 1966 and 1989.

30. The State Security Council was established in 1972 and "total defence" against a "total onslaught" became part of a pervasive ideological mindset. In the process the white electorate, including the rank and file of rural National Party supporters and (the whites only) parliament, were gradually losing any leverage on political power and were co-opted into a bureaucratic security state designed by hawks in ascendance.

31. *Paratus* (March 1974): 59.

32. M.J. Viljoen, "Die Ontstaan en Ontwikkeling van die Skoolkadette-stelsel in die RSA: Grepe uit die Geskiedenis en 'n Oorsig oor die Huidige Stelsel," *Scientia Militaria* 15 no. 3 (1985): 48.

33. *Paratus*, (March 1974): 59.

34. *Paratus* (February 1984): 34–35. Also see Viljoen, 45–46.

35. *Die Burger*, 28 April 1987, 10.

36. J. Young, *The Spirit of the Tower: The Grey 1856–2006* (Port Elizabeth: Grey High School and Junior School, 2006), 232.

37. S. Haw & R. Frame, *For Hearth and Home: The Story of Maritzburg College 1863–1988* (Pietermaritzburg: MC Publications, 1988), 434.

38. M.W. Phillips, *The End Conscription Campaign 1983–1988: A Study of White Extra-Parliamentary Opposition to Apartheid* (MA, University of South Africa, 2002), 74.

39. For a case study on (changing) political attitudes at one Afrikaans-speaking university, the University of Stellenbosch, and its effect on relations with the military, see Deon Visser and Ian Liebenberg, "Afrikaner Nationalism, Tertiary Military Education and Civil Discontent: Student Attitudes at an Afrikaans University, 1950–1989," ACTA: 34th Congress of the International Commission of Military History (Vol. II) entitled *Military Conflicts and Civil Populations: Total Wars, Limited Wars, Asymmetric Wars* (Rome: Italian Military Institute, 2009), 675–692, but especially 686, 689–691.

40. J. Gagiano, "Ruling Group Cohesion in South Africa: A Study of Political Attitudes among White University Students", in *Worlds of Difference: The Political Attitudes of White Students in South Africa. An IDASA Research Report*, ed. I. Liebenberg (Mowbray: IDASA, 1990), 21.

41. Gagiano, 21.

42. Gagiano, 29. Also compare S. Booysen, "Cohesion, Dissention and Contradiction in the Political World of South Africa's White Student Youth," in Liebenberg, 35–62.

43. Phillips, 6–7. Also see C. Lingle, "On the Real Costs of Military Conscription," *South African Journal of Economics* 57, no. 3: 178–183.

44. Phillips, 7.

45. P.H. Frankel, *Pretoria's Praetorians: Civil-Military Relations in South Africa* (Cambridge: Cambridge University Press, 1984), 135.

46.   See *The Hidden Hand, ed.* C. Schutte, I. Liebenberg & A. Minnaar (Pretoria: Human Sciences Research Council, 1998) for internal repression. For regional violence, see *Frontline Southern Africa: Destructive Engagement,* ed. P. Johnson & D. Martin (New York: Four Walls Eight Windows, 1988).

47.   For examples of arguments within this mindset, see G.A. Cruywagen, "Ek sê wat ek Wil! Waar Staan u mnr. Naudé?", *Ster,* 18 December 1970, 53; "Die Week van die Generaals" in *Die Brandwag,* 7 January 1977, 86ff; "Verdedigingsbegroting," *Die Brandwag,* 7 January 1977, 85; "Military Defensibility brings Stability," Byvoegsel/Supplement *Paratus,* September 1976, i; "Ons moet saamstaan en hard werk" (interview with Magnus Malan), Byvoegsel/Supplement *Paratus,* September 1976, xiv; "Kerk moet nooit primêre doel verwaarloos" (interview with the State President), *Die Kerkbode* (official newspaper of the Nederduits Gereformeerde Kerk), 16 March 1988, 16.

48.   John W. de Gruchy, *The Church Struggle in South Africa* (Cape Town: Fortress Press, 1979), 143. The Hammanskraal Declaration of 1974 by the South African Council of Churches should be seen in this context. "Thus the Hammanskraal Statement was not [only] a product of the peace churches; in fact it was not strictly a pacifist document. Fundamental to its logic was the 'just war' theory, a theory dependent on situational analysis, and one which no thorough pacifist would use to defend or promote his position." The inherent tension between principled/universal pacifism and those supporting a just war against an unjust government was to mark resistance to conscription in South Africa till the end.

49.   Compare De Gruchy, 142ff. See also Charles Villa-Vicencio, *Trapped in Apartheid: A Socio-Theoretical History of the English-Speaking Churches* (New York: Orbis Books, 1988), 156, 158–159. On this topic from a revisionist Calvinist point of view consult Allan Boesak, *Black and Reformed: Apartheid, Liberation and the Calvinist Tradition* (Johannesburg: Orbis Books, 1984), 39, 42–43.

50.   For a defence of conscription and a critique against conscientious objection to military service in the military forces under Nationalist Party rule, consult *Geloofsbesware teen Diensplig en Verbandhoudende Sake.* The document was issued by the Dutch Reformed Church elective leadership (Breë Moderatuur van die Nederduits Gereformeerde Kerk) (Pretoria, 1980). For an example of a practical manual for national servicemen, see Rob K. Gee, *AAANDAG! 'n Handleiding vir Christelik nasionale dienspligtiges* with a foreword by Dr Louw Alberts (Cape Town, 1974). Gee was at the time Director of the Unit for Action under the Armed Forces and based at Lenz Military Base.

51.   Seegers, 177. For a general overview, see Catholic Institute for International Relations & Pax Christi, *War and Conscience in South Africa: The Churches and Conscientious Objection* (London: 1982). The view of the Nederduitse Gereformeerde Kerk is contained in P. Potgieter, *Die Christen en Oorlog: 'n Bybelkor-kursus* (Wellington, 1981).

52.   The Amendment of the Defence Act made conscientious objection a crime punishable by a fine of R5 000 and/or imprisonment for up to five years. John Dugard, *Human Rights and the South African Legal Order* (New Jersey: Princeton University Press, 1978), 177.

53.   Seegers, 177.

54.   Some refer to the judicious mix of apartheid orientated nationalism, the rise of the security state, religious rationalisation for a strong state and technocratic legalism as "theologised nationalism". Villa-Vicencio, 140. The author expands on how such an ideology deeply influenced the notion of press freedom, individual rights and the role of the military, 140–143. Earlier the theologian Dawid Bosch described the convolution and use of religion to rationalise apartheid and white control as an emerging *civil religion.* Consult D.J. Bosch. "The Roots and Fruits of Afrikaner Civil Religion," in *New Faces of Africa: Essays in Honour of Ben Marais,* ed. W.G. Hofmeyer and W.S. Vorster (Pretoria: Unisa, 1984). Those critical of the white civil religion would recall that W.A. (Bill) de Klerk pointed out the close link between Protestantism and the evolution of the apartheid ideology long before the historian Hermann Giliomee, in a work entitled *The Puritans in Africa.* In the 1980s the supporters of the Kairos movement referred to "state theology" and an exiled South African poet amidst great controversy suggested that the apartheid leadership "moved God around like a Caspir" Afrikaans: "God soos 'n Caspir rondskuif" (a Caspir was an armoured personnel carrier that was used to subdue

unrest in the townships and was also used by the police unit, Koevoet, in northern Namibia during the border war).

55. Compare John Dugard and Anthony Matthews, *Freedom, State Security and the Rule of Law: Dilemmas of the Apartheid Society* (Cape Town: Juta, 1986).

56. Matthews, 158. See also Dugard.

57. See Dugard, 130ff, 155ff and 303ff, and Mathews, 269ff, 281ff and 284.

58. While noticeable in the Christian tradition, pacifism is not the domain of Christian believers only (M. Schmidt and Van der Walt, *Black Flame: The Revolutionary Class Politics of Anarchism and Syndicalism* (Edinburgh: AK Press, 2009), 204. Strong advocacy against all forms of pacifism was prevalent in early modern Europe. See Frank Tallet, *War and Society in Early-Modern Europe, 1495–1715* (London: Routledge, 1997), 238, 240–241. For a more basic text on the origins and complexities of pacifism, including non-Christian pacifism such as *satyāgraha* read "Pacifism and Nonviolent Movements" in *Encyclopaedia Britannica* (Macropedia, vol.13), (Tokyo, 1974), 845ff.

59. Such appeals were, and perhaps still are, not welcomed in a state that reflected authoritarian tendencies. In fact, numerous Western states still maintain chaplain services where chaplains wear the uniform of the military (the state's ultimate claim to power), fill out security clearances, and are paid by the state which make them by implication an officer of the state rather than the embodiment of God's calling (in a sense thus using religion in uniform to support the state, in a way the Chaplain as Commissar).

60. See for example *Afrikaners tussen die Tye*, ed. B. Lategan & H. Müller (Bramley: Taurus, 1990.)

61. Even before the Belhar Confession a core group of pastors and theologians within the "non-white" Dutch Reformed Church or *susterskerke* played an important role in highlighting church unity against apartheid ideology. Shun Govender, "Een Belijdende Kerk in Zuid-Afrika?" in *Met de moed der hoop. Opstellen aangeboden aan Dr C.F. Beyers Naudé* (Baarn: Ten Have, 1985), 94ff. See also *Unity and Justice: The Witness of the Belydende Kring*, ed. Shun P. Govender (Braamfontein: Die Belydende Kring, 1984).

62. Marjorie Hope and James Young, *The South African Churches in a Revolutionary Situation*, (New York: Orbis, 1981), 91ff.

63. Frankel, 133.

64. K. Spink, *Black Sash: The Beginning of a Bridge in South Africa* (London: Metheun, 1991), 218–223.

65. The exact number of men who publicly objected (many on political grounds) in 1988 was 143. Ben Schoeman, "Regverdige Alternatiewe is Nodig", *Kampus Kruis* 1, no. 3 (16 Augustus 1988): 8. For another view along the same lines, see Sue Valentine, "Min dae brings no Happiness: Wide Support for Civilian Service", *Democracy in Action* (July/August 1990): 20.

66. For examples, see End Conscription Campaign, *End Conscription Campaign in Perspective*, June 1987.

67. See *Hawks and Doves – The Pro- and Anti-Conscription Press in South Africa*, ed. M. Graaf (Durban: Contemporary Cultural Studies Unit, University of Natal, 1988).

68. For more on this, see D. Conway, "'All these Long-Haired Fairies should be forced to do their Military Training. Maybe they will become Men'. The End Conscription Campaign, Sexuality, Citizenship and Military Conscription in Apartheid South Africa," *South African Journal on Human Rights* 20, (2004): 207–229.

69. *Jeugkrag* was funded by Military Intelligence as part of Project Essay. "For some Years", *TRC Report, Vol. 2*, 526. For *Jeugkrag*'s view on the ECC, see the undated pamphlet *Jeugkrag SA/Youth for SA*, 15. *Jeugkrag*'s chairperson was Martinus van Schalkwyk who lectured at the University of Stellenbosch in Political Science after a sojourn at the Randse Afrikaans University as a National Party coordinator and a student of politics. He became the last leader of the National Party and joined the ANC, who appointed him as minister of tourism.

70. The PSA published the *PSA Bulletin* at Stellenbosch with a regular stream of articles against communism and terrorism, the value of the free market and articles attempting to discredit the "left". The PSA, headed by Nicholas Myburgh among others, hosted a public meeting for a Unita

delegation consisting of "Brigadier" Tito Chingunji, Wambu Chindodo and G. Mozanga. *PSA Bulletin*, no. 2 (2 September 1986).

71. National Student Federation, "20 Years of Struggle: Unita in Angola" (1985).

72. Catholic Institute for International Relations, *Out of Step: War Resistance in South Africa* (London: Catholic Institute for International Relations, 1989), 104. See 114 for an anti-ECC leaflet distributed by the NSF.

73. *Beeld*, 3 August 1992, 2. Also see *TRC Report, Vol. 2*, 529.

74. M. Shear, *Wits: A University in the Apartheid Era* (Johannesburg: University of the Witwatersrand, 1996), 68. *TRC Report, Vol. 2*, 529. The NSF was run under Project Aristotle. It was one of the special projects the SAP embarked upon after being directed by the SSC to do so on 16 November 1985.

75. See H.W. van der Merwe, *Peacemaking in South Africa: A Life in Conflict Resolution* (Cape Town: Tafelberg, 2000.)

76. Compare Centre for Intergroup Studies, Workshop on Alternative National Service, 30–31 October 1989, Hohenhort Hotel, Constantia, Cape. Also see Centre for Intergroup Studies, *Conscientious Objection*, Occasional Paper, No. 8 (First published 1983, further editions 1984, 1989). Especially relevant are 42ff, 64ff and 82ff.

77. P. Hopkins, *Voëlvry: The Movement that Rocked South Africa* (Cape Town: Zebra, 2006), 9 and 14. Also see A. Grundlingh, "'Rocking the boat' in South Africa? Voëlvry Music and Afrikaans Anti-Apartheid Social Protest in the 1980s," *The International Journal of African Historical Studies* 37, no. 3 (2004): 483–514.

78. For examples, see *Die Suid-Afrikaan* 12 (December 1987): 34–37 and *Die Suid-Afrikaan* 17 (October/ November 1988): 16–19.

79. For *Vrye Weekblad*, see M. du Preez, "Oranje Blanje Blues: 'n Nostalgiese Trip", *Vrye Weekblad 88–94* (Cape Town: 2005.)

80. See the programme for Ordes-werkswinkel on 14–15 October 1988, *Wat kom na Apartheid? Die Vryheidsmanifes in Perspektief*. For the response to that, see the undated pamphlets of Kovsie Navorsingsgroep on the ANC/SAKP alliance, *Die Freedom Charter in Perspektief: Standpunte van die ANC/SAKP-Alliansie* and Nasionale Studente Federasie, *Breek deur na Ware Vryheid: Die Regte Vryheidsmanifes*.

81. *Beeld*, 19 January 1993, 6.

82. For a discussion of contemporary publications on the Border War, see I. Liebenberg, G. van der Westhuizen & T. du Plessis, "Through the Mirage: Retracing Moments of a War 'Up There',"
Scientia Militaria 38, no. 2(2010): 131–149.

83. See for instance the letter in *Beeld*, 21 January 2010, 20.

84. *The Star*, 28 October 2009, 15.

85. *The Star*, 28 October 2009, 15.

86. Seegers, 196.

87. *Beeld*, 20 March 1997, 16.

88. See the ezine *Smokebox*, issue 46 at http://www.smokebox.net/archives/what/morgan1206.html. Accessed on 6 June 2012.

Cuban Archives
Images of the Angolan War

Nairobi, January 1975

Convened by the head of state of Kenya, the heads of the various organisations meet an Angolan delegation. From right to left are Agostinho Neto of the MPLA, Holden Roberto of the FNLA, the President of Kenya and Johnathan (Jonas) Savimbi of UNITA.

10 November 1975

At Quifangondo, 22 kilometres from Luanda, Angolan-Cuban forces finally halted the foreign forces invading from the north. FNLA troops supported by Zairean soldiers, South African contingents, and mercenaries who had CIA support, were repelled alter advancing swiftly from the north.

23 November 1975

South African forces were forced into a hasty retreat at Ebo (some referred to the incident as the "Ebo gallop"). Left is a knocked-out Eland armoured car.

1975–1976

South African equipment damaged and captured during the South African invasion at Ebo.

December 1975

Young South African prisoners of war were presented to the international media in Luanda. All hopes for plausible deniability about South African intervention were now dashed, and the cooperation between South Africa, the CIA, the forces of Mobuto SeseSeko of Zaire and Holden Roberto's FNLA was now common knowledge within the international community.

6 January 1976

Risquet Jorge Valdes, representing the Government of Cuba in Angola during a visit to Negage after it had been captured by Angolan-Cuban troops. Behind, watching with binoculars, Prime Commander Abelardo Colome Ibarra, head of the Cuban troops in Angola.

February 1976

Angolan and Cuban soldiers entrenching in the immediate vicinity of Caxito. By this time the balance of power was swinging away from the invaders from the north.

February 1976

The bridge at Cuvo Cuive River was destroyed by South African forces.

February 1976

Cuban soldiers at the Longe River, Karma.

February 1976

Civilians entrenched in Caxito, north of Luanda, awaiting attacks from the FNLA, the Zaireans and South Africans. All members of society took part in the defence as invading forces moved in with CIA and South African support, from the north and south, advancing rapidly towards Luanda in an attempt to prevent an Angola that would become a member of the non-aligned movement rather than a client state of the West.

January/February 1976   The invasion from the South repelled. On 9 February, the hoisting of the Angolan flag in Huambo. On the 10th of February, Angolan forces entered Lobito and Benguela. On the 16th and 17th Sa de Bandeira and Mocamedes followed. The South African newspaper *Sunday Times* noted that "the speed of FAPLA's advance has taken everybody by surprise" (Gleijeses, 2002: 342).

January 1976
FAPLA and Allied forces enter Uige on their way to the border of Zaire following the defeat of the invaders at Quifangondo, Morro da Cal and the area of Caxito earlier on. In the north, the threat was now repulsed.

27 March 1976
Angolan and Cuban troops at Ruacana on the Angolan/ Namibian border after the retreat of the apartheid South African invading forces.

1976
Dr Pedro Luis Pedroso, second from right, along with other Cuban fighters after the capture of the city of Huambo.

March 1977   During a visit to Angola President Fidel Castro met with the president of SWAPO, Mr Sam Nujoma. Soviet veterans stated that SWAPO's military wing, the People's Liberation Army of Namibia (PLAN), was well trained and well disciplined.

6 September 1977
Talks between Angola and South Africa at Mozamedes.

4 May 1978

Collateral damage. On 4 May 1978, South African forces struck at Cassinga (Operation Reindeer) in an airborne operation preceded by aerial bombardments, claiming that it was a major SWAPO base. Six hundred civilians were killed, including 350 children. One of the victims (left) was photographed by the international media. The Cuban military archives contain numerous photos of civilian casualties.

March 1980
A downed South African Impala aircraft being inspected by Angolan and Cuban forces. A SWAPO combatant can also be observed here.

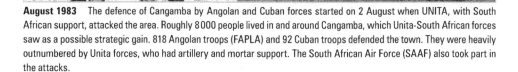

August 1983   The defence of Cangamba by Angolan and Cuban forces started on 2 August when UNITA, with South African support, attacked the area. Roughly 8 000 people lived in and around Cangamba, which Unita-South African forces saw as a possible strategic gain. 818 Angolan troops (FAPLA) and 92 Cuban troops defended the town. They were heavily outnumbered by Unita forces, who had artillery and mortar support. The South African Air Force (SAAF) also took part in the attacks.

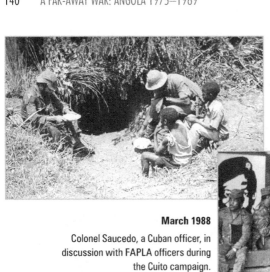

1987
Angolan and Cuban combatants on the Mozamedes-Menongue line sharing a meal with young boys from the community.

March 1988
Colonel Saucedo, a Cuban officer, in discussion with **FAPLA** officers during the Cuito campaign.

March 1988
Cuban armour in the vicinity of Cuito Cuanavale.

June 1988

The president of the Federation of Cuban Women, Vilma Espin, bidding farewell to the Anti-Aircraft Regiment, which was composed of women and was leaving for the South Front of Angola.

Cuban assessors and FAPLA combatants at Quifangondo.

Young Angolans at a recruitment post. Due to regular incursions by South African forces and the destabilisation effect of the rebel group Unita, headed by Jonas Savimbi, Angola had to implement conscription in 1981. Thanks to the policy of constructive engagement maintained by the USA, South African forces and Unita received leeway for their adventures in Angola.

Angolan forces made use of the Soviet SAM-2 anti-aircraft missile. First displayed in 1957 (code named Guideline by NATO), it was a dated piece of equipment by 1987. The SAM-2 was based on a rotatable platform and could be transported overland on a trailer by an articulated truck. Directing the missiles was by remote control or manually. The effective range was more than 30 kilometres and the missile could be used against all types of aircraft. The SAM-2, in combination with low-level anti-aircraft guns, such as the four-barrelled ZS-23 (23 mm calibre) formed part of a defensive umbrella that provided security before air superiority was established by the Angolan and Cuban forces.

Celebrations held the first year after the invasion by foreign forces were repelled on the Angolan front. Here Fidel Castro, Augostino Neto, Jorge Risquet and Lucia Lara, dynamic leader and strategist of the Angolan liberation struggle. Lara was later to say: "We were preparing for elections and for governance, but found ourselves embroiled in a war."

A group of Cuban combatants (or "internationalist forces" – *combatientes internacionalistas*). At the end of the campaign in 1976 around 38 000 Cuban soldiers, doctors and support personnel were deployed. During the SANDF incursion of 1987/1988 and the clashes around the Lomba River, Tumpo Triangle and Cuito Cuanavale, Cuban force deployment exceeded 50 000.

Russia
Images of a Far-Away War

FAPLA M-46 (130 mm) gun exercises, circa 1982.

FAPLA Zu-23 (23 mm) gun exercises, circa 1982.

Conscript sailor (radioman) Oleg Lazarev sits on BRDM-2 Matala near 11th FAPLA brigade, circa 1983.

Mulondo 1984. Soviet military advisors of the 19th brigade before anthills. Photo from archive of Colonel Soldatenko.

Exercises of FAPLA D-30 howitzer (122 mm) circa 1984. Photo from archive of Colonel Soldatenko.

Lt Colonel of artillery Vladimir Soldatenko in dug-out 2yh. FAPLA brigade, Kahama, circa 1984.

Lt Colonel of artillery, Vladimir Soldatenko, 2nd FAPLA brigade, writes a letter in a dug-out, Kahama, circa 1984.

Junior Lt Barabulyaiv sits on a T-34/85 tank in Angola, circa 1984.

Military interpreter Alexander Sergeev is preparing New Year pie. Cuito-Cuanava, on the eve of 1988.

Military interpreter Alexandex Shulga (right) sits on FAB-500 (500 kg bomb), Luena, circa 1987.

Military interpreter Igor Bakush in front of BTR-60PB before Operation Salute, October 1987.

Military interpreter Alexander Kalan next to an Engeza-50 Brazilian truck destroyed by a direct hit from a UNITA mine, 16th FAPLA brigade, 1987.

Military interpreter Alexander Sergeev of the 25th FAPLA brigade next to a Grad-1P (122 mm) recoilless rifle in December 1988 on the Shambinga River.

Warrant Officer Vladimir Dedeshko of the 2nd FAPLA Brigade with a Mosin carbine at Shangongo, circa 1988.

Military Interpreter Oleg Gritsuk of the 13th FAPLA Brigade at the end of 1987 at Cuito Cuanavale.

Maps

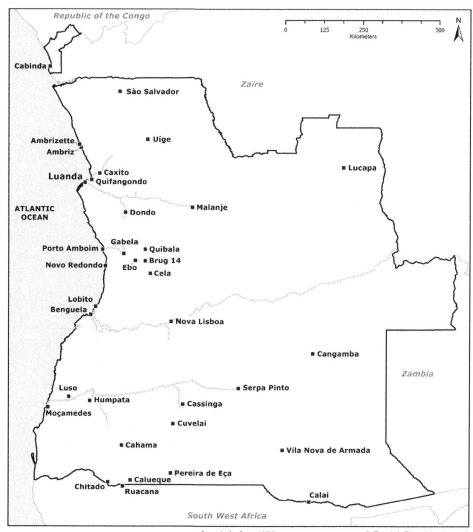

Angola before 1975.

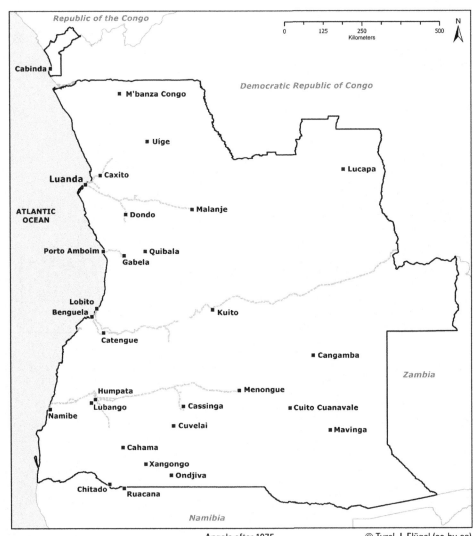

Angola after 1975.   © Tyrel J. Flügel (cc-by-sa)

Cuito Cuanavale: Map of the initial military situation with position of forces at Cuito Cuanavale and surroundings, 1987. SOURCE: Cabrera, M.R. *La Guerra de Angola*. La Habana: Editoria Politica, 1989 (Appendix).

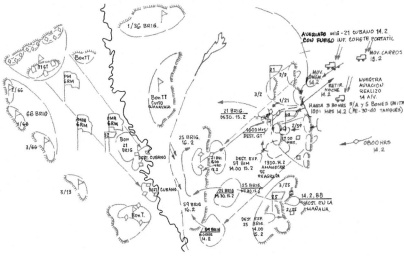

Cuito Cuanavale: The position of opposing forces on the 14th of February 1988.
SOURCE: Cabrera, M.R. *La Guerra de Angola*. La Habana: Editoria Politica, 1989 (Appendix).

COMBATE DEL DIA 23.3.88

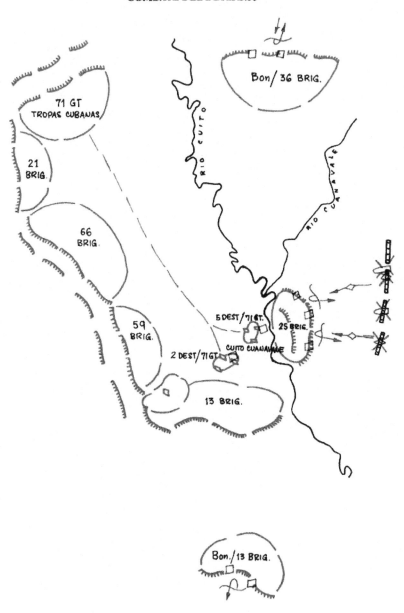

Map of the situation on the battlefield in the Cuito Cuanavale area on the 23rd of March 1988. The situation for the SADF became untenable. SOURCE: Cabrera, M.R. *La Guerra de Angola*. La Habana: Editoria Politica, 1989 (Appendix).

Dust, War, Far-away Theatres, Home fronts and Peace

Schutztruppe in German South West Africa (Deutsch-Südwest-Afrika) circa 1903.
SOURCE: Postcard, Swakopmund, 1998 (Author's collection).

Terrible twins – Cold War and Total Onslaught: Cover page of the *Pro Nat*, National Party mouthpiece, March 1978. The Red Bear – and Moscow – as omnipresence. SOURCE: Author's Archive.

For many white Namibians (Afrikaans: *Suidwesters*, derived from *Suidwes-Afrika*) UN Resolution 435 was a ploy to sever Namibia as the "fifth province" from South Africa and to undermine white power. Even the internal multi-ethnic Democratic Turnhalle Alliance (DTA) in Namibia was seen as the thin end of the wedge. SOURCE: Cover page of a book by Strauss, F.J. *SWA vir die Wolwe?* Windhoek: Eros Publishers, 1981 (Author's Archive).

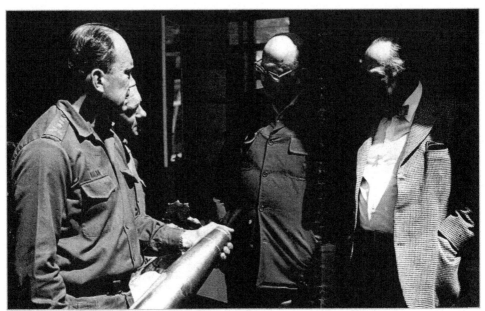

Three politicians and a general. From left to right: Magnus Malan, PW Botha and BJ Vorster. At the back left, Gen Constand Viljoen. SOURCE: Author's newspaper and photo collection (1976–1983).

After the withdrawal of the Cuban and South African forces from Angola the civil war continued for several years. Elections were held but Jonas Savimbi rejected the outcome of the elections and his Unita movement continued the insurgent war with intermittent help from various sources. With the killing of an isolated Savimbi on 22 February 2002 the war ended finally. Seen here are conscript FAPLA soldiers during signals training in the middle 1990s. SOURCE: Angolan Archives.

Operation Savannah; a South African 25-pounder (88 mm) gun in tow. On the left, an Eland armoured car with crew doing maintenance. During Savannah, the Eland (also referred to as "Noddy Car" by some) formed the backbone of the South African Defence Force (SADF) armoured capability. SOURCE: SANDF Documentation Centre, Pretoria.

South African cross-border operation. To the left can be seen a captured BM-21 multiple rocket launcher (MRL) with an anti-aircraft gun in tow. SOURCE: SANDF Documentation Centre, Pretoria.

A SADF recovery vehicle with a captured MPLA T-34/85 tank in tow. SOURCE: SANDF Documentation Centre, Pretoria.

A South African Air Force Puma helicopter landing against the backdrop of Mirage F1s at Air Force Base Waterkloof, Pretoria. SOURCE: *Radio & TV Dagboek*, 25 Julie–01 Augustus 1976.

Operational map of Angola with Russian inscriptions. SOURCE: Gennady Shubin.

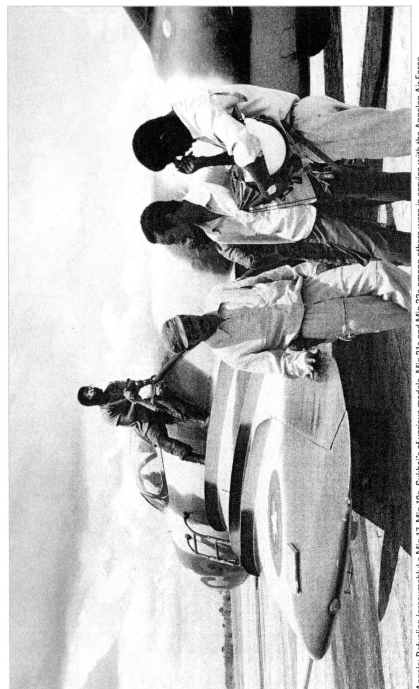

Angola: Refueling (presumably) a Mig 17. Mig 19s, Sukhoi's of various models, Mig 21s and Mig 23s among others were in service with the Angolan Air Force.
SOURCE: Angolan Archives.

Captured South African equipment at the war museum in Luanda. Among others in front two cannibalized Buffels, a Kwevoel truck and Eland armoured car. SOURCE: Ian Liebenberg.

Captured Eland armoured car, Military Museum, Luanda, 2007. SOURCE: Ian Liebenberg.

A member of the home guard (auxiliary forces) of Angola with a mural of President Agostinho
Neto in the background – middle 1980s. SOURCE: MPLA Archives.

State propaganda against the End Conscription Campaign distributed at Stellenbosch University circa 1986. SOURCE: Author's archive.

Independence Day, Namibia. Among others the leader of the unbanned ANC Mr Nelson Mandela later to become President of South Africa in 1994, with General Cintra Frias commander of the Cuban forces, to his immediate left and Jorge Risquet (with glasses) to his upper right. SOURCE: Tanja Hichert, 1990.

Freedom Monument, Windhoek, Namibia. SOURCE: Ian Liebenberg, 2009.

Editors Jorge Risquet and Hedelberto
Lopez Blanch during a lighter moment.
Cuban Military Archives, Havana, 2007.
SOURCE: Ian Liebenberg.

With Lucio Lara, influential leader and strategist of the MPLA
liberation movement. The politically astute Lara was to say later,
"We prepared for elections but was confronted by a civil war ..."
SOURCE: Paulo Lara (Gen).

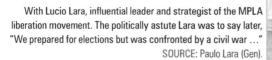

Editors Vladimir Shubin and Ian Liebenberg in discussion
with a South African colleague, Willem Schurink, 2007.
Pretoria. SOURCE: Mariaan Roos.

Editor Jorge Risquet, Havana, 2007.
SOURCE: Hedelberto Lopez Blanch.

Bibliography on the Border War

Gert van der Westhuizen

BOOKS

Abbott, P., Heitman, H. & Hannon, P. *Modern African Wars: South-West Africa*. Colchester: Osprey Publishing, 1991.

Adebajo, A. *UN Peacekeeping in Africa: From the Suez Crisis to the Sudan Conflicts*. Auckland Park: Jacana Media, 2011.

Africa Watch. *Accountability in Namibia*. New York: Africa Watch, 1992.

Alden, C. *Apartheid's Last Stand: The Rise and Fall of the South African Security State*. London: Macmillan Press, 1996.

Alexiev, A.R. *Unita and US Policy in Angola*. Santa Monica: Rand, 1987.

Allan, K., ed. *Paper Wars: Access to Information in South Africa*. Johannesburg: Wits University Press, 2009.

Andrew, R. *Buried in the Sky*. Sandton: Penguin Books, 2001.

Andrews, T.E. *The ABC of Military Associated Place and Street names in Pretoria and Environs*. Fort Klapperkop Military Museum, 1990.

Anonymous. *32 Bataljon/Battalion*. n.p.: June 1992.

Arnold, G. *Wars in the Third World since 1945*. 2nd ed. London: Cassell, 1995. First published in 1991.

Aron, R. *The Imperial Republic: The United States and the World, 1945-1973*. Cambridge: Winthrop, 1974.

Army Gymnasium. *The Army Gymnasium Annual 1968-1979*. n.p, n.d.

Asmal, K., Asmal, L. & Roberts, R.S. *Reconciliation through Truth: A Reckoning of Apartheid's Criminal Governance*. Cape Town/Johannesburg: David Philip in association with Mayibuye Books, 1996.

Attwood, W. *The Reds and the Blacks: A Personal adventure*. London: Hutchinson, 1967.

Baddock, P. *Images of War*. Durban: Graham Publishing, 1981.

Baker, D-P. & Jordaan, E., eds. *South Africa and Contemporary Insurgency: Roots, Practices, Prospects*. Claremont: UCT Press, 2010.

Bakkes, C. *Boskroniek (April-Junie 1977) Dagverhaal van 'n Grenssoldaat*. C.M. Waterkloofhoogte: Bakkes, 2008.

Bakkes, C.J. *Oepse Daisy*. Cape Town: Queillerie, 2011.

Baines, G. & Vale, P., eds. *Beyond the Border War: New Perspectives on Southern Africa's Late-Cold War Conflicts*. Pretoria: University of South Africa Press, 2008.

Barber, J. *South Africa's Foreign Policy 1945-1970*. London: Oxford University Press, 1973.

Barber, J. & Barratt, J. *South Africa's Foreign Policy*. Johannesburg: Southern Book Publishers, 1990.

Bark, D.L., ed. *The Red Orchestra. Vol. 2: The Case of Africa*. Stanford: Hoover Institution Press, 1988.

Barlow, E. *Executive Outcomes: Against all Odds*. Alberton: Galago, 2007.

Barnard, S.L., Van der Westhuizen, G.J. & Smit, I., eds. *Vrystaatse Artillerie: Geskiedenis van 6 Veldregiment*. Bloemfontein: Vrystaatse Artillerie, 1989.

Barnard, S.L. *Die Suid-Afrikaanse "Grensoorlog", 1966 tot 1989: Militêre Historici by die Kruispad*. Intreerede deur prof. S.L. Barnard, Departement Geskiedenis Universiteit van die Oranje-Vrystaat, 6 Oktober 1993, Bloemfontein: University of the Orange Free State, 1993.

Barnard, S.L. *Pantser in Aksie: 1 SDB 1933-1993*. Bloemfontein: 1 Spesiale Diensbataljon, 1993.

Barnard, L., ed. *Grensoorlog/Border War 1966-1989*. Special edition of *Journal for Contemporary History* 31, no. 3, December 2006.

Barnard, L., ed. *Grensoorlog/Border War 1966-1989, Deel 2/Part 2*. Special edition of *Journal for Contemporary History* 34, no. 1, February 2009.

Barnard, N. & Wiese, T. *Geheime Revolusie: Memoires van 'n Spioenbaas*. Kaapstad: Tafelberg, 2015.

Barns, T.A. *Angolan Sketches*. London: Methuen, 1928.

Batchelor, P., Kingma, K. & Lamb, G., eds. *Demilitarization and Peace-Building in Southern Africa, Vol. III*. London: Ashgate, 2004.

Batley, K. *A Secret Burden: Memories of the Border War by South African Soldiers who Fought in it*. Johannesburg & Cape Town: Jonathan Ball Publishers, 2007.

Becker, B., ed. *Speaking Out: Namibians Share their Perspectives on Independence*. Windhoek: Out of Africa Publishers, 2005.

Becker, D. *On Wings of Eagles: South Africa's Military Aviation History*. Durban: Walker Rumus, 1970.

Benard, E. & Twala, M. *Mbokodo. Inside MK – Mwezi Twala, a Soldier's Story*. Johannesburg: Jonathan Ball Publishers, 1994.

Bender, G., Coleman, J.S. & Sklar, R.L., eds. *African Crisis Areas and U.S. Foreign Policy*. Berkeley: University of California Press, 1985.

Benjamin, L. & Gregory, C., eds. *Southern Africa at the Crossroads? Prospects for Stability and Development in the 1990s*. Rivonia: Justified Press, 1992.

Bennett, E., Gamba, V. & Van der Merwe, D., eds. *ACT against Child Soldiers in Africa: A Reader*. Pretoria: Institute for Security Studies, 2000.

Bernstein, K. & Strasburg, T. *Frontline Southern Africa*. London: Christopher Helm, 1998.

Berridge, G.R. *South Africa, the Colonial Powers and 'African Defence': The Rise and Fall of the White Entente, 1948-1960*. New York: St. Martin's Press, 1992.

Biermann, H.H., ed. and comp. *The Case for South Africa as put forth in the Public Statements of Eric H. Louw Foreign Minister of South Africa*. New York: Mcfadden Books, 1963.

Birmingham, D. *Portugal and Africa*. Ohio University Research in International Studies, Africa Series no. 81. Athens, Ohio: Ohio University Press, 1999.

Birmingham, D. *Empire: Angola and its Neighbors in Africa*. Athens, Ohio: Ohio University Press, 2006.

Bissell, R.E. & Crocker, C., eds. *South Africa Into the 1980s*. Westview Special Studies on Africa, Boulder Colorado: Westview Press, 1979.

Blake, C. *Troepie: From Call-Up to Camps*. Cape Town: Zebra Press, 2009.

Blake, C. *From Soldier to Civvy: Reflections on National Service*. Cape Town: Zebra Press, 2010.

Blake, C. *Troepie Snapshots: Pictorial Recollections of the South African Border War*. Johannesburg: 30 Degrees South Publishers, 2011.

Boll, J., ed. *War: Interdisciplinary Investigations*. Papers presented at the 4th Global Conference – War, Virtual War and Human Security, Budapest, Hungary, 2 May-5 May 2007. Oxford: Inter-Disciplinary Press, 2008.

Bondil, N., ed. *Cuba: Art and History from 1868 to Today*. Montreal: The Montreal Museum of Fine Arts, 2009.

Bonsignore, E., managing ed. *Military Technology, 6 (9), 1982: The Military Balance 1982-83*. Bonn: Wehr & Wissen Verlag, n.d.

Bopela, T. & Luthuli, D. *Umkhonto we Sizwe: Fighting for a Divided People*. Alberton: Galaga Books, 2005.

Boraine, A. *A Country Unmasked*. Oxford: Oxford University Press, 2000.

Bosgra, S.J. & Van Krimpen, C. *Portugal and Nato*. 3rd revised ed. Amsterdam: Angola Comité, May 1972.

Bosman, H. *Eye in the Sky: A Brief History of the SA Police Service Air Wing*. Nelspruit: Freeworld Publications, 1998.

Botha, M. & Van Aswegen, A. *Beelde van Suid-Afrika: 'n Alternatiewe Rolprentoplewing*. Pretoria: Human Sciences Research Council, 1992.

Bothma, C. *Los af! 'n Terugblik op Nasionale Diensplig, deur die oë van 'n Dienspligtige*. Hermanus: Hemel & See Boeke, 2009.

Bothma, L.J. *Die Buffel Struikel. 'n Storie van 32 Bataljon en sy Mense*. Revised ed. Bloemfontein: L.J. Bothma, 2008.

Bothma, L.J. *Losbaadjiesak: Stories in die Langpad*. Bloemfontein: L.J. Bothma, 2009.

Bothma, L.J. *Anderkant Cuito: 'n Reisverhaal van die Grensoorlog*. Langenhovenpark: L.J. Bothma, 2011.

Bothma, L.J. *Vang 'n Boer: Die Stryd tussen Boer en Ovambo*. Langenhovenpark: L.J. Bothma, 2012.

Bottoman, W.W. *The Making of an MK Cadre*. Pretoria: LiNc Publishers, n.d.

Bouch, R.J. ed. *Infanterie in Suid-Afrika (1652-1976.)* Publication no. 5. Pretoria: South African Defence Force Documentation Service, 1977.

Boulden, Laurie H.& Edmonds, Martin. *The Politics of De-Mining: Mine Clearance in Southern Africa*. Johannesburg: The South African Institute of International Affairs, 1999.

Bozeman, A. *Conflict in Africa: Concepts and Realities*. Princeton: Princeton University Press, 1976.

Branquinho, L. *Fantasy Industry: Perceptions of the South African Special Forces in the Media*. Durban: Just Done Productions, 2006.

Brautigam, D. *The Dragon's Gift: The real story of China in South Africa*. Oxford: Oxford University Press, 2009.

Bravo, E. *After the Battle*. Havana & London: Granma/Nexus & Channel 4 Television, 1990.

Bravo, E. *Fidel: The Untold Story*. New York: First Run Features, 2001.

Bredin, M. *Blood on the Tracks: A Rail Journey from Angola to Mozambique*. (Corrected ed.) London: Picador, 1995.

Breytenbach, B. *The True Confessions of an Albino Terrorist*. London/Boston: Faber and Faber, 1984.

Breytenbach, C. *Savimbi's Angola*. Cape Town: Howard Timmins Publishers, 1980.

Breytenbach, J. *Forged in Battle*. Cape Town: Saayman & Weber, 1986 (2014).

Breytenbach, J. *They Live by the Sword: 32 'Buffalo' Battalion – South Africa's Foreign Legion*. Alberton: Lemur, 1990.

Breytenbach, J. *The Buffalo Soldiers: The Story of South Africa's 32-Battalion 1975-1993*. Alberton: Galago, 2002.

Breytenbach, J. *Eagle Strike! The Controversial Airborne Assault on Cassinga 04 May 1978*. Sandton: Manie Grove Publishing, 2008.

Breytenbach, J. *The Tempered Sword. Forged in Battle Revisited: Operation Savannah and the Birth of 32 Bn*. Sandton: Bushwarrior.com, 2011.

Breytenbach, J. *Eden's Exiles: One Soldier's Fight for Paradise*. Pretoria: Protea Book House, 2015. First published in 1997.

Brewer, J., ed. *Can South Africa Survive?* Johannesburg: Southern Book Publishers, 1989.

Bridgland, F. *Jonas Savimbi: A Key to Africa*. Edinburgh: Mainstream Publishing, 1986.

Bridgland, F. *The War for Africa: Twelve Months that Transformed a Continent*. Gibraltar: Ashanti Publishing, 1990.

Brittain, V. *Hidden Lives, Hidden Deaths: South Africa's Crippling of a Continent*. London: Faber and Faber, 1990. (First published in 1988.)

Brittain, V. *Death of Dignity: Angola's Civil War*. London: Pluto Press, 1998.

Brogan, P. *World Conflicts: Why and Where they are Happening*. London: Bloomsbury, 1989.

Brooks, A.J. *Tale Gunner: The Lighter Side of South African Military Life*. Johannesburg: 30 Degrees South Publishers, 2010.

Brown, R.K. *I am Soldier of Fortune: Dancing with Devils*. Pinetown/Oxford: 30 Degrees South/Casemate, 2013.

Buntman, F.L. *Robben Island and Prisoner Resistance to Apartheid*. Cambridge: Cambridge University Press, 2003.

Burleigh, M. *Small Wars, Far Away Places: The Genesis of the Modern World: 1945-1965*. London: Macmillan, 2013.

Burger, M. & Gould, C. *Secrets and Lies: Wouter Basson and South Africa's Chemical and Biological Warfare Programme*. Cape Town: Zebra Press, 2002.

Burness, D. *On the Shoulder of Marti: Cuban Literature on the Angolan War*. Colorado Springs: Three Continents Press, 1996.

Bushin, V. *Social Democracy and Southern Africa*. Moscow: Progress Publishers, 1989.

Butts, K.H. & Thomas, P.R. *The Geopolitics of Southern Africa: South Africa as Regional Superpower*. Boulder, Colorado: Westview, 1986.

Byron, Thomas J.J. *Elimination Theory: The Secret Covert Networks of Project Coast*. Baltimore: Publish America, 2004.

Cabot, J. *Strike Back at Terror*. Pretoria: Thelaw, 1987.

Callinicos, A. *South Africa between Reform and Revolution*. London: Bookmarks, 1988.

Campbell, K.M. *Soviet Policy towards South Africa*. Basingstoke & London: Macmillan, 1986.

Cann, J.P. *Counterinsurgency in Africa: The Portuguese Way of War 1961-1974*. Solihull: Helion & Company, 2012.

Cann, J.P. *The Flechas: Insurgent Hunting in Eastern Angola, 1965-1974*. Africa@War Volume 11. Solihull/Pinetown: Helion & Company/30 Degrees South, 2013.

Cannon, T. *Revolutionary Cuba*. New York: Thomas Y. Crowell, 1981.

Cantón, N.J. *History of Cuba: The Challenge of the Yoke and the Star*. Havana: SI-MAR S.A. Publishing House, 2000.

Castro, F. *Fidel Castro Speeches 1984-85: War and Crisis in the Americas*. New York: Pathfinder Press, 1985.

Castro, F. (with Ramonet, I.) *My Life*. London: Allen Lane, 2007.

Catholic Institute for International Relations & Pax Christi. *War and Conscience in South Africa: The Churches and Conscientious Objection*. London: Catholic Institute for International Relations & Pax Christi, 1982.

Catholic Institute for International Relations & British Council of Churches. *Namibia in the 1980s. A Future for Namibia 1*. 2nd ed. London: Catholic Institute for International Relations & British Council of Churches, 1986.

Catholic Institute for International Relations. *Out of Step: War Resistance in South Africa*. London: Catholic Institute for International Relations, 1989.

Cawthra, G. *Brutal Force: The Apartheid War Machine*. London: International Defence and Aid Fund for South Africa, 1986.

Cawthra, G, *Policing South Africa: The South African Police & the Transition from Apartheid*. London/Cape Town: Zed Books & David Philip, 1993/1994.

Cawthra, G., Kraak, G. & O'Sullivan G., eds. *War and Resistance: Southern African Reports*. London: Macmillan Press, 1994.

Chaliand, G. *The Struggle for Africa: Conflict and the Great Powers*. New York: St Martin's Press, 1982.

Chapman, P. *A Cook's Tour of Duty: South African Army Service Corps (1978-1980)*. Durban: Just Done Productions, 2006.

Chidester, D. *Shots in the Streets: Violence and Religion in South Africa*. Cape Town: Oxford University Press, 1992.

Chomsky, N. *Hegemony or Survival: America's Quest for Global Dominance*. London: Penguin Books, 2007.

Cliffe, L. *The Transition to Independence in Namibia*. Boulder, Colorado: Lynne Rienner, 1994.

Clingman, S. *Birthmark*. Auckland Park: Jacana, 2015.

Cock, J. & Nathan, L., eds. *War and Society: The Militarisation of South Africa*. Cape Town & Johannesburg: David Philip, 1989.

Cock, J. *Colonels & Cadres: War & Gender in South Africa*. Cape Town: Oxford University Press, 1991.

Cock, J. & Mckenzie, P., eds. *From Defence to Development: Redirecting Military Resources in South Africa*. Cape Town/Ottawa: David Philip/International Development Research Centre, 1998.

Coetzee, A. & Polley, J. *Crossing Borders: Writers meet the ANC*. Bramley: Taurus, 1990.

Coetzee, H. *Duits-Wes-Afrika: Dorsland, Oorlog en Moord*. Boordfontein: Rosslyn-Pers, 2008.

Coetzee, P. *Special Forces "Jam Stealer"*. n.p.: African Publisher, 2008.

Coetzee, P. *Verkennings Kommandos: Ons Vergeet nie. Die Biografie van 'n Spesialis wat gedien het in Spesiale Magte en die Suid-Afrikaanse Weermag*. n.p.: Peet Coetzee, 2010. (Afrikaans version of *Special Forces "Jam Stealer"*.)

Coetzer, J.P.J. *Gister se Dade Vandag se Oordeel*. Pretoria: J.P. van der Walt, 2000.

Coghlan, M. *History of the Umvoti Mounted Rifles*. Durban: Just Done Productions, 2012.

Coker, C. *The United States and South Africa, 1968-1985: Constructive Engagement and its Critics*. Durham, North Carolina: Duke University Press, 1986.

Conway, D. *Masculinities, Militarisation and the End Conscription Campaign: War Resistance in Apartheid South Africa*. Johannesburg: Wits University Press, 2012.

Cooper, A.D., ed. *Allies in Apartheid: Western Capitalism in Occupied Namibia*. London: Macmillan Press, 1988.

Chalmers, T., ed. *The Military Balance in Africa 1976*. Durban: Tom Chalmers Enterprises for World Airnews, n.d.

Charlsworth, M. *Revolution in Perspective: People Seeking Change – 1775 to the Present Day*. n.p.: Peter Lowe, 1972.

Christian Children's Fund. (English translation by Mary Daly.) *Free to Play in Peace: Angola's War Seen through the Eyes of its Children*. Richmond, Virginia/Luanda: Christian Children's Fund, 2002.

Cilliers, J. & Reichardt, M., eds. *About Turn: The Transformation of the South African Military and Intelligence*. Halfway House: Institute for Defence Policy, 1995.

Cilliers, J., ed. *Dismissed: Demobilisation and Reintegration of Former Combatants in Africa*. Halfway House: Institute for Defence Policy, 1995.

Cilliers, J., ed. *Continuity in Change: The SA Army in Transition*. Institute for Security Studies Monograph Series, no. 26. Halfway House: Institute for Security Studies, August 1998.

Cilliers, J. & Dietrich, C. *Angola's War Economy: The Role of Oil and Diamonds*. Pretoria: Institute of Security Studies (ISS), 2000.

Ciment, J. *Angola and Mozambique: Postcolonial Wars in Southern Africa*. New York: Facts on File Inc., 1997.

Claridge, D.R. *A Spy for all Seasons: My Life in the CIA*. New York: Scribner, 1997.

Cloete, B. *Pionne*. Garsfontein: Publiself, 2005. Hermanus: Hemel en See Boeke, 2009.

BOOKS

Cowell, A. *Killing the Wizards: Wars of Power and Freedom from Zaire to South Africa*. New York: Simon & Schuster, 1992.

Crocker, C.A. *High Noon in Southern Africa: Making Peace in a Rough Neighbourhood*. Johannesburg: Jonathan Ball, 1992.

Crook, L. *Young's Field: A History of the Anti-Aircraft School*. n.p.: Anti-Aircraft School/10 Anti-Aircraft Regiment Kimberley, 1991.

Cronjé, G. & Cronjé, S. *The Workers of Namibia*. London: International Defence & Aid Fund, 1979.

Cronjé, M.J. *In die Weermag: Ons vir jou Suid-Afrika*. Braamfontein: Evangelie Uitgewers, 1977.

Cruise, A. *Louis Botha's War: The Campaign in German South-West Africa, 1914-1915*. Cape Town: Zebra Press, 2015.

Cruywagen, D. *Brothers in War and Peace: Constand and Abraham Viljoen and the Birth of the new South Africa*. Cape Town: Zebra Press, 2014.

Cruywagen, R. *What's News?* Tygervallei: Naledi, 2012.

Cushing, L. *iRevolución: Cuban Poster Art*. San Francisco: Chronicle Books, 2003.

Dale, R. 2014. *The Namibian War of Independence, 1966-1989: Diplomatic, Economic and Military Campaigns*. Jefferson: McFarland & Company, Inc. Publishers.

Davidson, B., Slovo, J. & Wilkinson, A.R. *Southern Africa – The New Politics of Revolution*. Harmondsworth: Penguin Books, 1976.

Davidson, Basil. *The People's Cause: A History of Guerrillas in Africa*. Longman Studies in African History. Harlow/Essex: Longman/Burnt Mill, 1981.

Davies, J.E. *Constructive engagement? Chester Crocker & American Policy in South Africa, Namibia & Angola*. Oxford/ Auckland Park/Athens, Ohio: James Currey/Jacana Media/ Ohio University Press, 2007.

Davis, S. *Apartheid's Rebels: Inside South Africa's Hidden War*. Craighall: AD Donker, 1988. First published by Yale University Press, 1987.

Davey, M. *The Bondelzwarts Affair: A Study of the Repercussions, 1922-1959*. Pretoria: Communications of the University of South Africa, C31, 1961.

De Klerk, W.A. *Drie Swerwers oor die Einders*. 3rd improved ed. Cape Town: Nasionale Boekhandel, 1962.

De Klerk, W.A. *Drie Swerwers in Suidwes*. Johannesburg: Perskor-uitgewery, 1971.

De Kock, E. & Gordin, J. *A Long Night's Damage: Working for the Apartheid State*. Saxonwold: Contra Press, 1998.

De Oliveira, R.S. *Magnificent and beggar land: Angola since the civil war*. Auckland Park: Jacana, 2015.

Delaney, J. & Greenough, J. *Staying Alive: The Paratrooper's Story*. Oxford/Grand Rapids, Michigan: Monarch Books, 2004.

Department of Foreign Affairs of the Republic of South Africa. *Owambo*. n.p.: Department of Foreign Affairs of the Republic of South Africa, 1971.

De Spinola, A. *Portugal en die Toekoms*. Johannesburg: Perskor-uitgewery, 1974.

Deutschsman, D., ed. *Changing the History of Africa: Angola and Namibia*. Melbourne: Ocean Press, 1989.

De Villiers, C.F., Metrowich, F.R. & Du Plessis, J.A. *Die Kommunisme in Aksie*. Pretoria: Department of Information, 1975.

De Villiers, D. & De Villiers, J. *P.W. Botha: Vegter en Hervormer*. Cape Town: Tafelberg, 1989.

De Vries, R. *Eye of the Storm*. Tygerberg: Naledi Publishers, 2013.

De Vries, F. (Translated by Bezuidenhout, Z.) *Rigting Bedonnerd: Op die Spoor van die Afrikaner Post-'94*. Cape Town: Tafelberg, 2012.

De Vries, R. *Mobiele Oorlogvoering: 'n Perspektief vir Suider-Afrika*. Menlopark: F.J.N. Harman Uitgewers, 1987.

De Vries, R. *Eye of the Firestorm: Strength Lies in Mobility*. Tyger Valley: Naledi, 2013.

De Witt, J.H.J. *8 SA Infanteriebataljon/Infantry Battalion*. Upington: 8 SA Infantry Battalion, 1983.

Diedericks, A. *Journey without Boundaries*. Durban: Just Done Productions, 2007.

Dierks, K. *Chronology of Namibian History: From Pre-Historical Times to Independent Namibia*. 2nd updated and revised ed. Windhoek: Namibia Scientific Society, 2002. First published in 1999.

Dobell, L. *SWAPO's Struggle for Namibia: War by other Means*. Basel: Basel Namibia Studies, 1998.

Dorning, W.A. *A Short History of 1 Special Service Battalion/'n Kort Kroniek van 1 Spesiale Diensbataljon, 1933-1983*. n.p.: Military Information Bureau, South African Defence Force, n.d.

Dreyer, R. *Namibia and Angola: The Search for Independence and Regional Security, 1966-1988*. Geneva: Graduate Institute for International Studies, 1988.

Drechsler, H. 1966. *Let us Die Fighting: The Struggle of the Herero and Nama against German Imperialism (1884-1915)*. Berlin: Akademie-Verlag, 1966.

Du Pisani, A. *SWA/Namibia: The Politics of Continuity and Change*. Johannesburg: Jonathan Ball, 1986.

Du Pisani, A. *Beyond the Barracks: Reflections of the Role of the SADF in the Region*. Braamfontein: Occasional Paper, South African Institute of International Affairs, February 1988.

Du Plooy, S. *Wonderwerke op die Grens*. Cape Town: Lux Verbi, 1985.

Du Preez, L. *Ek en my Soldaat*. Cape Town: Lux Verbi, 1987.

Du Preez, M. *Dwars: Mymeringe van 'n Gebleikte Afrikaan*. Cape Town: Zebra Press, 2009.

Du Preez, S. *Avontuur in Angola: Die Verhaal van Suid-Afrika se Soldate in Angola 1975-1976*. Pretoria: J.L. van Schaik, 1989.

Durand, A. *Zulu Zulu Golf: Life and Death with Koevoet*. Cape Town: Zebra Press, 2011.

Durand, A. *Zulu Zulu Foxtrot: To Hell and Back with Koevoet*. Cape Town: Zebra Press, 2012.

Du Toit, A. *Namibië: Heimweë na 'n Vreemde Land*. Pretoria: J.P. van der Walt, 1991.

Du Toit, R. & Claassen, R. (compilers.) *Rooiplaas! 1 Valskermbataljon*. Tygervallei: Naledi, 2015.

El-Khawas, M.A. & Cohen, B. *The Kissinger Study of Southern Africa: National Security Study Memorandum 39 (Secret)*. Westport: Lawrence Hill & Company, 1976.

Els, P. *We Fear Naught but God: The Story of the South African Special Forces "The Recces"*. Johannesburg: Covos-Day, 2000. (With CD: *The Recces*, by Lourens Fourie.)

Els, P.J. *Ongulumbashe: Where the Bushwar began*. Wandsbeck: Reach Publishers, 2007.

Els, P.J. *We Conquer from Above: Ex Alto Vincimus: the History of 1 Parachute Battalion, 1961-1991*. Valhalla: PelsA Books, 2010.

Els, P.J. *Four SADF Operations*. Pretoria: PelsA Books, 2010.

Emmett, T. *Popular Resistance and the Roots of Nationalism in Namibia, 1915-1966*. Schlettwien, Basel: Basel Namibia Studies 4, 1999.

Engels, E. *Riemvasmaak: Hartland, Harde Land*. Hermanus: Hemel & See Boeke, 2005.

Fauvet, P. & Mosse, M. *Carlos Cardoso: Telling the Truth in Mozambique*. Cape Town: Double Storey, 2006.

Feinstein, A. *In Conflict*. Windhoek: New Namibia Books, 1998.

Feinstein, A. *Battle Scarred: Hidden Costs of the Border War*. Cape Town: Tafelberg, 2011.

Field, R. *Alex la Guma: A Literary & Political Biography*. Auckland Park: Jacana Media, 2010.

Fig, David. *Uranium Road: Questioning South Africa's Nuclear Direction*. Johannesburg: Jacana, 2005.

First, R. *South West Africa*. Harmondsworth: Penguin Books, 1971.

Flint, L. *God's Miracles versus Marxist Terrorists: The Epic True Story of the Men and Victims who Fought the Rhodesian and South West African Wars*. Clocolan: Meesterplan Publishers, 1985.

Forsyth, O. *Agent 407: A South African Spy Breaks Her Silence*. Johannesburg/Cape Town: Jonathan Ball Publishers, 2015.

Foster, D., Haupt, P. & De Beer, M. *The Theatre of Violence: Narratives of Protagonists in the South African Conflict*. Cape Town: Institute for Justice and Reconciliation, 2005.

Forty, J. *Defining Moments: Modern War*. Rochester, Kent: Grange Books, 2005.

Fourie, B. *Brandpunte: Agter die Skerms met Suid-Afrika se Bekendste Diplomaat*. Cape Town: Tafelberg, 1991.

Fowler, B., ed. *Pro Patria*. Halifax: Sentinal Projects, 1995/Durban: Just Done Productions, 2006.

Fowler, B. *Grensvegter? South African Army Psychologist*. Halifax: Sentinel Projects, 1996.

Frankel, P.H. *Pretoria's Praetorians: Civil-Military Relations in South Africa*. Cambridge: Cambridge University Press, 1984.

Fraser, C.A. *Revolusionêre Oorlogvoering: Grondbeginsels van Opstandbekamping*. Pretoria: South African Defence Force, 1958.

Fraser, I. *My Own Private Orchestra*. Johannesburg: Penguin Books, 1993.

Frederickse, J. *South Africa: A Different Kind of War – From Soweto to Pretoria*. Johannesburg: Ravan Press, 1986.

Gann, L.H. & Duignan, P. *South Africa: War? Revolution? Peace?* Cape Town: Tafelberg, 1979. First published in 1978.

Gee, R.K. *AAANDAG! 'n Handleiding vir Christelik nasionale dienspligtiges*. Cape Town: SAJVC Literatuur, 1974.

Geldenhuys, D. *South Africa's Search for Security since the Second World War*. Johannesburg: Occasional Paper, South African Institute of International Affairs, September 1978.

Geldenhuys, D. *The Neutral Option and Sub-Continental Solidarity: A Consideration of Foreign Minister Pik Botha's Zurich Statement of 7 March 1979*. Johannesburg: Occasional paper, South African Institute of International Affairs, March 1979.

Geldenhuys, D. *Some Foreign Policy Implications of South Africa's "Total National Strategy", with Particular Reference to the "12-Point Plan"*. Braamfontein: The South African Institute of International Affairs, March 1981.

Geldenhuys, D. *What do we Think? A Survey of White Opinion on Foreign Policy Issues*. Braamfontein: Occasional Paper, The South African Institute of International Affairs, November 1982.

Geldenhuys, D. *The Diplomacy of Isolation: South African Foreign Policy Making*. Johannesburg: Macmillan South Africa, published for The South African Institute of International Affairs, 1984.

Geldenhuys, J. *Dié wat Wen: 'n Generaal se Storie uit 'n Era van Oorlog en Vrede*. Pretoria: J.L. van Schaik, 1993.

Geldenhuys, J. (Translated by A. Geldenhuys.) *A General's Story from an Era of War and Peace*. Johannesburg: Jonathan Ball Publishers, 1995.

Geldenhuys, J. *Dié wat Gewen het: Feite en Fabels van die Bosoorlog*. Pretoria: Litera Publikasies, 2007.

Geldenhuys, J., comp. *Ons was Daar: Wenners van die Oorlog om Suider-Afrika*. Pretoria: Kraal-Uitgewers, n.d.

George, E. *The Cuban Intervention in Angola, 1965-1991: From Che Guevera to Cuito Cuanavale*. London: Frank Cass, 2005.

Gevisser, M. *Portraits of Power: Profiles in a Changing South Africa*. Cape Town: David Philip/Mail & Guardian, 1996.

Gewald, J-B. *Herero Heroes: A Socio-Political History of the Herero of Namibia 1890-1923*. Oxford: James Currey, 1999.

Giacobetti, F. (Translated by Chanterelle Translations.) *Che's Compañeros: Witnesses to a Legend*. Paris: Assouline, n.d.

Gillmore, G. *Pathfinder Company. 44 Parachute Brigade: The Philistines*. Johannesburg: 30 Degrees South, 2010.

Giniewski, P. *Die stryd om Suidwes-Afrika*. Kaapstad: Nasionale Boekhandel, 1966.

Gleijeses, P. *Conflicting Missions: Havana, Washington, Pretoria*. Alberton: Galago,2003.

Gleijeses, P. *The Cuban Drumbeat. Castro's Worldview: Cuban Foreign Policy in a Hostile World. What was Communism? 2*. London: Seagull, Books, 2009.

Gleijesis, P. *Visions of Freedom: Havana, Washington, Pretoria and the Struggle for Southern Africa, 1976-1991*. Johannesburg: Wits University Press, 2013.

Goldblatt, I. *History of South West Africa from the Beginning of the Nineteenth Century*. Cape Town: Juta, 1971.

Gott, R. *Cuba: A New History*. New Haven/London: Yale Nota Bene/Yale University Press, 2005.

Graaf, Michael, ed. *Hawks and Doves – The Pro- and Anti-Conscription Press in South Africa*. Durban: Contemporary Cultural Studies Unit, University of Natal, 1988.

Greef, J. *A Greater Share of Honour*. Durban: Just Done Productions, 2008.

Green, G. *Stand at Ease*. Wandsbeck: Reach Publishers, 2009.

Greyling, R.J. *Terrorisme: Die Feite*. Pretoria: J.L. van Schaik, 1985.

BOOKS

Grim, F. *Gepoogde Verkragting van Suid-Afrika*. Kempton Park: Aksie Morele Standaarde & Hart-Uitgewers, 1975. First published in 1974.

Grové, W. *Die Padkaart van 'n Speurder: My Storie*. Tygervallei: Naledi, 2012.

Grundy, K.W. *The Rise of the South African Security Establishment: An Essay on the Changing Locus of State Power*. Johannesburg: South African Institute of International Affairs, Bradlow Series, no.1, 1983.

Grundy, K.W. *Soldiers without Politics: Blacks in the South African Armed Forces*. Berkeley: University of California Press, 1983.

Grundy, K.W. *The Militarization of South African Politics*. Oxford: Oxford University Press, 1988. (Paperback reprint with corrections and a new postscript to the original 1986 edition).

Gumaräes, F. *The Origins of the Angolan Civil War: Foreign Intervention and Domestic Political Conflict*. London: Macmillan, 1998.

Gutteridge, W. & Spence, J.E. *Violence in Southern Africa*. London: Frank Cass, 1997.

Haarhoff, D. *The Wild South-West: Frontier Myths and Metaphors in Literature set in Namibia, 1760-1988*. Johannesburg: Witwatersrand University Press, 1991.

Hall, J. *Weep for Africa: A Rhodesian Light Infantry Paratrooper's Farewell to Innocence*. Pinetown/Solihull: 30 Degrees South/Helion & Company, 2014.

Hamann, H. *Days of the Generals*. Cape Town: Zebra Press, 2001.

Hammond, P. *In the Killing Fields of Mozambique*. Cape Town: Frontline Fellowship, 1998.

Hanlon, J. *Apartheid's Second Front: South Africa's War against its Neighbours*. Harmondsworth: Penguin Special, Penguin Books, 1986. (Abridged version of *Beggar your Neighbours*.)

Hanlon, J. *Beggar your Neighbours: Apartheid Power in Southern Africa*. London/Bloomington: Catholic Institute for International Relations/James Currey/Indiana University Press, 1987.

Harman, F.N.J., ed. *Ons vir jou Suid-Afrika*. Pretoria & Cape Town: HAUM, 1979.

Harper-Ronald, J. & Budd, G. *Sunday Bloody Sunday: A Soldier's War in Northern Ireland, Rhodesia, Mozambique and Iraq*. Alberton: Galagao, 2009.

Harrison, P. *South Africa's Top Sites: Struggle*. Kenilworth: Spearhead, 2004.

Hart, K. & Lewis, J., eds. *Why Angola Matters: Report of a Conference held at Pembroke College, Cambridge, March 21-22, 1994*. Cambridge: African Studies Centre, 1995.

Hartmann, W., Silvester, J. & Hayes, P., eds. *The Colonising Camera: Photographs in the Making of Namibian History*. 2nd impression. Cape Town: University of Cape Town Press, 2001. (First published in 1998.)

Hayes, P., Silvester, J., Wallace, M. & Hartmann, W., eds. *Namibia under South African Rule: Mobility & Containment 1915-45*. Oxford: James Currey, 1998.

Heitman, H.R. (translated by L. van Blommenstein.) *Die Suid-Afrikaanse Krygsmag*. Johannesburg: Central News Agency/Bison Books, 1985.

Heitman, H.R. & Dorning, W.A., comp. *Steeds Kampioene: Suid-Afrikaanse Weermag 1912-1987/Still Champions: South African Defence Force 1912-1987*. Durban: Walker-Ramus Trading Co on behalf of the Directorate Public Relations of the South African Defence Force, n.d.

Heitman, H.R. *South African Arms & Armour: A Concise Guide to Armaments of the South African Army, Navy and Air Force*. Cape Town: Struik Publishers, 1988.

Heitman, H.R. (translated by C. Malherbe.) *Krygstuig van Suid-Afrika: 'n Kort Gids oor die Krygstuig van die Suid-Afrikaanse Leër, Vloot en Lugmag*. Cape Town: Struik Publishers, 1988.

Heitman, H.R. *War in Angola: The Final South African Phase*. Gibraltar: Ashanti Publishing, 1990.

Heitman, H.R. *Modern African Wars (3): South-West Africa. Men-at-arms 242*. Oxford: Osprey Publishing, 1991.

Henderson, L.W. *Angola: Five Centuries of Conflict*. Ithaca: Cornell University Press, 1979.

Hendrikz, A. *Sheena Duncan*. Cape Town: Tiber Tree Press, 2015.

Herbstein, D. & Evenson, J. *The Devils are Among Us: The War for Namibia*. London/New Jersey: Zed Books, 1989.

Heunis, J. *Die Binnekring: Terugblikke op die Laaste Dae van Blanke Regering*. Johannesburg/Cape Town: Jonathan Ball, 2007.

Heywood, A. *The Cassinga Event: An Investigation of the Records*. Windhoek: National Archives of Namibia, 1994.

Hiemstra, R.C. *Die Wilde Haf*. Cape Town: Human & Rousseau, 2001.

Hodges, T. *Angola: From Afro-Stalinism to Petro-Diamond Capitalism*. Bloomington: Indiana University Press, 2001.

Hofmeyr, S. *Mense van my Asem*. Cape Town: Zebra Press, 2008.

Holt, C. *At Thy Call we did not Falter: A Frontline Account of the 1988 Angolan War, as Seen through the Eyes of a Conscripted Soldier*. Cape Town: Zebra Press, 2005.

Houman, P. & McQuillan, S. *The Mini-Nuke Conspiracy: Mandela's Nuclear Nightmare*. London/Boston: Faber and Faber, 1995.

Hooper, J. *Koevoet!* Johannesburg: Southern Book Publishers, 1988.

Hooper, J. *Koevoet!* Rugby, Warwickshire: GG Books, 2012.

Hooper, J. *Beneath the Visiting Moon: Images of Combat in Southern Africa*. Massachusetts: Lexington Books, Lexington, 1990.

Hooper, J. *Bloodsong! An Account of Executive Outcomes in Angola*. London: HarperCollins, 2002.

Horrell, M. *South-West Africa*. Johannesburg: South African Institute of Race Relations, 1967.

Hough, M. & Van der Merwe, M., eds. *Selected South African Strategic Perceptions*. University of Pretoria: Institute for Strategic Studies, 1988.

Hugo, G. *Africa Will Always Break Your Heart*. Durban: Just Done Productions, 2007.

Ignatyev, O. *Secret Weapon in Africa*. Moscow: Progress Publishers, 1977.

International Defence and Aid Fund for Southern Africa. *Namibia: The Facts*. London: International Defence and Aid Fund for Southern Africa, 1989.

International Institute for Strategic Studies. *The Military Balance 1975-1976*. London: International Institute for Strategic Studies, 1975.

International Institute for Strategic Studies. *The Military Balance 1978-1979*. London: International Institute for Strategic Studies, 1978.

Isaacs, J. & Downing, T. *Cold War: For 45 Years the World Held its Breath*. London: Bantam Press, 1998.

James, W.M. A. *Political History of the Civil War in Angola, 1974-1990*. London. Transaction Publishers, 2011.

Jansen, A. *Eugene de Kock: Sluipmoordenaar van die Staat*. Kaapstad: Tafelberg, 2015.

Jaster, R. *South Africa in Namibia: The Botha Strategy*. Lanham: University Press of America, 1985.

Jaster, R. *The Defence of White Power: South African Foreign Policy under Pressure*. Basingstoke: MacMillan, 1988.

Jenny, H. (Translated by Patricia & Heinrich Eichbaum.) *South West Africa: Land of Extremes*. Windhoek: South West African Scientific Society, 1976.

Johnson, P. & Martin, D. *Destructive Engagement: Southern Africa at War*. Harare: Zimbabwe Publishing House for the Southern African Research and Documentation Centre, 1986.

Johnson, P. & Martin, D. *Frontline Southern Africa: Destructive Engagement*. New York: Four Walls Eight Windows, 1988.

Jooste, L. *Die Kuns van Oorlog: 'n Inleiding tot Militêre Kuns in Suid-Afrika*. Pretoria: Militêre Informasieburo SAW, n.d.

Joubert, E. *Die Nuwe Afrikaan: 'n Reis deur Angola*. Cape Town: Tafelberg, 1974.

Joubert, J. *'n Dagboek vir die Grenssoldaat*. Pretoria: Daan Retief Publishers, 1983.

Jurgens, R. *The Many Houses of Exile*. Weltevreden Park: Covos Day, 2000.

Kamongo, S. & Bezuidenhout, L. *Shadows in the Sand: A Koevoet Tracker's Story of an Insurgency War*. Pinetown: 30 Degrees South Publishers, 2011.

Kane-Berman, J. *Political Violence in South Africa*. Johannesburg: South African Institute of Race Relations, 1993.

Kapelaanslektuurkommissie van die Afrikaanse Kerke. *Die Woord vir Elke Dag*. n.p., n.d.

Kaplan, J. *The Dressing Station: A Surgeon's Chronicle of War and Medicine*. New York: Grove Press, 2001.

Kapteijns, L., Richters, A. & Richters, J.M. *Mediations of Violence in Africa: Fashioning New Futures from Contested Pasts*. n.p.: Brill Academic Pub, 2010. (Originally published in Leiden, The Netherlands.)

Kapuscinski, R. (Translated by Brand, W.R. & Mroczkowska-Brand, K.) *Another Day of Life*. London: Picador/Pan Books, 1988.

Kasrils, R. *"Armed and Dangerous." My Undercover Struggle against Apartheid*. Oxford: Heinemann Educational, 1993.

Katjavivi, J. *Undisciplined Heart*. Athlone/Windhoek: Modjadi Books/Tigereye Publishing, 2010.

Katjavivi, P.H. *A History of Resistance in Namibia*. Reprint. London: James Currey, 1989.

Keable, K., ed. *London Recruits: The Secret War against Apartheid*. Pontypool: Merlin Press, 2012.

Kemper, H.L. *With my Head held High. A True Tale of Struggle, Perseverance and the Search for Meaning: Mike Greeff's Story*. Cape Town: Quantum Publishers, 2010.

Kirkwood Branch of the Southern Cross. *Trakteer die Troepe/Treat the Troops*. Roodepoort: CUM Books, 1983.

Kitchen, H. & Clough, M. *The United States and South Africa: Realities and Red Herrings*. Washington: CSIS, 1984.

Kleynhans, A.S.J. *Die Stryd teen Terreur in SWA/Namibië*. Windhoek: South West African Territorial Force, Public Relations Department of the South West African Territorial Force, 1988.

Klinghoffer, A.J. *The Angolan War: A Study of Soviet Policy in the Third World*. Boulder, Colorado: Westview, 1980.

Kobo, J. *Waiting in the Wing*. Milton Keynes: Word Publishing, 1994.

Kommissie vir Sosiale Studies van die Amerikaanse Vereniging vir die Verdediging van die Tradisie, Familie en Private-Eiendom (TPF). *Die Volle Waarheid omtrent SWAPO: Idealistiese Christene en Helde van Vryheid en Geregtigheid of Instrumente van Internasionale Kommunistiese Aggressie*. Silverton: Distributed in South Africa as a Special Edition of *Candidas*, newsletter of the SA Catholic Defence League, 1984.

Konig, B. *Namibia: The Ravages of War. South Africa's Onslaught on the Namibian People*. London: International Defence & Aid Fund for Southern Africa, 1983.

Korff, G. *19 with a Bullet: A South African Paratrooper in Angola*. Johannesburg: 30 Degrees South Publishers, 2009.

Kotzé, D.A. *Pleeg ons Politieke Geweld?* Cape Town & Pretoria: Human & Rousseau, 1984.

Kruger, C., comp. *Suid-Afrikaanse Oorlogskuns in Beeld/South African Images of War*. Johannesburg: South African Museum of Military History, April 1990.

Labuschagne, R. *On South Africa's Secret Service: An Undercover Agent's Story*. Alberton: Galago, 2002.

Lamprecht, D. *Tannie Pompie se Oorlog: In die Driehoek van die Dood*. Kaapstad: Tafelberg, 2015.

Landsberg, C. *The Diplomacy of Transformation: South African Foreign Policy and Statecraft*. Johannesburg: Pan Macmillan South Africa, 2010.

L'Ange, G. *Urgent Imperial Service: South African Forces in German South West Africa 1914-1915*. Rivonia: Ashanti Publishing, 1991.

Laurence, P. *Death Squads: Apartheid's Secret Weapon*. London: Penguin Books, 1990.

Legum, C. *After Angola: The War over Southern Africa*. London: Rex Collins, 1976.

Legum, C. *The Battlefields of Southern Africa*. New York: Africana Publishing Company, 1988.

Leonard, R. *South Africa at War: White Power and the Crisis in South Africa*. Craighall: AD Donker, 1985. (South African edition of original 1983 publication.)

Lewis, A. *Terreur in Christus' Naam: Bijdrage tot de Kennis van een Gedeelte van de Eigentijdse Kerkgeschiedenis met Name ten aansien van Zuidelijk Afrika*. Pretoria: Christian League of Southern Africa, 1978.

Leys, C. & Saul, J.S. *Namibia's Liberation Struggle: The Two-Edged Sword*. London: James Currey, 1995.

BOOKS

Leys, C. & Brown, S., eds. *Histories of Namibia: Living through the Liberation Struggle – Life Histories*. London: The Merlin Press, 2004 and 2005.

Liebenberg, I., Van der Westhuizen, G., Lortan, F. & Nel, F.B.O., eds. *The Long March: The Story of the Struggle for Liberation in South Africa*. Pretoria: Kagiso-Haum Publishers, 1994.

Liebenberg, I. & Roefs, M. *Demobilisation and its Aftermath, II: Economic Reinsertion of South Africa's Demobilised Military Personnel*. Institute for Security Studies Monograph Series, no. 61. Pretoria: Institute for Security Studies, August 2001.

Little, I.C. *Above Board and Under Cover: A Voyage through sometimes Murky Waters*. Durban: Just Done, 2009.

Lord, D. *Fire, Flood and Ice: Search and Rescue Missions of the South African Air Force*. Johannesburg: Covos Books, 1998.

Lord, D. *Standby! South African Air Force Search and Rescue*. Updated edition of *Fire, Flood and Ice: Search and Rescue Missions of the South African Air Force*. Johannesburg: 30 Degrees South Publishers, 2010.

Lord. D. *Vlamgat: The Story of the Mirage F1 in the South African Air Force*. Johannesburg: 30 Degrees South Publishers, 2000.

Lord, D. *From Fledgling to Eagle: The South African Air Force during the Border War*. Johannesburg: 30 Degrees South Publishers, 2008.

Louw, C. *Ope Brief aan Willem de Klerk*. Dainfern: Uitgewery Praag, n.d.

Louw, C. *Boetman en die Swanesang van die Verligtes*. Cape Town: Human & Rousseau, 2001.

Louw, M.H.H., ed. *National Security: A Modern Approach*. Institute for Strategic Studies, University of Pretoria, 1978.

Louw, W. *Owambo*. Sandton: Southern African Freedom Foundation, n.d.

Lubowski, M. & Van der Vyfer, M. *Anton Lubowski: Paradox of a Man*. Strand: Queillerie, n.d.

Lubbe, L. *Van Ovamboland tot Masjonaland*. n.p.: Louis Lubbe, 2014.

Ludi, G. *Operation Q-018*. Cape Town: Nasionale Boekhandel, 1969.

Lush, D. *Last Steps to Uhuru: An Eyewitness Account of Namibia's Transition to Independence*. Windhoek: New Namibia Books, 1993.

Maier, K. *Angola: Promises and Lies*. Rivonia: William Waterman Publications, 1996.

Malan, J.S. *Opmars van die Antichris*. Pietersburg: Filadelfia-uitgewers, 1983.

Malan, M. *My Lewe saam met die SA Weermag*. Pretoria: Protea Boekhuis, 2006.

Mandela, N. & Castro, F. *How Far We Slaves Have Come! South Africa And Cuba In Today's World*. New York: Pathfinder, 1991.

Mannall, D. *Battle on the Lomba 1987: The Day a South African Armoured Battalion Shattered Angola's Last Mechanised Offensive – A Crew Commander's Account*. Solihull: Helion & Company, 2014.

Manning, R. *"They Cannot Kill Us All": An Eyewitness Account of South Africa Today*. Boston: Houghton Mifflin Company, 1987.

Manong, S. *If We Must Die. An Autobiography of a Former Commander of uMkhonto we Sizwe*. n.p.: Nkululeko Publishers, 2015.

Marais, C. & Du Toit, J. *A Drink of Dry Land*. Cape Town: Struik Publishers, 2006.

Marais, J. *Tydbom: 'n Polisieman se Ware Verhaal*. Cape Town: Tafelberg, 2010.

Marais, N. *The Political Dimension of the Settlement Phase during a Revolutionary War*. Institute for Strategic Studies, University of Pretoria, 1982.

Marcum, J. *The Angolan Revolution, Volume I: The Anatomy of an Explosion (1959-1962)*. Massachusetts: Massachusetts Institute of Technology Press, 1969.

Marcum, J. *The Angolan Revolution, Volume 2: Exile Politics and Guerrilla Warfare (1962-1976)*. Massachusetts: Massachusetts Institute of Technology Press, 1978.

Marjay, F. (Photographs by Weisweiler, H.) *Angola*. Lisbon: Livraria Bertrand, 1961.

Marks, B. *Our South African Army Today*. Cape Town/Johannesburg: Purnell, 1979.

Martin, D. & Phyllis, J., eds. *Destructive Engagement: Southern Africa at War*. Harare: Zimbabwe Publishing House, 1986.

Massie, R.K. *Loosing the Bonds: The United States and South Africa in the Apartheid Years*. New York: Nan A. Talese, 1997.

Matloff, J. *Fragments of a Forgotten War*. London: Penguin Books, 1997.

Matthee, C.F., comp. *8 SA Infanterie Bataljon/Infantry Battalion*. Upington: 8 SA Infantry Battalion, 1981.

Matthysen, P., Kalkwarf, M. & Huxtable, M. *"Recce": A Collector's Guide to the History of the South African Special Forces*. Johannesburg: 30 Degrees South Publishers, 2010.

Matthysen, P., ed. *Parabats on the Border: The War Diaries of 1 Parachute Battalion 22/02/77-25/06/1977*. Johannesburg: Marc Norman Publishing, 2010.

McAleese, P. *No Mean Soldier: The Story of the Ultimate Professional Soldier in the SAS and Other Forces*. London: Cassell Military Paperbacks, 2003. (Reprint.) Originally published in 1993.

McAllion, H. *Killing Zone: A Life in the Paras, the Recces, the SAS and the RUC*. London: Bloomsbury, 1996.

McKinley, D. *The ANC and the Liberation Struggle*. London/Chicago: Pluto Press,1997.

McRae, D. *Under our Skin: A White Family's Journey through South Africa's Darkest Years*. London: Simon & Schuster, 2012.

McWilliams, J.P. *Armscor: South Africa's Arms Merchant*. London: Brassey's, 1989.

McWilliams, M. *Battle for Cassinga: South Africa's Controversial Cross-Border Raid, Angola 1978*. (Africa at War, Vol. 3.) Pinetown: 30 Degrees South, 2011.

Meiring, P. *Kroniek van die Waarheidskommissie: Op Reis deur die Verlede en die Hede na die Toekoms van Suid-Afrika*. Vanderbijlpark: Carpe Diem Books, 1999.

Melber, H. *Our Namibia: A Social Studies Textbook*. Great Britain: Zed Books, 1983.

Melber, H., comp. *Our Namibia: A Social Studies Textbook*. London: Zed Books, 1986.

Melber, H. *Namibia: A Decade after Independence*. Windhoek: NEPRU, 2000.

Melber, H., ed. *Limits to Liberation in Southern Africa: The Unfinished Business of Democratic Consolidation*. Cape Town: Human Sciences Research Council, 2003.

Melber, H., ed. *Re-Examining Liberation Namibia: Political Culture since Independence*. Uppsala: Nordic Africa Institute, 2003.

Melber, H. *Understanding Namibia: The Trials of Independence*. Auckland Park: Jacana, 2014.

Meli, F. *South Africa Belongs to Us: A History of the ANC*. Harare: Zimbabwe Publishing House, 1988.

Mendes, P.R. (Translated by Landers, C.) *Bay of Tigers: A Journey through War-Torn Angola*. Johannesburg & Cape Town: Jonathan Ball, 2003.

Meredith, Martin. *Fischer's Choice: A Life of Bram Fischer*. Johannesburg & Cape Town: Jonathan Ball, 2002.

Merrett, C. *A Culture of Censorship: Secrecy and Intellectual Repression in South Africa*. Cape Town/Pietermaritzburg/ Macon, Georgia: David Philip/University of Natal Press/ Mercer University Press, 1994.

Mertens, A. *South West Africa and its Indigenous Peoples*. London: Collins,1977. (Revised edition.)

Metrowich, F.R. *Africa Survey: Essays on Contemporary African Affairs*. Pretoria: FAA Popular Series no. 1, Foreign Affairs Association, 1975.

Metrowich, F.R., ed. *African Freedom Annual 1979*. Sandton: Southern African Freedom Associaton.

Middlemas, K. *Cabora-Bassa: Engineering and Politics in Southern Africa*. London: Weidenfeld & Nicolson, 1975.

Miescher, G. (comp.) *Guide to the Swapo Collection in the Basler Afrika Bibliographien*. Basel: Basler Afrika Bibliographien, Namibia Resource Centre & Southern African Library, 2006.

Mills, G. *The Wired Model: South Africa, Foreign Policy and Globilisation*. Cape Town: The South African Institute of International Affairs/Tafelberg, 2000.

Mills, G. & Williams, D. *7 Battles that Shaped South Africa*. Cape Town: Tafelberg, 2006.

Minnaar, A. Liebenberg, I. and Schutte, C., eds. *Hidden Hand: Covert Operations in South Africa*. Pretoria: Human Sciences Research Council (HSRC)/Friedrich Nauman Foundation/Institute for Democracy in South Africa (IDASA), 1994.

Minter, W. *King Solomon's Mines Revisited: Western Interests and the Burdened History of Southern Africa*. New York: Basic Books, 1986.

Minter, W. *Portuguese Africa and the West*. New York: Monthly Review Press, 1972.

Minter, W. *Apartheid's Contras: An Inquiry into the Roots of War in Angola and Mozambique*. London/New Jersey: Witwatersrand University Press/Zed Books, 1994.

Mockler, A. *The New Mercenaries*. London: Sidgwick & Jackson, 1985.

Molnar, T. *South West Africa: The Last Pioneer Country*. New York: Fleet Publishing Corporation, 1966.

Monin, L. & Gallimore, A. *The Devil's Gardens: A History of Landmines*. London: Pimlico, 2002.

Moorcraft, P. *Africa's Super Power*. Johannesburg: Sygma/Collins, 1981.

Moorcraft, P. L. *Guns and Poses: Travels with an Occasional War Correspondent*. Albury Guildford, Surrey: Millstream Press, 2001.

Moorcraft, P. *Inside the Danger Zones: Travels to Arresting Places*. Johannesburg & Cape Town: Jonathan Ball Publishers, 2011.

Moorsom, R. *Walvis Bay – Namibia's Port*. London: International Defence and Aid Fund (IDAF) for Southern Africa/ United Nations Council for Namibia, 1984.

Morison, D. *The USSR and Africa*. London & New York: Oxford University Press, 1964. Issued under the auspices of the Institute of Race Relations, London and the Central Asian Research Centre.

Morris, M. *Terrorism: The First Full Account in Detail of Terrorism and Insurgency in Southern Africa*. Cape Town: Howard Timmins, 1971.

Morris, M. *Armed Conflict in Southern Africa: A Survey of Regional Terrorisms from their Beginnings to the Present, with a Comprehensive Examination of the Portuguese Position*. Cape Town: Jeremy Spence, 1974.

Morris, M. *Apartheid: An Illustrated History*. Cape Town & Johannesburg: Jonathan Ball, 2012.

Morris, P. *Back to Angola: A Journey from War to Peace*. Cape Town: Zebra Press, 2014.

Mudge, D. *Dirk Mudge: Enduit vir 'n Onafhanlike Namibië*. Pretoria: Protea Boekhuis, 2015.

Müller, J.A. *"The Inevitable Pipeline into Exile": Botswana's role in the Namibian Liberation Struggle*. Basel: Basler Afrika Bibliographien/Namibia Resource Centre & Southern African Library, 2012.

Namakulu, O.O. *Armed Liberation Struggle: Some Accounts of PLAN's Combat Operations*. Gamsberg Macmillan: Windhoek, 2004.

Namhila, E.N. *The Price of Freedom*. Windhoek: New Namibia Books, 1997.

Namhila, E N. *Kaxumba kaNdola. Man and Myth: The Biography of a Barefoot Soldier*. Basel: Basler Afrika Bibliographien, 2005.

Naón, A.E. & Merizalde, L.D. *SWA/Namibia: Dawn or Dusk?*. n.p.: A.E. Naón, 1989.

Nathan, L. *Marching to a Different Drum: A Description and Assessment of the Formation of the Namibian Police and Defence Force*. Bellville: Centre for Southern African Studies, University of the Western Cape, 1991.

Newitt, M. *Portugal in Africa: The Last Hundred Years*. London: C. Hurst & Co, 1981.

Ngculu, J. *The Honour to Serve: Recollections of an MK Soldier*. Claremont: David Philip Publishers, 2010.

Ngurare, E.T., Seibeb, H.H. & Swartbooi, B.C., eds. *The Politics of Apologetics*. Windhoek: !Namib Publishers, 2009.

Nicol, M. *The Invisible Line: The Life and Photography of Ken Oosterbroek 1962-1994*. Roggebaai/Parklands: Kwela Books in association with Random House, 1998.

Nixon, R. *Selling Apartheid: South Africa's Global Propaganda War*. Auckland Park: Jacana, 2015.

Nothling, C.J., ed. *Ultima Ratio Regum*. Pretoria: Publication no. 8, South African Defence Force Military Information Bureau, 1987.

BOOKS

Nothling, C.J. & Martins, Du P. *History of the South African Air Force (1920-1990)*. Pretoria: Directorate Public Relations, South African Defence Force, 1990.

Nothling, C.J. & Becker, D., comps. *The Pride of the Nation (A Short History of the South African Air Force, 1920-1995)*. Pretoria: South African Air Force, 1995.

North, J. *Freedom Rising*. 2nd ed. with a new epilogue. New York: New American Library, 1986. First published in 1985.

Nortje, P. *32 Battalion: The Inside Story of South Africa's Elite Fighting Unit*. Cape Town: Zebra Press, 2003.

Nortje, P. *The Terrible Ones: A Complete History of 32 Battalion. Vol. I*. Cape Town: Zebra Press, 2012.

Nortje, P. *The Terrible Ones: A Complete History of 32 Battalion. Vol. II*. Cape Town: Zebra Press, 2012.

Nortje, P. *The Battle of Savate: 32 Battalion's Greatest Operation*. Cape Town: Zebra Press, 2015.

Norval, M. *Death in the Desert: The Namibian Tragedy*. Washington: Selous Foundation Press, 1989.

Nunes, F. *Altered States*. Durban: Just Done Productions, 2010.

Nussey, W. *Watershed – Angola and Mozambique: A Photo History: The Portuguese Collapse in Africa, 1974-1975*. Solihull/Pinetown: Helion & Company/30 Degrees South, 2014.

O'Linn, B. *Namibia: The Sacred Trust of Civilization – Ideal and Reality*. Windhoek: Gamsberg Macmillan Publishers, 2003.

Oliver, B.J. *The Strategic Significance of Angola*. Institute for Strategic Studies, University of Pretoria, 1984.

Olusaga, D. & Erichsen, C.W. *The Kaiser's Holocaust: Germany's Forgotten Genocide and the Colonial Roots of Nazism*. London: Faber and Faber, 2010.

Omotoso, K. *Woza Africa!/Come on Africa: Music goes to War*. Johannesburg: Jonathan Ball, 1997.

Onslow, Sue, ed. *Cold War in Southern Africa: White Power, Black Liberation*. London & New York: Cold War History Series, Routledge, 2009.

Organization of Angolan Women. (Translated by Holness, M.) *Angolan Women: Building the Future*. London/Luanda: Zed Books/Organization of Angolan Women, 1984.

Orpen, N. *Cape Town Rifles Dukes*. Cape Town: Cape Town Rifles Dukes Regimental Council, 1984.

Orpen, N. *Total Defence: The Role of Commandos in the Armed Forces of South Africa*. Cape Town: Nasionale Boekhandel, 1967.

Orr, W. *From Biko to Basson: Wendy Orr's Search for the Soul of South Africa as a Commissioner of the TRC*. Saxonwold: Contra Press, 2000.

Otto, W. *Die Spesiale Diensbataljon (1933-1973)*. Pretoria: Central Documentation Service, South African Documentation Service, Publication no. 2, 1973.

Pahad, A. *Insurgent Diplomat: Civil Talks or Civil War?* Johannesburg: Penguin Books, 2014.

Papenfus, T. *Pik Botha en sy Tyd*. Pretoria: Litera, 2010.

Paterson, H.R. & Levin, M. *Through Desert, Veld and Mud: A History of 15 Maintenance Unit 1899-1999*. Durban: 15 Maintenance Unit, 2002.

Paul, M. *Parabat*. Johannesburg: My Book Productions, 2008.

Pauw, J. *In the Heart of the Whore: The Story of Apartheid's Death Squads*. Halfway House: Southern Book Publishers, 1991.

Pauw, J. *Into the Heart of Darkness: Confessions of Apartheid's Assassins*. Johannesburg: Jonathan Ball, 1997.

Pawson, L. *In the Name of the People: Angola's Forgotten Massacre*. London: I.B. Tauris, 2014.

Payne, R.J. *Opportunities and Dangers of Soviet-Cuban Expansion: Towards a Pragmatic US Policy*. Albany: State University of New York Press, 1988.

Pearce, J. *An Outbreak of Peace: Angola's Situation of Confusion*. Claremont: David Philip, 2005.

Pienaar, S. *Getuie van Groot Tye*. Cape Town: Tafelberg, 1980.

Pienaar, S. *South Africa and International Relations between the Two World Wars*. Johannesburg: Witwatersrand University Press, 1987.

Pike, H.R. *A History of Communism in South Africa*. Germiston: Christian Mission International of South Africa, 1985.

Pitta, R., Fannell J. & McCouaig, S. *South African Special Forces. Elite Series 47*. London: Osprey Publishing, 1993.

Polack, P. *The Last Hot Battle of the Cold War: South Africa vs. Cuba in the Angolan Civil War*. Pinetown/Oxford: 30 Degrees South/Casemate, 2014.

Polakow-Suransky, S. *The Unspoken Alliance: Israel's Secret Relationship with Apartheid South Africa*. Auckland Park: Jacana Media, 2010.

Pool, G. *Die Herero-Opstand 1904-1907*. Cape Town/Pretoria: Hollandsch Afrikaansche Uitgewers Maatschappij, 1979.

Porto, J.G. & Parsons, I. *Sustaining the Peace in Angola: An Overview of Current Demobilisation Disarmament and Reintegration*. Pretoria: Institute for Security Studies, Monograph Series no. 83, April 2003.

Porto, J.G., Parsons, I. & Alden, C. *From Soldiers to Citizens: The Social, Economic and Political Reintegration of Unita Ex-Combatants*. Pretoria: Institute for Security Studies, Monograph Series no. 130, March 2007.

Potgieter, D. *Totale Aanslag: Apartheid se Vuil Truuks Onthul*. Cape Town: Zebra Press, 2007.

Pretorius, J.W.F. *Suidwes-Afrika: 'n Eenheidstaat, Swart Meerderheidsregering en 'n Geïntegreerde Gemeenskap sonder dat die Volkere daaroor Ooreengekom het*. Windhoek: J.W.F. Pretorius, Februarie 1989.

Prinsloo, T.F., ed. *Lugmaggimnasium Gedenkblad 1952-1977/Air Force Gymnasium Memorial Album 1952-1977*. n.p.: Air Force Gymnasium, n.d.

Puren, J. & Pottinger, B. *Mercenary Commander*. Alberton: Galago, 1986.

Purkitt, H.E. & Burgess, S.F. *South Africa's Weapons of Mass Destruction*. Bloomington & Indianapolis: Indiana University Press, 2005.

Qunta, C., ed. *Women in Southern Africa*. Braamfontein: Skotaville Publishers, 1987.

Rabe, J.C., comp. *Die Geskiedenis van Genieskool 1940-1990/ School of Engineers, the History*. n.p., 1990.

Ramonet, I., ed. *Fidel Castro: My Life*. London: Allen Lane, 2006.

Ratcliffe, J. *Terreno Occupado*. Johannesburg: Warren Siebrits, 2008.

Ractliffe, J. *As terras do fim do mundo. The Lands of the End of the World*. Cape Town: Michael Stevenson, 2010.

Ramsden, T. *Border-Line Insanity: A National Serviceman's Story*. Alberton: Galago, 2009.

Reid-Daly, R. *Staying Alive: A Southern African Survival Handbook*. Rivonia: Ashanti Publishing, 1990.

Renwick, R. *Mission to South Africa: Diary of a Revolution*. Johannesburg: Jonathan Ball, 2015.

Retief, B. *Humour in SA Uniform*. Johannesburg: Perskor, 1990.

Rich, P.B., ed. *The Dynamics of Change in Southern Africa*. New York: St Martin's Press, 1994.

Richards, D. & Mills, G., eds. *Victory among People: Lessons from Countering Insurgency and Stabilising Fragile States*. London/Marshalltown: Royal United Services Institute for Defence and Security Studies/Brenthurst Foundation, 2011.

Riley, E. *Major Political Events in South Africa 1948-1990*. Oxford/New York: Facts on File, 1991.

Robbins, D. *On the Bridge of Goodbye: The Story of South Africa's Discarded San Soldiers*. Johannesburg/Cape Town: Jonathan Ball, 2007.

Roherty, J.M. *State Security in South Africa: Civil-Military Relations under P.W. Botha*. Armonk, New York: M.E. Sharpe, 1992.

Romain, T. *Blind Date at a Funeral: Memories of Growing Up in South Africa*. Cape Town: Penguin Books, 2015.

Ron, T. & Golan, T. *Angolan Rendezvous: Man and Nature in the Shadow of War*. Johannesburg: 30 Degrees South Publishers, 2010.

Roos, S.G. *Geestelike Weerbaarheid teen Ideologiese Terrorisme*. Pretoria: NG Kerkboekhandel Transvaal, 1979.

Rossouw, P.J. *Die Christen en Kommunisme*. n.p.: Die Bybelkorrespondensie- en skolingskursusse van die Nederduitse Gereformeerde Kerk, 1983.

Rotberg, R.I. *Suffer the Future: Policy Choices in Southern Africa*. Cambridge, Massachusetts/London: Harvard University Press, 1980.

Rotberg, R.I., ed. *Namibia: Political and Economic Prospects*. Lexington, MA: Lexington Books, 1983.

Rupiya, M., ed. *Evolutions & Revolutions: A Contemporary History of Militaries in Southern Africa*. Pretoria: Institute for Security Studies, 2005.

Russell, A. *Big Men, Little People: Encounters in Africa*. London: Macmillan, 1999.

Ryan, J. *One Man's Africa*. Johannesburg/Cape Town: Jonathan Ball, 2002.

SA Army Headquarters. *Revolusionêre Oorlogvoering teen die RSA/Revolutionary Warfare against the RSA*. SA Army Headquarters, n.p., n.d.

Saayman, J. & Venter, P. *Namibia Mirror. Independence: 21 March 1990*. Windhoek: Gamsberg Macmillan, 1990.

Saphire, H. & Saunders, C. *Southern African Liberation Struggles: New Local, Regional and Global Perspectives*. Claremont: UCT Press, 2013.

Sanders, J. *Apartheid's Friends: The Rise and Fall of South Africa's Secret Service*. London: John Murray, 2006.

Sarkin-Hughes, J. *Carrots and Sticks: The TRC and the South African Amnesty Process*. Antwerp: Intersentia Publishers, 2004.

Sarkin, J. *Germany's Genocide of the Herero: Kaizer Wilhelm II, His General, His Settlers, His Soldiers*. London/Cape Town: James Currey/UCT Press, 2010.

Saunders, C., ed. *Perspectives on Namibia: Past and Present*. Cape Town: Occasional Paper 4, Centre for African Studies, University of Cape Town, 1983.

Schoeman, R. *Weermagstories: Dienspligtiges Verbreek die Stilte*. Kaapstad: Lux Verbi, 2014.

Scholtz, L. *The SADF in the Border War, 1966-1989*. Cape Town: Tafelberg, 2013.

Scholtz, G.D. *Suid-Afrika en die Wêreldpolitiek 1652-1952*. Johannesburg: Voortrekkerpers, 1954.

Scholtz, J.J.J., comp. *Vegter en Hervormer: Grepe uit die Toesprake van P.W. Botha*. Cape Town: Tafelberg, 1988.

Scheepers, M. *Striking inside Angola with 32 Battalion*. Solihull/Pinetown: Helion & Company/30 Degrees South Publishers, 2012.

Schleicher, H.G. & Schleicher, I. (Translated by Ringleb, B. & Ringleb, K.) *Special Flights to Southern Africa: The GDR and Liberation Movements in Southern Africa*. Harare: Southern Africa Printing and Publishing House, 1998.

Schutte, C., Liebenberg, I. & Minnaar, A., eds. *The Hidden Hand: Covert Operations in South Africa*. 2nd revised edition. Pretoria: Human Sciences Research Council, 1998.

Seegers, A. *The Military in the Making of Modern South Africa*. London/New York: IB Tauris Publishers, 1996.

Seidman, A. & Seidman, N. *U.S. Multinationals in Southern Africa*. Dar es Salaam: Tanzania Publishing House, 1977.

Seiler, J., ed. *Southern Africa Since the Portuguese Coup*. Westview Special Studies on Africa, Boulder Colorado: Westview Press, 1980.

Serfontein, J.H.P. *Namibia?* Randburg: Fokus Suid Publishers, 1976.

Shaw, G. *The Cape Times: An Informal History*. Cape Town: David Philip, 1999.

Shay, R, & Vermaak, C. *The Silent War*. Salisbury: Galaxie Press, 1972. First published in 1971.

Shelton, G., Monyue, D., Pullinger, A., Simmonds, M. & Williams, R. *Demobilisation and its Aftermath, I: A Profile of South Africa's Demobilised Military Personnel*. Institute for Security Studies Monograph Series no. 59, Pretoria: Institute for Security Studies, August 2001.

Shipanga, A. & Armstrong, S. *In Search of Freedom: The Andreas Shipanga Story*. Gibraltar: Ashanti Publishing,1989.

Shityawete, H. *Never Follow the Wolf: The Autobiography of a Namibian Freedom Fighter*. London: Kliptown Books, 1990.

Shubin, G., comp. & ed. (Translated by Sidorov, P.) *The Oral History of Forgotten Wars: The Memoirs of Veterans of the War in Angola*. Moscow: Memories, 2007.

Shubin, G. & Tokarev, A., eds. (Translated by Reilly, T. & Sidorov, P.) *Bush War: The Road to Cuito Cuanavale. Soviet Soldiers' Accounts of the Angolan War*. Auckland Park: Jacana Media, 2011.

Shubin, G. Zhdarkin, I., Barabulya, V. & Kuznetsova-Timonova, A. (eds.) Translated by Tamara Reilly. *Cuito Cuanavale: Frontline Accounts by Soviet Soldiers*. Auckland Park: Jacana, 2014.

BOOKS

Shubin, V. *ANC: A View from Moscow*. Auckland Park: Jacana Media, 2008. First published in 1999 by Mayibuye Books.

Shubin, V. *The Hot "Cold War"*. London/Scottsville: Pluto Press/University of KwaZulu-Natal Press, 2008.

Simons, H.J. *Struggles in Southern Africa for Survival and Equality*. Basingstoke: Macmillan, 1997.

Sisulu, E. *Walter & Albertina Sisulu: In our Lifetime*. Claremont: David Philip, 2002.

Slipchenko, S. (Translated by Garb, P.) *In Southern Africa*. Moscow: Progress Publishers, 1987.

Smith, I. *Mad Dog Killers: The Story of a Congo Mercenary*. Pinetown: 30 Degrees South Publishers, 2012.

Smith, S. *Front Line Africa: The Right to a Future. An Oxfam Report on Conflict and Poverty in Southern Africa*. Oxford: Oxfam, 1990.

Snow, P. *The Star Raft: China's Encounter with Africa*. London: Weidenfeld and Nicolson, 1988.

Snyman, P.H.R. *Beeld van die SWA Gebiedsmag*. Pretoria: Public Relations South African Defence Force, 1989.

Soggot, D. *Namibia: The Violent Heritage*. London: Rex Collins, 1986.

Sonderling, S. *Bushwar/Bosoorlog/Buschkrieg*. Windhoek: Eyes Publishing, 1980.

Sopa, A., ed. *Samora: Man of the People*. Maputo: Maguezo Editores, 2001.

South African Defence Force. *South African Defence Force Yearbook/Suid-Afrikaanse Weermag Jaarboek 1985*. Edupress.

South African Defence Force. *Die Suid-Afrikaanse Weermag Jaarboek/The South African Defence Force Yearbook 1987*. Durban: Walker-Ramus.

South African Defence Force. *South African Defence Force Review*. Durban: Walker-Ramus Trading Co. SA (Pty) Ltd., 1989.

SWA/Namibia Information Services. *Teeninsurgensie – 'n Lewenswyse*. Windhoek: SWA/Namibia Information Services, January 1980.

Soule, A., Dixon, G. & Richards, A. *The Wynand du Toit Story*. Johannesburg: Hans Strydom Publishers, 1987.

Spaarwater, M. *A Spook's Progress: From Making War to Making Peace*. Cape Town: Zebra Press, 2012.

Spence, J.E. *The Strategic Significance of South Africa*. London: Royal United Services Institution, 1970.

Spence, J.E. *The Political and Military Framework*. London: The Study Group on External Investment in South Africa and Namibia (South-West Africa), African Publications Trust, 1975.

Spence, J.E. *The Soviet Union, the Third World and Southern Africa*. Pretoria: South African Institute of International Affairs, 1988.

Spies, F.J. du T. (In co-operation with Du Preez, S.J.) *Operation Savannah, Angola 1975-1976*. Pretoria: Directorate Public Relations, South African Defence Force, 1989.

Stander, S. *Like the Wind: The Story of the South African Army*. Cape Town: Saayman & Weber, 1985.

Stapleton, T. *A Military History of South Africa: From the Dutch-Khoi Wars to the End of Apartheid*. Santa Barbara, California: Praeger Security International, 2010.

Stassen, N. *Afrikaners in Angola 1928-1975*. Pretoria: Protea Boekhuis, 2009.

Steenkamp, N.S. *Die Hoop Groei Weer: Oor die Dood van 'n Soldaat*. Pretoria: J.L. Van Schaik, 1991.

Steenkamp, N.S. (Klasie). *Die Grensoorlog in ons Binnekant: Hanteer Verlies Gelowig*. Helderview: Benedic Books, 2012.

Steenkamp, W. *Adeus Angola*. Cape Town: Howard Timmins, 1976.

Steenkamp, W. *Borderstrike! South Africa into Angola*. Durban/Pretoria: Butterworth Publishers, 1983.

Steenkamp, W. *South Africa's Border War 1966-1989*. Gibraltar: Ashanti Publishing, 1989.

Steenkamp, W. *Freedom Park: Roots and Solutions*. Durban: Just Done Publications, 2007.

Stevens, J. *A Namibian Canvas*. Randburg: Truth House Publishing, 2003.

Steyn, D. & Söderlund, A. *Iron Fist from the Sea: South Africa's Seaborne Raiders 1978-1988*. Solihull/Rugby: Helion & Company/GG Books UK, 2014.

Steyn, H., Van der Walt, R. & Van Loggerenberg, J. *Armament and Disarmament: South Africa's Nuclear Weapons Experience*. Pretoria: Network Publishers, 2003.

Stiff, P. *Taming the Landmine*. Alberton: Galago, 1986.

Stiff, P. *Nine Days of War*. 2nd ed. Alberton: Lemur Books, 1991. First published in 1991.

Stiff, P. *Warfare by Other Means: South Africa in the 1980s and 1990s*. Alberton: Galago, 2001.

Stiff, P. *The Silent War: South African Recce Operations 1969-1994*. 2nd ed. Alberton: Galago, 2001. First published in 1999.

Stiff, P. *The Covert War: Koevoet Operations Namibia 1979-1989*. Alberton: Galago, 2004.

Stockwell, J. *In Search of Enemies: A CIA Story*. New York: Norton, 1978.

Strauss, F.J. *SWA vir die Wolwe?* Windhoek: Eros Publishers, 1981.

Strydom, L. *Rivonia – Masker af!* Johannesburg: Voortrekkerpers, 1964.

Sutton-Pryce, T. *Zimbabwe: A Model for Namibia: A Comparison of Events in Zimbabwe-Rhodesia 1979-1980 with the Situation in SWA in 1989*. Pretoria: Academica,1989.

Swanepoel, P.C. *Polisie-Avonture in Suidwes-Afrika*. n.p,: Voortrekkerpers, n.d.

Swanepoel, T.C. *Really inside BOSS: A Tale of South Africa's Late Intelligence Service (And something about the CIA)*. Pretoria: P.C. Swanepoel, April 2008. Reprint. First published in 2007.

Taylor, J. *A Whisper in the Reeds: "The Terrible Ones" – South Africa's 32 Battalion at War*. London: Helion Publishers, 2013.

Texeira, B. *The Fabric of Terror: Three Days in Angola*. Cape Town/Pretoria: Human & Rousseau, 1965.

Thallon, W. *Devil Incarnate: A Depraved Mercenary's Lifelong Swathe of Destruction*. Edinburgh/London: Mainstream Publishing, 2001.

Thiro-Beukes, E., Beukes, A., and Beukes, H.S.J. *Namibia: A Struggle Betrayed*. Rehoboth, Namibia: Akasia Drukkery, 1986.

Thompson, J.H. *An Unpopular War: From Afkak to Bosbefok –
Voices of South African National Servicemen*. Cape Town:
Zebra Press, 2006.

Thornberry, C. *A Nation is Born: The Inside Story of Namibia's
Independence*. Windhoek: Gamsberg Macmillan, 2004.

Timerman, J. (Translated by Talbot, T.) *Cuba: A Journey*. London:
Picador,1994.

Tomaselli, K. *The Cinema of Apartheid: Race and Class in South
African Film*. New York/Chicago: Smyrna Press, 1988.

Totemeyer, G., Kandeta, V. & Werner, W. *Namibia in Perspective*.
Windhoek: Council of Churches in Namibia, 1987.

Turner, J.W. *Continent Ablaze: The Insurgency Wars in Africa 1960
to the Present*. Johannesburg: Jonathan Ball Publishers,
1998.

Turok, B. *The ANC and the turn to the Armed Struggle, 1950-1970*.
Auckland Park: Jacana Media, 2010.

Turton, A. *Shaking Hands with Billy*. Durban: Just Done
Productions, 2010.

Tvetden, I. *Angola: Struggle for Peace and Reconstruction*. London:
WestView Press/Harper Collins, 1997.

Tyson, H., ed. *Conflict and the Press: Proceedings of The Star's
Centennial Conference on the Role of the Press in a Divided
Society*. Johannesburg: Argus Printing & Publishing
Company, 1987.

Tyson, H. *Editors under Fire*. Wynberg/Sandton: Random House,
1993.

Uys, I. *Cross of Honour*. Germiston: Uys Publishers, 1992.

Uys, I. *Bushman Soldiers: Their Alpha and Omega*. Germiston:
Fortress Publishers, 1993.

Uys, I. *Bushmen Soldiers: The History of 31, 201 & 203 Battalions
during the Bush War, 1974-1990*. Solihull/Rugby: Helion &
Company/GG Books UK, 2014.

Uys, I. *Enduring Valour. South Africa's Cross of Honour*. Solihull/
Rugby: Helion & Company/GG Books UK, 2014.

Van der Berg, D. *Charlie's Omega*. Durban: Just Done Productions,
2007.

Van der Merwe, G. *Diensplig/National Service '83*. Sandton:
Gordon Publishing, n.d.

Van der Merwe, G. *Diensplig/National Service '84*. Sandton:
Gordon Publishing, n.d.

Van der Merwe, G. *Diensplig/National Service '86*. Sandton:
Gordon Publishing, n.d.

Van der Merwe, G. *Diensplig/National Service 1988*. Sandton:
Gordon Publishing, n.d.

Van der Merwe, J. *Trou tot die Dood toe: Die Suid-Afrikaanse
Polisiemag*. Dainfern: Uitgewery Praag, 2010.

Van der Spuy, D.C., comp. *Amnesty for Terrorism*. South African
Bureau of National and International Communication:
Simondium Publishers, March 15, 1978. Second edition
July 15, 1978.

Van der Waag, I. *A Military History of Modern South Africa*. Cape
Town: Jonathan Ball Publishers, 2015.

Van der Waals, W.S. *Portugal's War in Angola 1961-1974*. Rivonia:
Ashanti Publishing, 1993/ Pretoria: Protea Book House,
2011.

Van der Walt, N. *Bos toe! 'n Storie oor die Laaste Fase van
die Grensoorlog soos Beleef deur 'n Junior Offisier van
32-Bataljon*. Swartkops: Nico van der Walt, 2007.

Van der Walt, R. Steyn, H. & Van Loggerenberg, J. *Armament and
Disarmament: South Africa's Nuclear Experience*. 2nded.
London: iUniverse, 2005.

Van Heerden, R. & Hudson, A. *Four Ball One Tracer: Commanding
Executive Outcomes in Angola and Sierra Leone*. Pinetown:
30 Degrees South Publishers, 2012.

Van Huyssteen, C.N.L. *The Lonely Grave in the Fish River Canyon*.
Roodepoort: CUM Books, 1983. First published in 1981.

Van Jaarsveld, A.S., ed. *Militêre Geneeskunde in Suid-Afrika
(1913-1983)*. Pretoria: Publication no. 7, Military Information
Bureau, South African Defence Force, 1983.

Van Rensburg, W. *SWA/Namibian Border War – Major Military
and Political Incidents: 1959-1989*. Durban: Just Done
Productions & Publications, 2013.

Van Rooyen, P. *Agter 'n Eland Aan*. Cape Town/Pretoria: Quellerie
Publishers, 1995.

Van Wyk, A. *Honoris Crux: Ons Dapperes/Our Brave*. Cape Town:
Saayman & Weber, 1982.

Van Wyk, A. *Honoris Crux: Ons Dapperes/Our Brave II*. Cape Town:
Saayman & Weber, 1985.

Van Wyk, A. *Dirk Mudge Reënmaker van die Namib*. Pretoria: J.L.
van Schaik, 1999.

Van Wyk, A. *Die Roem en die Rou: Stories agter Honoris Crux*.
Pretoria: Litera Publications, 2008.

Veloso, J. (translated by Fauvet, P.) *Memories at Low Altitude: The
Autobiography of a Mozambican Security Chief*. Cape Town:
Zebra Press, 2012. First published in Portuguese in 2006.

Venter, A.J. (photographs by Breytenbach, C.) *The Terror Fighters:
A Profile of Guerrilla Warfare in Southern Africa*. Cape Town/
Johannesburg: Purnell, 1969.

Venter, A.J. *Terroris: 'n Ooggetuieverslag*. Cape Town: Tafelberg,
1971.

Venter, A.J. *Portugal's Guerrilla War: The Campaign for Africa*.
Cape Town: John Malherbe Publishers, 1973.

Venter, A.J. *War in Africa*. Cape Town/Pretoria: Human &
Rousseau, 1973.

Venter, A.J. *Africa Today*. Johannesburg: Macmillan South Africa,
1975.

Venter, A.J. *The Zambesi Salient: Conflict in Southern Africa*.
London: Robert Hale, 1975.

Venter, A. J. *Black Leaders of Southern Africa*. Randburg: Siesta
Publications, 1976.

Venter, A.J. *Vorster's Africa: Friendship and Frustration*.
Johannesburg: Ernest Stanton Publishers, 1977.

Venter, A.J., ed. *Challenge: Southern Africa within the African
Revolutionary Context: An Overview*. Gibraltar: Ashanti
Publishing, 1989.

Venter, A. J. *War in Angola*. Tuen wan, Hong Kong: Concord
Publishers, 1992.

Venter, A.J. *War Dog: Fighting other People's Wars*. Havertown,
Pennsylvania: Xasemate, 2003.

Venter, A.J. (in association with Badenhorst, N.P. & Victor, P.
L.) *How South Africa Built Six Atom Bombs and then
Abandoned its Nuclear Weapons Programme*. Kyalami
Estate: Ashanti Publishing, 2008.

Venter, A.J. *War Stories by Al J. Venter and Friends: Up Close and
Personal in Third World Conflicts*. Pretoria: Protea Book
House, 2011.

BOOKS

Venter, A.J. *Gunship Ace: The Wars of Neall Ellis, Helicopter Pilot and Mercenary*. Pretoria: Protea Book House, 2012.

Venter, A.J. *Mercenaries: Putting the World to Right with Hired Guns*. Pinetown/Oxford: 30 Degrees South/Casemate, 2014.

Venter, A.J. *Portugal's Guerrilla Wars in Africa: Lisbon's Three Wars in Angola, Mozambique and Portuguese Guinea 1961-74*. Solihull: Helion & Company, 2013.

Venter, A.J., Ellis, N. & Wood, R. *The Chopper Boys: Helicopter Warfare in Africa*. n.p.: Greenhill Books, n.d.

Venter, G.M. & Van der Westhuizen, D.C. *Diensplig Sonder Sukkel*. Pretoria: Erroll Marx Publishers, 1982.

Venter, P. & Venter, G.S. *Ek was Daar*. Vishoek: Hamba Straight Uitgewers,1995.

Venter, P.C. *Tussen Tiers: SA oorlogshelde*. Pretoria: Folio, 1983.

Verbaan, M. *Hearts and Mines: Tales of a Lost Colony and other Namibian Graffiti*. Windhoek: Free Press of Namibia, 1992.

Villa-Vicenco, C. *Civil Disobedience and Beyond: Law, Resistance and Religion in South Africa*. Cape Town: David Philip, 1990.

Volker, W., ed. *Army Signals in South Africa: The Story of the South African Corps of Signals and its Antecedents*. Pretoria: Veritas Books, 2010.

Volker, W., ed. *Signal Units of the South African Corps of Signals and Related Services*. Pretoria: Veritas Books, 2010.

Volker, W., ed. *9C – Nine Charlie! Army Signallers in the Field: The Story of the Men and Women of the South African Corps of Signals, and their Equipment*. Pretoria: Veritas Books, 2010.

Warren, M.H.H. *In the Name of God: Defending Apartheid*. n.p.: Michael 'Double-H', 2012.

Webb, S. *Ops Medic: A National Serviceman's Border War*. Alberton: Galago, 2008.

Weigert, S.L. *Angola: A Modern History, 1961-2002*. London: Palgrave Macmillan, 2011.

Weyl, N. *Traitor's End: The Rise and Fall of the Communist Movement in South Africa*. Cape Town & Johannesburg: Tafelberg Uitgewers, 1970.

Welz, M. *Breyten en die Bewaarder: Die Breytenbachverhoor Junie-Julie 1977*. Johannesburg: McGraw-Hill, 1977.

Wiarda, H.J. *Transcending Corporatism? The Portuguese Corporative System and the Revolution of 1974*. Colombia: University of South Carolina Institute of International Studies, 1976.

Williams, D. *On the Border: The White South African Military Experience 1965-1990*. Cape Town: Tafelberg, 2008.

Williams, D. *Springboks, Troepies and Cadres: Stories of the South African Army, 1912-2012*. Cape Town: Tafelberg, 2012.

Wilkens, M. *Chopper Pilot: The Adventures and Experiences of Monster Wilkins*. Nelspruit: Freeworld Publications, African Aviation Series no. 6, 2000.

Wilsworth, C. *First in Last out: The South African Artillery in Action 1975-1988*. Johannesburg: 30 Degrees South Publishers, 2010.

Wingrin, D. *Tumult in the Clouds: Stories from the South African Air Force 1920-2010*. Pinetown/Solihull: 30 Degrees South Publishers/Helion & Company, 2012.

Wolfers, M. & Bergerol, J. *Angola in the Frontline*. London: Zed Press, 1983.

Wolvaardt, P. *A Diplomat's Story: Apartheid and Beyond 1969-1998*. Alberton: Galago, 2005.

Woods, K.J. *The Kevin Woods Story: In the Shadow of Mugabe's Gallows*. Johannesburg: 30 Degrees South Publishers, 2007.

Woodward, B. *Veil: The Secret Wars of the CIA 1981-1987*. New York: Pocket Books, 1988.

Wright, B. *Troopie Days. No. 1*. Johannesburg/Cape Town: Perskor Publishers, 1990. First published in 1989.

Wylie, D. *Art + Revolution: The Life and Death of Thami Mnyele South African Artist*. Auckland Park: Jacana Media, 2008.

Ya Nangolo, M. & Sellstrom, T. *Kassinga: A Story Untold*. Windhoek: Namibia Book Development Council, 2005.

Ya-Otto, J., Gjerstad, O. & Mercer, M. *Battlefront Namibia: An Autobiography*. Westport, Connecticut: Lawrence Hill & Company, 1981.

Yeats, C. *Prisoner of Conscience: One Man's Remarkable Journey from Repression to Freedom*. London: Rider Books, 2005.

BOOKS (SPANISH AND PORTUGUESE)

The following are examples. The list is not exhaustive.

Blanch, H.L. *Historias Secretas de Medicos Cubanos*. La Habana: Memoria. Centro Cultural. Pable de la Torriente Brau, 2005.

Cabrera, M.R. La *Guerra de Angola*. La Habana: Editoria Politica, 1989.

FAPLA. *FAPLA: Baluarte de paz em Angola*. Luanda: Editoria Luanda, 2002.

Hernandez,T. H. *Trueno Justiciero: Mis campanis en ciela Angolana*. La Habana: Memoria, 2005.

Lara, L. *Itinerário do MPLA através de documentos e anotações: Um amplo movimento, Vol 1* (second edition). Luanda: LitoTipo, 1998.

Roca, E. Angola: *Contribuicao ao Estude de Nacionalismo Moderno Angola* (period de 1950-1964). Vol. 1. Luanda: Kilombelombe, 2002.

Roca, E. Angola: *Contribuicao ao Estude de Nacionalismo Moderno Angola* (period de 1950-1964). Vol. 2. Luanda: Kilombelombe, 2002.

SWAPO: Departemento de Informação e Publicade, SWAPO da Namibia. *Nasce Uma Nação: A Luta de Libertação da Namibia*. London: Zed Press, 1985.

BOOKS (RUSSIAN)

Titles in phonetic Russian followed by English translation.

Kuzhetsova-Timonova, A., Tokarev, A., Zhdarkin, I. & Shubin, G. *Vospominanya veyetanov voiny v Angole I drugih lokalnyh konfliktov [Memoirs of veterans war in Angola and other local conflicts]*. Moscow: Memories Publishers, 2011.

Shubin, G., Kuznetsova-Timonova, A., Zhdarkin, I., Barabulya, V & Babushkin, D. *Zabytaya grazhdanskaya voina v Angole: Vospomonanyua ochevidtsev (Izdanie vtoroe ispravlennoe I dopolnennoe) [Forgotten civil war in Angola: Memoirs of eyewitnesses]*, Vol. 1 (second revised edition). Moscow: Memories Publishers, 2015.

Shubin, G., Kuznetsova-Timonova, A., Zhdarkin, I., Barabulya, V. & Babushkin, D. *Zabytaya grazhdanskaya voina v Angole: Vospomonanyua ochevidtsev (Izdanie vtoroe ispravlennoe I dopolnennoe) [Forgotten civil war in Angola: Memoirs of eyewitnesses].* Vol. 2 (second revised edition). Moscow: Memories Publishers, 2015.

Shubin, G., Zhdarkin, I. & Barabulya, V. *Vospominaniya sovetskih I rossiskih veteranov ob Angole: Informatsia s elektronnoi ploshcadki rossiskogo souza veteranov Angoly [Memoirs of Soviet and Russian veterans about Angola – Information from Site of Russian Angola veteran's Union].* Moscow: Memories Publishers, 2014.

Shubin, G. (editor) & Chernetsov, E. *Samye pamyatnye dni. The most memorable days.* Moscow: Memories Publishers, 2013.

Tokarev, A. & Shubin, G. *Vospominaniya neposredstrvennyh uchastnikov I ochevidtsev gtrazhdanskoi voiny v Angole: Ustnaua Istoriya vabytyh voin. [Reminicenses of direct participants and eye-witnesses of civil war in Angola: An oral history of forgotten wars].* Moscow: Memories Publishers, 2009.

ARTICLES AND CHAPTERS IN BOOKS

Adams, G. "Cuba and Africa: The International Politics of the Liberation Struggles, a Documentary History." *Latin American Perspectives* 7, no. 1 (1981): 108-125.

Ajulu, R. & Cammack, D. "Lesotho, Botswana, Swaziland: Captive States," in *Destructive Engagement: Southern Africa at War* edited by Johnson, P. & Martin, D. Harare: Zimbabwe Publishing House for the Southern African Research and Documentation Centre, 1986. 139-170; and *Frontline Southern Africa: Destructive Engagement* edited by Johnson, P. & Martin, D. New York: Four Walls Eight Windows, 1988. 191-232.

Alao, A. "A Comparative Evaluation of the Armed Struggle in Namibia, South Africa and Zimbabwe." *Terrorism and Political Violence* 8, no. 4 (Winter 1996): 58-77.

Alao, A. "A Comparative Evaluation of the Armed Struggle in Namibia, South Africa and Zimbabwe," in *Violence in Southern Africa* edited by Gutteridge, W. & Spence, J.E. London: Frank Cass, 1997. 58-77.

Albright, D.E. "The USSR, its Communist Allies, and Southern Africa." *Munger Africana Library Notes* 55 (November 1980): 4-29.

Alden, C. "Mozambique: An Abiding Dependency," in *Southern Africa at the Crossroads? Prospects for Stability and Development in the 1990s,* edited by Benjamin, L. & Gregory, C. Rivonia: Justified Press, 1992. 75-102.

Alden, C. "Political Violence in Mozambique: Past, Present and Future," in *Violence in Southern Africa* edited by Gutteridge, W. & Spence, J.E. London: Frank Cass, 1997. 40-57.

Alexander, M. "The Militarisation of White South African Society, 1948-1994," *Scientia Militaria, South African Journal of Military Studies* 30, no. 2 (2000): 267-289.

Anonymous. "The SA Catering Corps and the School of Catering/ Die SA Spysenierskorps en Spyseniersskool," in *Suid-Afrikaanse Weermag Oorsig 1990/South African Defence Force Review 1990* edited by De La Rey, A. Durban: Directorate Public Relations, SADF/Walker-Ramus Trading Co, n.d. 333-351.

Archer, S. "Defence Expenditure and Arms Procurement in South Africa," in *War and Society: The Militarisation of South Africa* edited by Cock, J. & Nathan, L. Cape Town & Johannesburg: David Philip, 1989. 244-259.

Baines, G. "'South Africa's Vietnam?' Literary History and Cultural Memory of the Border War," *South African Historical Journal* 49 (2003): 172-192.

Baines, G. "'South Africa's Vietnam?' Literary History and Cultural Memory of the Border War." *Safundi: The Journal of South African and American Comparative Studies* 13/14: 1-21.

Baines, G. "Introduction: Challenging the Boundaries, Breaking the Silences," in *Beyond the Border War: New Perspectives on Southern Africa's Late-Cold War Conflicts* edited by Baines, Gary & Vale, Peter. Pretoria: University of South Africa Press, 2008. 1-21.

Baines, G. "Blame, Shame or Reaffirmation? White Conscripts Reassess the Meaning of the 'Border War' in Post-Apartheid South Africa," *Interculture* 5, no. 3 (October 2008): 214-227.

Baines, G. "Conflicting Memories, Competing Narratives and Complicating Histories: Revisiting the Cassinga Controversy," *Journal of Namibian Studies* 6 (2009): 7-26.

Baines, G. "The Life of a Uniformed Technocrat turned Securocrat," *Historia* 54, no. 1 (2009): 314-327.

Baines, G. "Site of Struggle? The Freedom Park Fracas and the Divisive Legacy of South Africa's Border War/Liberation Struggle," *Social Dynamics* 35, no. 2 (September 2009): 330-344.

Baines, G. "SADF Soldiers' Stories," *Journal of Namibian Studies* 5 (2009): 7-25.

Baines, Gary. "The Saga of South African POWs in Angola, 1975-1982," *Scientia Militaria, South African Journal of Military Studies* 40, no. 2 (2012): 102-141.

Baines, G. "Vietnam Analogies and Metaphors: The Cultural Codification of South Africa's Border War." *Safundi: The Journal of South African and American Studies,* Special Issue: *Beyond Rivalry: Literature/History, Fiction/Non-fiction* 13, no. 1-2 (2012): 73-90.

Baines, G. "A Battle for Perceptions: Revisiting the Cassinga Controversy in Southern Africa," in *A Natural Inclination: The Massacre throughout History* edited by Dwyer, P. & Ryan, L. New York: Berghahn, 2013.

Baines, G. "Trauma in Transition: Representing Psychological Problems of South African War Veterans," http://*wwwmcc.murdoch.edu.au/trauma/docs/baines_g.pdf*

Baker, D.G. "Retreat from Challenge: White Reactions to Regional Events Since 1974," in *Southern Africa Since the Portuguese Coup.* Westview Special Studies on Africa, Boulder Colorado: Westview Press, 1980. 155-167.

Barber, S. "The View from Washington – US Policy towards South Africa," in *Challenge: Southern Africa within the African Revolutionary Context. An overview* edited by Venter, A.J. Gibraltar: Ashanti Publishing, 1989. 91-106.

Barnard, S.L. "'n Historiese Oorsig van die Gewapende Konflik aan die Noordgrens van SWA/Namibië 1966-1989," *Acta Academica* 23, no. 1 (March 1991): 102-127.

Barnard, S.L. "Enkele Fasette van die Problematiek van die Akademikus by die Skryf van Suid-Afrikaanse Kontemporêre Militêre Geskiedenis," *Militaria* 22, no. 4 (1992): 54-59.

BOOKS

ARTICLES & CHAPTERS

Barnard, L. "Die Gebeure by Cassinga, 4 Mei 1978 – 'n Gevallestudie van die Probleme van 'n Militêre Historikus," *Historia* (May 1996): 88-99.

Barnard, S.L. "Life on the Border: A Socio/Historic Study of the Members of the South African Air Force during the 'Bush War', 1966-89," *Journal for Contemporary History* 27, no. 1 (2002): 35-47.

Barnard, L. "The 'Forgotten War': The Challenge on doing Research on the so-called 'Border War'/Die 'Vergete Oorlog': Die Uitdaging om Historiese Navorsing oor die Grensoorlog te doen," in *Research Report/Navorsingsverslag University of the Free State/Universiteit van die Vrystaat/Yunivesithi ya Freistata* edited by Pienaar, A. & De Lange, A. Centenary Edition/Eeufeesuitgawe, 2003. 171-174.

Barnard, L. "Die Suid-Afrikaanse Lugmag se Optrede tydens Operasie Savannah – Relevant of 'n Noodsaaklike Ergernis?" *Journal for Contemporary History* 28, no. 2 (September 2003): 66-80.

Barnard, L. "Die Suid-Afrikaanse Lugmag se Aandeel in die Militêre Optrede tydens die Suid-Afrikaanse Weermag se Aanval op Cassinga, 4 Mei 1978," *Journal for Contemporary History* 28, no. 2 (September 2003): 81-96.

Barnard, L. "The Controversy of the Battle of Cassinga. Does the Media Provide the Final Answer?" *Journal for Contemporary History* 29, no. 3 (December 2005): 184-198.

Barnard, L. "Die Suid-Afrikaanse Lugmag (SALM) se Optrede in die Teaters Angola en Rhodesië (circa 1966-1974) as Aanloop tot die Grensoorlog," in *Grensoorlog/Border War 1966-1989* edited by Barnard, L. *Journal for Contemporary History* 31, no. 3 (December 2006): 74-90.

Barnard, L. "The Battle of Cassinga, 4 May 1978: A Historical Reassessment. Part 1: The Course of the Battle and Ensuing Controversy," in *Grensoorlog/Border War 1966-1989* edited by Barnard, L. *Journal for Contemporary History* 31, no. 3 (December 2006): 131-146.

Barnard, L. "The Battle of Cassinga, 4 May 1978: A Historical Reassessment. Part 2: Interviews with two SADF Soldiers," in *Grensoorlog/Border War 1966-1989* edited by Barnard, L. *Journal for Contemporary History* 31, no. 33 (December 2006): 147-160.

Barnard, L. "Enkele Aantekeninge oor die Militêre Struktuur en Prosesse van die Suid-Afrikaanse Lugmag (SALM) gedurende die Grensoorlog, in *Grensoorlog/Border War 1966-1989* edited by Barnard, L. *Journal for Contemporary History* 31, no. 3 (December 2006): 215-232.

Barnard, L. "The South African Air Force's Transport Aircraft: Acquisition and Utilisation during the Border War," in *Grensoorlog/Border War 1966-1989* edited by Barnard, L. *Journal for Contemporary History* 31, no. 3 (December 2006): 233-250.

Barnard, L. "The Role of the South African Air Force (SAAF) during the SADF's Cross-Border Operations in Angola, 1978-1981: A Historical Exploration," in *Grensoorlog/Border War 1966-1989* edited by Barnard, L. *Journal for Contemporary History* 31, no. 3 (December 2006): 267-282.

Barnard, L. "The Role of the South African Air Force (SAAF) during the SADF's Cross-Border Operations in Angola, November 1981-1982: A Historical Exploration," in *Grensoorlog/Border War 1966-1989, Deel 2/Part 2* edited by Barnard, L. *Journal for Contemporary History* 34, no. 1 (February 2009): 181-195.

Barnard, L. "Die Suid-Afrikaanse Lugmag se Finale Onttrekking uit die Teater van Suid-Angola en Noord-Namibië – Die Einde van 'n Era," in *Grensoorlog/Border War 1966-1989, Deel 2/Part 2* edited by Barnard, L. *Journal for Contemporary History* 34, no. 1 (February 2009): 196-206.

Barnard, L. "Cross-Border Operations of the SAAF in Angola: 1987-1989. Prelude to the Final Stages of the War, in *Grensoorlog/Border War 1966-1989, Deel 2/Part 2* edited by Barnard, L. *Journal for Contemporary History* 34, no.1 (February 2009): 223-236.

Barnard, L. "Die Suid-Afrikaanse Lugmag se Optrede in die Teaters van Noord-Namibië en Suid-Angola 1983-1985: 'n Historiese Verkenning," in *Grensoorlog/Border War 1966-1989, Deel 2/Part 2* edited by Barnard, L. *Journal for Contemporary History* 34, no. 1 (February 2009): 266-280.

Barnard, W.S., ed. "Kompas op SAW/Namibië," in *Vereniging vir Geografie, Spesiale Publikasie, no. 5* (1985): 190-206.

Batchelor, P. "South Africa's Arms Industry: Prospects for Conversion," in *From Defence to Development: Redirecting Military Resources in South Africa* edited by Cock, J. & Mckenzie, P. Cape Town/Ottawa: David Philip/International Development Research Centre, 1998. 97-121.

Batley, K. "The Language of Landscape: The Border Terrain in the Writing of South African Troops," *English Usage in South Africa* 23, Pretoria: Unisa University Press, 1992.

Batley, K. "Documents of Life: South African Soldiers' Narratives of the Border War," in *Beyond the Border War: New Perspectives on Southern Africa's Late-Cold War Conflicts* edited by Baines, G. & Vale, P. Pretoria: University of South Africa Press, 2008.

Becker, Heike. "Remaking our Histories: The Liberation War in Post-Colonial Namibian Writing," in *Beyond the Border War: New Perspectives on Southern Africa's Late-Cold War Conflicts* edited by Baines, G. & Vale, P. Pretoria: University of South Africa Press, 2008. 281-301.

Beckett, I. "Portuguese Africa," in *War in Peace: An Analysis of Warfare since 1945* edited by Thompson, R. London: Orbis Publishing, 1981. 152-157.

Beinart, W. "Political and Collective Violence in Southern African Historiography," *Journal of Southern African Studies* 18, no. 3 (1992): 455-486.

Bench, B. "'Constructive Engagement': The Confused Art of Regional Foreign Policy," in *South African Review II*, South African Research Service. Johannesburg: Ravan Press, 1984. 197-210.

Bender, G.J. "American Policy toward Angola: A History of Linkage," in Bender, G., Coleman, J.S. & Sklar, R.L., eds. *African Crisis Areas and U.S. Foreign Policy.* Berkeley/Los Angeles/London: University of California Press, 1985. 110-128.

Bender, G.J. "Peacemaking in Southern Africa: The Luanda Pretoria Tug-of-War." *Third World Quarterly* 11, no. 2 (April 1989): 15-30.

Beri, H.M.L. "Continuing Struggle in Namibia." *Strategic Analysis* 6, no. 1 (February 1983): 679-683.

Berridge, G.R. "The Role of the Superpowers," in *Can South Africa Survive?* edited by Brewer, J. Johannesburg: Southern Book Publishers, 1989. 9-35.

Birmingham, D. "Angola Revisited," *Journal of Southern African Studies* 15, no. 1 (1988): 1-14.

Birmingham, D. "Angola," in *A History of Post-Colonial Lusophone Africa* edited by Chabal, P. et al. London: Hurst & Company, 2002. 137-184.

Bissell, R.E. "How Strategic is South Africa?" in Bissell, R.E. & Crocker, C., eds. *South Africa Into the 1980s.* Westview Special Studies on Africa, Boulder Colorado: Westview Press, 1979. 209-231.

Bissell, R.E. "Soviet Military Aid to Africa," *Journal of Contemporary African Studies* 1, no. 1 (October 1981): 1-18.

Blight, J.P. & Weiss, T.G. "Must the Grans still Suffer? Some Thoughts on Third World Conflicts after the Cold War," *Third World Quarterly* 13, no. 2 (1992): 229-253.

Bonate, L.J.K. "Muslims and the Liberation Struggle in Northern Mozambique," in *Southern African Liberation Struggles: New Local, Regional and Global Perspectives* edited by Saphire, H. & Saunders, C. Claremont: UCT Press, 2013. 58-75.

Boshoff, W. "Die Repatriasie van die Ebo-4: Die Lokalisering en Opgrawing van die Grafte van vier Suid-Afrikaanse Soldate in die Ebo-distrik, Kwanza Sul, Angola, 1975-2012,"*Journal for Contemporary History* 37, no. 2 (December 2012): 1191-223.

Botha, C. "Internal Colonisation and an Oppressed Minority? The Dynamics of Relations between Germans and Afrikaners against the Background of Constructing a Colonial State in Namibia, 1884-1990," *Journal of Namibian Studies* 2 (2007): 7-50.

Botha, C.R. "South Africa's Total Strategy in the Era of Cold War, Liberation Struggles and the uneven Transition to Democracy," *Journal of Namibian Studies* 4 (2008): 75-111.

Bredenkamp, I. & Wessels, A. "A Historical Perspective on the Influence of the Military Environment on Chaplaincy, with Special Reference to the Namibian War of Independence, 1966-1989," *Journal for Contemporary History* 34, no. 2 (June 2009): 105-125.

Bredenkamp, I. & Wessels, A. "The South African Military Chaplaincy Service and Transformation, c. 1990-1998," *Journal for Contemporary History* 36, no. 3 (December 2011): 101-124.

Bredenkamp, I. & Wessels, A. "Die Suid-Afrikaanse Kapelaansdiens (SAKD) en Staatsbeleid tydens die Grensoorlog, 1966-1989," *Acta Theologica* 31, no. 1 [online]: 1-19.

Bredenkamp, I. & Wessels, A. "A Historical Perspective on South African Military Chaplaincy and Cold War Ideologies during the Border War, 1966-1989," in *Journal for Contemporary History*, 38 (2), December 2013, pp. 46-69.

Breytenbach, J. "Airborne Assault on Cassinga Base, 4 May 1978," in *Grensoorlog/Border War 1966-1989, Deel 2/Part 2* edited by Barnard, L. *Journal for Contemporary History* 34, no. 1 (February 2009): 141-163.

Breytenbach, W. "South Africa within the African Revolutionary Context", in *Challenge: Southern Africa within the African Revolutionary Context. An Overview* edited by Venter, A.J. Gibraltar: Ashanti Publishing, 1989. 63-90.

Breytenbach, W. "Cuito Cuanavale Revisited: Same Outcomes, Different Consequences," *African Insight* 27, no. 1 (1997): 61-67.

Bridgland, F. "Angola and the West," in *Challenge: Southern Africa within the African Revolutionary Context. An Overview* edited by Venter, A.J. Gibraltar: Ashanti Publishing, 1989. 117-145.

Brinkman, I. "Angolan Civilians in Wartime, 1961-2002," in *Daily Lives of Civilians in Wartime Africa: From Slavery Days to Rwandan Genocide* edited by Laband, J. Scottsville: University of KwaZulu-Natal Press, 2007. 169-194.

Britain, V. "Cuba and Southern Africa," *New Left Review* 172 (1988): 117-124.

Britain, V. "Eighteen Years Later, Speaking to Lucio Lara," *African Communist* 143 [online].

Brown, D.M. "Images of War: Popular Fiction in English and the War on South Africa's Borders," *English Academy Review* 4, no. 1 (January 1987): 53-66.

Brown, S. "Diplomacy by Other Means – SWAPO's Liberation War," in *Namibia's Liberation Struggle: The Two-Edged Sword* edited by Leys, C. & Saul, J.S. London: James Currey, 1995. 19-39.

Burness, D. "Angolan Writing – An Arm of Liberation," in *Critical Perspectives on Lusophone Literature from Africa* edited by Burness, D. Boulder, Colorado: Lynne Rienner, 1981. 50-55.

Callister, G. "Patriotic Duty or Resented Imposition? Public Reactions to Military Conscription in White South Africa, 1952-1972," *Scientia Militaria, South African Journal of Military Studies* 35, no. 1 (2007): 46-67.

Cammack, D. "South Africa's War of Destabilisation," in *South African Review 5* compiled and edited by Moss, G. & Obery, I. Johannesburg: Ravan Press & Southern African Research Service, 1989. 191-208.

Campbell, H. "The Military Defeat of the South Africans in Angola," *Monthly Review* 40, no. 11 (1989): 1-15.

Campbell, H. "Cuito Cuanavale," in *The Oxford Companion to Politics of the World* edited by Crahan, M.E. et al. New York: Oxford University Press, 2001. 187-188.

Campbell, K.M. "Southern Africa in Soviet foreign policy," in *Adelphi Papers* 227 (1987): 3-77.

Cawthra, G. "Guns or Butter? Growth, Development and Security," in *From Defence to Development: Redirecting Military Resources in South Africa* edited by Cock, J. & Mckenzie, P. Cape Town/Ottawa: David Philip/International Development Research Centre, 1998. 25-40.

Cerrebka, Z. "The Effects of Militarization of Africa on Human Rights," *Africa Today* (1st and 2nd Quarters 1987).

Cobbett, W. "Apartheid's Army and the Arms Embargo," in *War and Society: The Militarisation of South Africa* edited by Cock, J. & Nathan, L. Cape Town & Johannesburg: David Philip, 1989. 232-243.

Cock, J. "Introduction," in *War and Society: The Militarisation of South Africa* edited by Cock, J. & Nathan, L. Cape Town & Johannesburg: David Philip,1989. 13.

Cock, J. "Manpower and Militarisation: Women and the SADF," in *War and Society: The Militarisation of South Africa* edited by Cock, J. & Nathan, L. Cape Town & Johannesburg: David Philip, 1989. 51-66.

Cock, J. "Political Violence," in *People and Violence in South Africa* edited by McKendrick, B. & Hoffmann, W. Cape Town: Oxford University Press, 1990. 45-72.

ARTICLES & CHAPTERS

Cock, J. "Introduction," in *From Defence to Development: Redirecting Military Resources in South Africa* edited by Cock, J. & Mckenzie, P. Cape Town/Ottawa: David Philip/International Development Research Centre, 1998. 1-24.

Cock, J. "Light Weapons Proliferation: The Link between Security and Development," in *From Defence to Development: Redirecting Military Resources in South Africa* edited by Cock, J. & Mckenzie, P. Cape Town/Ottawa: David Philip/International Development Research Centre, 1998. 122-147.

Cock, J. "Militarism and Women in South Africa", in *Review of African Political Economy*, 45/46, 1989. 50-64.

Coetzee, A. "Literature and Crisis: One Hundred Years of Afrikaans Literature and Afrikaner Nationalism," in *Rendering Things Visible: Essays on South African Literary Culture* edited by Trump, M. Johannesburg: Ravan Press, 1990.

Coetzee, J. "Rewolusionêre Oorlog en Teeninsurgensie," in *Nasionale Veiligheid en Strategie met Spesifieke verwysing na die RSA* edited by Hough, M. Institute for Strategic Studies, University of Pretoria, Publication no. 10, 1981.

Cohen, B. "US Imperialism and Southern Africa," *Review of African Political Economy* 9 (May-August 1978): 82-88.

Coker, C. "South Africa and the Soviet Union," in *Challenge: Southern Africa within the African Revolutionary Context. An Overview* edited by Venter, A.J. Gibraltar: Ashanti Publishing, 1989. 306-322.

Colvin, C. "'Brothers and Sisters, Do not be Afraid of me': Trauma, History and the Therapeutic Imagination in the new South Africa," in *Contested Pasts: The Politics of Memory* edited by Hodgkin, K. & Radstone, S. London: Routledge, 2003. 153-167.

Conradie, D. "Achievements of the SADF 1961-1982," *Scientia Militaria, South African Journal of Military Studies* 13, no. 2 (1983): 51-56.

Conway, Daniel. "'Somewhere on the Border – of Credibility': The Cultural Construction and Contestation of 'the Border' in White South African Society," in *Beyond the Border War: New Perspectives on Southern Africa's Late-Cold War Conflicts* edited by Baines, G. & Vale, P. Pretoria: University of South Africa Press, 2008. 75-93.

Cooper, A.D. "Introduction I: Prelude to a Revolution," in *Allies in Apartheid: Western Capitalism in Occupied Namibia* edited by Cooper, A.D. London: Macmillan Press, 1988. 1-7.

Cooper, A.D. "The United States and Namibia: A Failure of Leadership," in *Allies in Apartheid: Western Capitalism in Occupied Namibia* edited by Cooper, A.D. London: Macmillan Press, 1988. 175-192.

Cooper, A.D. "Conclusion: Namibia and the Challenge of International Law," in *Allies in Apartheid: Western Capitalism in Occupied Namibia* edited by Cooper, A.D. London: Macmillan Press, 1988. 193-196.

Conway, D. "'All these Long-Haired Fairies should be Forced to do their Military Training. Maybe they will become Men.' The End Conscription Campaign, Sexuality, Citizenship and Military Conscription in Apartheid South Africa," *South African Journal on Human Rights* 20 (2004): 207-229.

Cooper, C. "The Militarisation of the Bantustans: Control and Contradictions," in *War and Society: The Militarisation of South Africa* edited by Cock, J. & Nathan, L. Cape Town & Johannesburg: David Philip, 1989. 174-187.

Craig, D. "Screening the Border War, 1971-88," *Kleio* 36 (2004): 28-46.

Craig, D. "'Total Justification': Ideological Manipulation and South Africa's Border War," in *Beyond the Border War: New Perspectives on Southern Africa's Late-Cold War Conflicts* edited by Baines, G. & Vale, P. Pretoria: University of South Africa Press, 2008. 56-74.

Cramer, C. "War and Peace in Angola and Mozambique," *Journal of Southern African Studies* 22, no. 3 (1996): 481-490.

Crocker, C.A. "Current and Projected Military Balances in Southern Africa," in Bissell, R.E. & Crocker, C., eds. *South Africa Into the 1980s*. Westview Special Studies on Africa, Boulder Colorado: Westview Press, 1979. 71-105.

Crocker, C.A. "South Africa: Strategy for Change," *Foreign Affairs* 59, no. 2 (Winter 1980/81): 323-351.

Cullinan, S. "Military Policy and the Namibian Dispute," in *South African Review I: Same Foundations, New Facades?* Southern African Research Service. Johannesburg: Ravan Press, 1983. 33-41.

Dale, R. "The Armed Forces as an Instrument of South African Policy in Namibia," *Journal of Modern African Studies* 18, no. 1 (1980): 57-71.

Dale, R. "Achieving Namibia's Independence: The Realities of International and Regional Politics, 1915-1990," *Journal for Contemporary History* 17, no. 1 (June 1992): 36-51.

Dale, R. "Namibia Liberata," *African Studies Review* 49, no. 1 (2006): 124-128.

Dale, R. "A Comparative Reconsideration of the Namibian Bush War, 1966-89," *Small Wars and Insurgencies* 18, no. 2. 196-215.

Daniel, John. "Racism, the Cold War and South Africa's Regional Security Strategies 1948-1990," in *Cold War in Southern Africa: White Power, Black Liberation* edited by Onslow, Sue. London & New York: Routledge, Cold War History Series, 2009. 35-54.

Daniels, C. "The Struggle for Indigenous People's Rights," in *Re-Examining Liberation Namibia: Political Culture since Independence* edited by Melber, H. Uppsala: Nordic Africa Institute, 2003. 47-68.

Davidson, B. "Walking 300 Miles with Guerrillas through the Bush of Eastern Angola," *Munger Africana Library Notes* 6 (April 1971).

Davies, R. & O'Meara, D. "Total Strategy in Southern Africa: An Analysis of South African Regional Policy since 1978," *Journal of Southern African Studies* 11, no. 2 (April 1985): 183-211.

Davies, R. "South African Regional Policy Post-Nkomati: May 1985-December 1986," in *South African Review 4* compiled and edited by Moss, G. & Obery, I. Johannesburg: Ravan Press & Southern African Research Service, 1987. 341-355. (Second impression 1989.)

Davies, R. "The SADF's Covert War against Mozambique," in *War and Society: The Militarisation of South Africa* edited by Cock, J. & Nathan, L. Cape Town & Johannesburg: David Philip, 1989. 103-115.

Davies, R. "South African Regional Policy before and after Cuito Cuanavale," in *South African Review 5* compiled and edited by Moss, G. & Obery, I. Johannesburg: Ravan Press & Southern African Research Service, 1989. 166-180.

De Beer, D. "The Netherlands and Namibia: The Political Campaign to End Dutch Involvement in the Namibian Uranium Trade," in *Allies in Apartheid: Western Capitalism in Occupied Namibia* edited by Cooper, A.D. London: Macmillan Press, 1988. 124-135.

De Beer, K.J. "The Total Onslaught on the Republic of South Africa as Bastion of the Free Western World," *Journal for Contemporary History* 12, no. 1 (April 1987): 28-48.

De St. Jorre, J. "South Africa: Up against the World," *Foreign Policy* 28 (Autumn 1977): 53-85.

De Visser, L.E. "Winning Hearts and Minds in the Namibian Border War," *Scientia Militaria, South African Journal of Military Studies* 39, no. 1 (2011): 85-100.

De Vries, J.J.P. & Swart, S. "The South African Defence Force and Horse Mounted Infantry Operations, 1974-1985," *Scientia Militaria, South African Journal of Military Studies* 40, no.3 (2012): 398-428.

De Wet, F. and Liebenberg, I. "Militarised Politics, Economic Consequences and the Implosion of State Legitimacy in South Africa," in *Reflections on War: Preparedness and Consequences* edited by Potgieter, T & Liebenberg, I. Stellenbosch: Sun Media, 2012. 65-90.

Dobell, L. "Review Article–Namibia's Transition under the Microscope: Six Lenses," *Journal of Southern African Studies* 21, no. 3 (1995): 529-535.

Dobell, L. "SWAPO in Office," in *Namibia's Liberation Struggle: The Two-Edged Sword* edited by Leys, C. & Saul, J.S. London: James Currey, 1995. 171-195.

Dobell, L. "Silence in Context: Truth and/or Reconciliation in Namibia," *Journal of Southern African Studies* 23, no. 2 (June 1977): 372-373.

Domínguez, J.I. "Cuba's Civil-Military Relations in Comparative Perspective: Looking Ahead to a Democratic Regime," in *Looking Forward: Comparative Perspectives on Cuba's Transition* edited by Pérez-Stable, M. Notre Dame, Indiana: University of Notre Dame Press, 2007. 47-71.

Doning, W.A. & Heitman, H.R. "The Joint Monitoring Commission," *Militaria* 18, no. 1 (1988): 1-27.

Dosman, E. "Countdown to Cuito Cuanavale: Cuba's Angolan Campaign," in *Beyond the Border War: New Perspectives on Southern Africa's Late-Cold War Conflicts* edited by Baines, G. & Vale, P. Pretoria: University of South Africa Press, 2008. 207-228.

Drewett, M. "Battling over Borders: Narratives of Resistance to the South African Border War Voiced through Popular Music," *Social Dynamics* 29, no. 1 (Summer 2003): 78-98.

Drewett, M. "The Construction and Subversion of Gender Stereotypes in Popular Cultural Representations of the Border War," in *Beyond the Border War: New Perspectives on Southern Africa's Late-Cold War Conflicts* edited by Baines, G. & Vale, P. Pretoria: University of South Africa Press, 2008. 94-119.

Du Pisani, A. "South Africa in Namibia: Variations on a Theme," *International Affairs Bulletin* 10, no. 3 (1986): 6-18.

Du Pisani, A. "Namibia: The Historical legacy," in *Namibia in Perspective* edited by Totemeyer, G., Kandetu, V. & Werner, W. Windhoek: Council of Churches in Namibia, 1987. 13-26.

Du Pisani, A. "Namibia: Impressions of Independence," in *The Dynamics of Change in Southern Africa* edited by Rich, P.B. New York: St Martin's Press, 1994. 199-217.

Du Pisani, A. "State and Society under South African Rule," in *State, Society and Democracy: A Reader in Namibian Politics* edited by Keulder, C. Gamsberg: Macmillan, 2000. 49-67.

Du Pisani, A. "The Role of the Military in the Formation and Consolidation of the Namibian State," in *Demilitarization and peace-building in Southern Africa, Vol. III* edited by Batchelor, P., Kingma, K. & Lamb, G. Aldershot: Ashgate, 2004. 65-87.

Du Pisani, A. "Memory Politics" in *Where others Wavered. The Autobiography of Sam Nujoma. My Life in SWAPO and my Participation in the Liberation Struggle of Namibia, Journal of Namibian Studies* 1 (2007): 97-107.

Du Plessis, T., Van der Westhuizen, G. & Liebenberg, I. "The Willing and the not so Willing: Conscription and Resistance to Compulsory Military Service in South Africa, 1968-1989," *Journal for Contemporary History* 37, no. 2 (December 2012): 143-164.

Du Preez, S. "Operasie Savannah – Dagboek van Kapt. J.A. Laubscher," *Militaria* 20, no. 2 (1990): 5-27.

Dzinesa, G. & Rupiya, M. "Promoting National Reconciliation and Regional Integration: The Namibian Defence Force from 1990-2005," in *Evolutions & Revolutions: A Contemporary History of Militaries in Southern Africa* edited by Rupiya, M. Pretoria: Institute for Security Studies, 2005. 199-234.

Ellis, S. "War in Southern Africa: Some Implications for the Environment," in *The Hidden Hand: Covert Operations in South Africa* edited by Schutte, C., Liebenberg, I. & Minnaar, A. 2nd revised edition. Pretoria: Human Sciences Research Council, 1998. 439-456.

Emmett, T. "Popular Resistance in Namibia, 1920-1925," in *Resistance and Ideology in Settler Societies. Southern African Studies, Volume 4* edited by Lodge, T. Johannesburg: Ravan Press, 1986. 6-48.

Erichsen, E., Hogberg, B. & Tostensen, A. "Scandinavia and Namibia: Contradictions of Policies and Actions," in *Allies in Apartheid: Western Capitalism in Occupied Namibia* edited by Cooper, A.D. London: Macmillan Press,1988. 136-155.

Erichsen, C.W. "Shoot to Kill: Photographic Images in the Namibian Liberation/Bush War," *Kronos* 27 (February 2001): 158-182.

Esterhuyse, A. "The Strategic Contours of the South African Military Involvement in Namibia and Angola during the 1970/1980s," in *Grensoorlog/Border War 1966-1989, Deel 2/Part 2* edited by Barnard, L. *Journal for Contemporary History* 34, no. 1 (February 2009): 16-35.

Esterhuyse, A. & Jordaan, E. "The South African Defence Force and Counterinsurgency, 1966-1990," in *South Africa and Contemporary Insurgency: Roots, Practices, Prospects* edited by Baker, D-P. & Jordaan, E. Claremont: UCT Press, 2010. 104-124.

Evans, G. "Classrooms of War: The Militarisation of White South African Schooling," in *War and Society: The Militarisation of South Africa* edited by Cock, J. & Nathan, L. Cape Town & Johannesburg: David Philip, 1989. 283-297.

ARTICLES & CHAPTERS

Evans, M. "Restructuring: The Role of the Military," in *South African Review I: Same Foundations, New Facades?* Southern African Research Service. Johannesburg: Ravan Press, 1983. 42-49.

Evans, M. & Phillips, M. "Intensifying Civil War: The Role of the South African Defence Force," in *State, Resistance and Change in South Africa* edited by Frankel, P., Pines, N. & Swilling, M. Johannesburg: Southern Book Publishers, 1988, 1989.

Fauvet, P. "Angola: The Rise and Fall of Nito Alves," *Review of African Political Economy* 9 (May-August 1978): 88-104.

Ferreira, C. "Vrou van die Grensbewaker," in *Bokbaai & Boegoe: Die Verfynde Vrou* edited by Jonkheid, E. Pretoria: Daan Retief Publishers,1981.

Ferreira, R. & Liebenberg, I. "The Impact of War on Angola and South Africa: Two Southern African Case Studies," in *Grensoorlog/Border War 1966-1989* edited by Barnard, L. *Journal for Contemporary History* 31, no. 3 (December 2006): 42-73.

Fig, D. "Apartheid's Nuclear Arsenal: Deviation from Development," in *From Defence to Development: Redirecting Military Resources in South Africa* edited by Cock, J. & Mckenzie, P. Cape Town/Ottawa: David Philip/International Development Research Centre, 1998. 163-180.

Fig, D. "In the Dark: Seeking Information about South Africa's Nuclear Energy Programme," in *Paper Wars: Access to Information in South Africa* edited by Allan, K. Johannesburg: Wits University Press, 2009. 56-87.

Fokkens, A.M. "The Suppression of Internal Unrest in South West Africa (Namibia) 1921-1933," *Scientia Militaria, South African Journal of Military Studies* 40, no. 3 (2012): 109-146.

Foltz, W.J. "United States Policy Toward South Africa: Is One Possible?" in Bender, G., Coleman, J.S. & Sklar, R.L., eds. *African Crisis Areas and U.S. Foreign Policy.* Berkeley/Los Angeles/London: University of California Press, 1985. 32-63.

Fourie, D. "The Climate of Security," in *South Africa – The Road Ahead* edited by Jacobs, G. Johannesburg: Jonathan Ball Publishers, 1986. 178-190.

Fourie, D. "African Military Potential – Into the Nineties," in *Challenge: Southern Africa within the African Revolutionary Context. An Overview* edited by Venter, A.J. Gibraltar: Ashanti Publishing, 1989. 436-469.

Fourie, D. "Decline and Fall: Why the South African Civilian Defence Secretariat was Dissolved in 1966," *Scientia Militaria, South African Journal of Military Studies* 40, no. 3 (2012): 40-70.

Fourie, D.F.S. "Revolusionêre Oorlogvoering," in *Konflik en Orde in Internasionale Verhoudinge* edited by Barnard, L.D. Johannesburg: Perskor-uitgewery, 1978. 182-196.

Fourie, S.M. "Van Mobilisering na Transformasie: Die Era van Suid-Afrika se Militêre Hoogbloei met die Vaaldriehoekse Samelewing (1974-1994) as Konsentrasieveld," *Scientia Militaria, South African Journal of Military Studies* 30, no. 2 (2000): 291-308.

Fourie, S.M. & Tempelhoff, J.W.N. "Die Era van Suid-Afrika se Militêre Hoogbloei (1974-1994) met die Vaaldriehoekse Samelewing as Konsentrasieveld," *Historia* 46, no. 2 (November 2001): 503-518.

Gear, S. "Now that the War is Over. Ex-Combatants Transition and the Question of Violence: A Literature Review," *Violence and Transition Series* 8 (2002): 1-163.

Gear, Sasha. "The Road Back: Psycho-Social Strains of Transition for South Africa's Ex-Combatants," in *Beyond the Border War: New Perspectives on Southern Africa's Late-Cold War Conflicts* edited by Baines, G. & Vale, P. Pretoria: University of South Africa Press, 2008. 245-266.

Geldenhuys, D. "South African Reactions to the Nkomati Accord: A House Divided," *Journal of Contemporary African Studies* 4, nos. 1/2 (October 1984/April 1985): 179-213.

Geldenhuys, J. "The Power Struggle in South Africa," in *South Africa – The Road Ahead* edited by Jacobs, G. Johannesburg: Jonathan Ball Publishers, 1986. 191-200.

Gewald, J. "Who Killed Clemens Kapuuo?" *Journal of Southern African Studies* 30, no. 3 (September 2004): 559-576.

Gibson, D. "Untold Stories and Disconnectedness: The Dilemma of Conscript Veterans of the Bush War," *Werkwinkel* 4, no.1 (2009): 71-102.

Gibson, D. "'The *Balsak* in the Roof': Bush War Experiences and Mediations as related by White South African Conscripts," in *Mediations of Violence in Africa: Fashioning New Futures from Contested Pasts* edited by Kapteijns, L. & Richters, A. n.p.: Wits University Press, 2010. 211-245.

Gleijeses, P. "Moscow's Proxy? Cuba and Africa 1975-1988," *Journal of Cold War Studies* 8, no. 2 (Spring 2006): 3-51.

Gleijeses, P. "Cuba and the Independence of Namibia," *Cold War History* 7, no.2 (May 2007): 285-303.

Gleijeses, P. "From Cassinga to New York: The Struggle for the Independence of Namibia," in *Cold War in Southern Africa: White Power, Black Liberation* edited by Onslow, Sue. London & New York: Routledge, Cold War History Series, 2009. 201-224.

Gordon, R.J. "The Impact of the Second World War on Namibia," *Journal of Southern African Studies. Special Issue: Namibia: Africa's Youngest Nation* 19, no.1 (March 1993): 147-165.

Gordon, R. "'Oh Shucks, Here Comes UNTAG!' Peace-Keeping as Adventure in Namibia," *Beyond the Border War: New Perspectives on Southern Africa's Late-Cold War Conflicts* edited by in Baines, G. & Vale, P. Pretoria: University of South Africa Press, 2008. 229-244.

Gould, C. "The Nuclear Weapons History Project," in *Paper Wars: Access to Information in South Africa* edited by Allan, K. Johannesburg: Wits University Press, 2009. 88-121.

Graham, M. "Cold War in Southern Africa," *Africa Spectrum* 45, no. 1 (2010): 131-139.

Green, R.H. & Thompson, C.B. "Political Economies in Conflict: SADCC, South Africa and sanctions," in *Destructive Engagement: Southern Africa at War* edited by Johnson, P. & Martin, D. Harare: Zimbabwe Publishing House for the Southern African Research and Documentation Centre, 1986. 245-280; and in *Frontline Southern Africa: Destructive Engagement* edited by Johnson, P. & Martin, D. New York: Four Walls Eight Windows, 1988. 339-386.

Greig, I. "East Germany's Drive for Influence in Africa," *ISSUP Strategic Review* (June 1985): 19-26.

Grest, J. "Mozambique since the Nkomati Accord," in *South African Review 4* compiled and edited by Moss, G. & Obery, I. Johannesburg: Ravan Press & Southern African Research Service, 1987. 356-372. (Second impression 1989.)

Grest, J. "Mozambique after Machel," in *South African Review 5* compiled and edited by Moss, G. & Obery, I. Johannesburg: Ravan Press & Southern African Research Service, 1989. 209-226.

Grest, J. "The South African Defence Force in Angola," in *War and Society: The Militarisation of South Africa* edited by Cock, J. & Nathan, L. Cape Town & Johannesburg: David Philip, 1989. 116-132.

Griffiths, R.J. "Democratisation and Civil-Military Relations in Namibia, South Africa and Mozambique," *Third World Quarterly* 17, no. 3 (1996): 473-486.

Grossmann, A.M. "Lost in Transition: The South African Military and Counterinsurgency", in *Small Wars & Insurgencies* 19, no. 4 (2008): 541-572.

Grossmann, A.M. "The South African Military and Counterinsurgency: An Overview," in *South Africa and Contemporary Insurgency: Roots, Practices, Prospects* edited by Baker, D-P. & Jordaan, E. Claremont: UCT Press, 2010. 83-103.

Grundlingh, A. "Oorlog en Onrus: Vertolkings van Resente Suid-Afrikaanse Militêre Geskiedenis," *South African Historical Journal* 23 (1990): 155-167.

Grundy, K.W. "The New Role of South Africa's Security Establishment: Centralization of State Power and the Centrality of the South African Security Establishment," *Munger Africana Library Notes* 75 (March 1985).

Hackland, B., Murray-Hudson, A. & Wood, B. "Behind the Diplomacy: Namibia, 1983-5," *Third World Quarterly* 8, no. 1 (January 1986): 51-77.

Hale, F. "Baptist Ethics of Conscientious Objection to Military Service in South Africa: The Watershed case of Richard Steele," *Acta Theologica* 2 (2005): 18-44.

Halperin, N. "The Cuban Role in Southern Africa," in Seiler, J., ed. *Southern Africa Since the Portuguese Coup.* Westview Special Studies on Africa, Boulder Colorado: Westview Press, 1980. 25-43.

Hamilton, R.G. "Class, Race and Authorship in Angola," in *Marxism and African Literature* edited by Gugelberger, G.M. Trenton, New Jersey: Africa World Press, 1986. 136-149.

Hanekom, L. "Melvin Beneke: 'Ons vir jou, Suid-Afrika' – 'n Verhaal uit die Angolese Grensoorlog, 1987," in *Kinderhelde van die Vrystaat* edited by Hanekom, L. Hammanskraal: Unibook-Uitgewers, 1988. 76-84.

Hanlon, J. "Introduction to Section 4: Relations with Southern Africa," in *South African Review 4* compiled and edited by Moss, G. & Obery, I. Johannesburg: Ravan Press & Southern African Research Service, 1987. 332-340. (Second impression, 1989.)

Hansson, D. "Changes in Counter-Revolutionary State Strategy in the Decade 1978 to 1989," in *Towards Justice? Crime and State Control in South Africa: Contemporary South African Debates* edited by Hansson, D. & Smit, D. V-Z. Cape Town: Oxford University Press, 1990. 28-62.

Hatzky, C. "'Os Bons Colonizadores': Cuba's Educational Mission in Angola, 1976-1991," *Safundi: The Journal of South African and American Studies* 9, no. 1 (January 2008): 53-68.

Henderson, R.D. "South African Intelligence under De Klerk," in *About Turn: The Transformation of the South African Military and Intelligence* edited by Cilliers, J. & Reichardt, M. Halfway House: Institute for Defence Policy, 1995. 140-171.

Henrichsen, D., Miescher, G., Rizzo, L. & Silvester, J. "Posters Act: Namibian Poster Action and the Photographic Poster Archive," in *Kronos*, 35, November 2009, pp. 159-174.

Henriksen, T.H. "Namibia: A Comparison with Anti-Portuguese Insurgency," *The Round Table* 70, no. 278 (April 1980): 184-194.

Heitman, H.R. "Equipment of the Border War," in *Grensoorlog/Border War 1966-1989* edited by Barnard, L. *Journal for Contemporary History* 31, no. 3 (December 2006): 91-111.

Heitman, H.R. "The Other Edge of Asymmetry: South Africa's Bush War Strategy," in *Grensoorlog/Border War 1966-1989, Deel 2/Part 2* edited by Barnard, L. *Journal for Contemporary History* 34, no. 1, (February 2009): 1-15.

Hendrik, C. "Sam Nujoma: Portrait of a SWAPO Leader," *Munger Africana Library Notes* 61, (September 1981): 11-16.

Heywood, L. "Towards an Understanding of Modern Political Ideology in Africa: The Case of the Ovimbundu of Angola," *Journal of Modern African Studies* 36, no. 1 (1998): 139-167.

Hodges, T. "How the MPLA Won in Angola," in *After Angola: The War over Southern Africa* edited by Legum, C. London: Rex Collins, 1976. 45-64.

Holloway, A.F. "Congressional Initiatives on South Africa," in Bender, G., Coleman, J.S. & Sklar, R.L., eds. *African Crisis Areas and U.S. Foreign Policy.* Berkeley/Los Angeles/London, University of California Press, 1985. 89-94.

Holness, M. "Angola: The Struggle Continues," in *Destructive Engagement: Southern Africa at War* edited by Johnson, P. & Martin, D. Harare: Zimbabwe Publishing House for the Southern African Research and Documentation Centre, 1986. 73-110; and in *Frontline Southern Africa: Destructive Engagement* edited by Johnson, P. & Martin, D. New York: Four Walls Eight Windows, 1988. 101-152.

Howe, H.M. "The South African Defence Force and Political Reform," *The Journal of Modern African Studies* 32 (1994): 29-51.

Hull, G. "South Africa's Propaganda War: A Bibliographic Essay," *African Studies Review* 22, no. 3 (December 1979): 79-98.

Hurlich, S. "Canadian Transnational Corporations in Namibia: An Economic and Political Overview," in *Allies in Apartheid: Western Capitalism in Occupied Namibia* edited by Cooper, A.D. London: Macmillan Press, 1988. 39-78.

Hyslop, J. "Introduction to Section I: The State and Politics," in *South African Review 5* compiled and edited by Moss, G. & Obery, I. Johannesburg: Ravan Press & Southern African Research Service, 1989. 1-15.

Hyslop, J. "War Envy," in *Load Shedding: Writing on and over the Edge of South Africa* edited by McGregor, L. & Nuttall, S. Johannesburg & Cape Town: Jonathan Ball Publishers, 2009. 107-125.

Hunter, J. "No Man's Land of Time: Reflections on the Politics of Memory and Forgetting in Namibia," in *Beyond the Border War: New Perspectives on Southern Africa's Late-Cold War Conflicts* edited by Baines, G. & Vale, P. Pretoria: University of South Africa Press, 2008. 302-321.

Igreja, V. "Testimonies of Suffering and Recasting the Meanings of Memories of Violence in Post-War Mozambique," in *Mediations of Violence in Africa: Fashioning New Futures from Contested Pasts* edited by Kapteijns, L. & Richters, A. n.p.: Wits University Press, 2010. 141-172.

ARTICLES &
CHAPTERS

Innes, D. "Imperialism and the National Struggle in Namibia," *Review of African Political Economy* 9 (May-August 1978): 45-59.

Ionescu, M.E. "Romania and South African Liberation Movements: The Cold War Relationship, 1969-1977," in *Regions, Regional Organisations and Military Power* edited by Potgieter, T., Esterhuyse, A. & Liebenberg, I. Stellenbosch: Sun Media, 2008. 81-88.

Isby, D. "The Strategic Significance of Southern Africa in the 1990s," in *Challenge: Southern Africa within the African Revolutionary Context. An Overview* edited by Venter, A.J. Gibraltar: Ashanti Publishing, 1989. 21-30.

Israel, M. "Counter-Exile Activities: Covert Action in the United Kingdom," in *The Hidden Hand: Covert Operations in South Africa* edited by Schutte, C., Liebenberg, I. & Minnaar, A. 2nd revised ed. Pretoria: Human Sciences Research Council, 1998. 343-362.

Israel, M. "South African War Resisters and the Ideologies of Return from Exile," *Journal of Refugee Studies* 15, no. 1 (2002): 26-42.

Jacobs, C.J. "Die Problematiek in die Navorsing van Kontemporêre Krygsgeskiedenis in Suid-Afrika," *Militaria* 23, no. 2 (1993): 20-27.

Jacobs, C.J. "A Chronicle of South African Warfare1488-1994," in *South African Military Yearbook 1997*. Pretoria: South African Military History Consultants, 1997. 33-59.

Jacobs, C.J. "The Forward Defence Strategy of the South African Defence Force (SADF), 1978-1989," in *Grensoorlog/Border War 1966-1989* edited by Barnard, L. *Journal for Contemporary History* 31, no. 3 (December 2006): 23-41.

Jacobs, C.J. "Conflict between South Africa and Mozambique, 1975-1989, within the Framework of the Cold War and Regional Tensions," in *Grensoorlog/Border War 1966-1989, Deel 2/Part 2* edited by Barnard, L. *Journal for Contemporary History* 34, no. 1 (February 2009): 281-297.

Jaffee, G. "The Southern African Development Coordination Conference (SADCC)," in *South African Review I: Same Foundations, New Facades?* Southern African Research Service. Johannesburg: Ravan Press, 1983. 23-32.

Jansen van Rensburg, W. "Standoff Attacks by PLAN on South African Security Force Bases during the SWA/Namibian 'Bush War'". *Journal for Contemporary History* 38, no. 1 (June 2013): 255-292.

Jaster, R.S. "The 1988 Peace Accords and the Future of South-Western Africa," *Adelphi Papers* 253 (Autumn 1990): 1-76.

Jochelson, K. & Buntman, F. "Shopping for War: An Analysis of Consumerist Militarism," in *War and Society: The Militarisation of South Africa* edited by Cock, J. & Nathan, L. Cape Town & Johannesburg: David Philip, 1989. 298-306.

Johnson, P. & Martin, D. "Mozambique: Victims of Apartheid," in *Frontline Southern Africa: Destructive Engagement* edited by Johnson, P. & Martin, D. New York: Four Walls Eight Windows, 1988. 1-56.

Jordaan, E. "The Role of South African Armour in South-West Africa/Namibia and Angola: 1975-1989," in *Grensoorlog/Border War 1966-1989* edited by Barnard, L. *Journal for Contemporary History* 31, no. 3 (December 2006): 161-186.

Jooste, L. "Die Stand van Suid-Afrikaanse Militêre Geskiedenis oor die SA Weermag se Betrokkenheid in Suidwes-Afrika en Angola: 1966 tot 1989," *Militaria* 23, no. 2 (1993): 9-18.

Jury, B. "Boys to Men: Afrikaans Alternative Popular Music 1986-1990," *African Languages and Cultures* 9, no. 2 (1996): 99-109.

Kaden, R. "'This will Help in Healing our Land': Remembering and Forgetting Quatro in Post-Apartheid South Africa," *Journal for Contemporary History* 37, no. 1 (June 2012): 101-122.

Kagan-Guthrie, Z. "Chester Crocker and the South African Border War, 1981-1989: A Reappraisal of Linkage," *Journal of Southern African Studies* 35, no. 1 (March 2009): 65-80.

Kapp, P.H. "Die Koue Oorlog: Die Wêreld se Langste Oorlog?/The Cold War: The World's Longest War?" *Scientia Militaria, South African Journal of Military Studies* 27(1997): 106-120.

Kasrils, Ronnie. "Cuito Cuanavale, Turning Point in the Struggle against Apartheid," *African Communist*, no. 185, First 7 Second Quarters (May 2008): 54-60.

Ketelo, B., Maxongo, A., Tshona, Z., Massango, R. & Mbeno, L. "A Miscarriage of Democracy: The ANC Security Department in the 1984 Mutiny in Umkhonto we Sizwe," *Searchlight South Africa, A Marxist Journal of Southern African Studies* 5 (July 1990): 35-65.

Khwela, G.C. "The Clausewitzian and Heuristic Evolution of the ANC's Armed Struggle: A Dependent Pillar of the South African Revolution," *Scientia Militaria, South African Journal of Military Studies* 30, no. 2 (2000): 309-328.

Khwela, G.C. "Umkhonto weSizwe's Contribution to the Defence of the African Revolution in Angola," *Journal for Contemporary History* 28, no. 2 (September 2003): 107-123.

Killingray, D. "War and Society in Africa since 1800," *South African Historical Journal* 25 (November 1991): 131-153.

Kitazawa, Y. "Japan's Illegal Uranium Contracts with Namibia," in *Allies in Apartheid: Western Capitalism in Occupied Namibia* edited by Cooper, A.D. London: Macmillan Press, 1988. 114-123.

Kleyn, W. "Die Rol van die Suid-Afrikaanse Weermag in Natuur- en Omgewingsbewaring," *Scientia Militaria, South African Journal of Military Studies* 18, no.1 (1988): 28-38.

Kondlo, K.K.M. "'In the Twilight of the Azanian Revolution'. Leadership Diversity and its Impact on the PAC during the Exile Period (1962-1990)," *Journal for Contemporary History* 30, no. 1 (June 2005): 25-43.

Koornhof, H.E. "Works of Fiction: Current South African War Literature," in *War and Society: The Militarisation of South Africa* edited by Cock, J. & Nathan, L. Cape Town & Johannesburg: David Philip, 1989. 275-282.

Kynoch, G. "The 'Transformation' of the South African Military," *The Journal of Modern African Studies* 34, no. 3 (1996): 441-457.

Labuschagne, P. "Monuments and Meaning Making: Freedom Park and the Bumpy Road to Reconciliation and Nation-Building in South Africa," *Journal for Contemporary History* 37, no. 1 (June 2012): 158-170.

Lamb, G. "Militarization's Long Shadow: Namibia's Legacy of Armed Violence," *The Economics of Peace and Security Journal* 1, no. 2 (2006): 30-37.

L'Ange, G. "Countries in the Cross-Fire," in *Challenge: Southern Africa within the African Revolutionary Context. An Overview* edited by Venter, A.J. Gibraltar: Ashanti Publishing, 1989. 323-354.

Landman, R. "A Politically Incorrect War," in *Off Camera* edited by Landman, R. Cape Town: Double Storey, 2003. 53-61.

Lari, A. "Returning Home to Normal Life? The Plight of Displaced Angolans," *ISS Paper*, no. 85, (February 2004): 1 -14.

Lass, H.R. "Internasionale Terreur en Stedelike Terrorisme," in *Konflik en Orde in Internasionale Verhoudinge* edited by Barnard, L.D. Johannesburg: Perskor-uitgewery, 1978. 197-215.

Leao, A. & Rupiya, M. "A Military History of the Angolan Armed Forces from the 1960s Onwards – As Told by Former Combatants," in *Evolutions & Revolutions: A Contemporary History of Militaries in Southern Africa* edited by Rupiya, M. Pretoria: Institute for Security Studies, 2005. 7-42.

Legum, C. "A Study of Foreign Intervention in Angola," in *After Angola: The War over Southern Africa* edited by Legum, C. London: Rex Collins, 1976. 7-44.

Legum, C. "South Africa in the Contemporary World," in *The Apartheid Regime: Political Power and Racial Domination* edited by Price, R.M. & Rosberg, C.G. Berkeley: Institute of International Studies, University of California, 1980. 281-296.

Le Roux, L. "The Post-Apartheid South African Military: Transforming with the Nation," in *Evolutions & Revolutions: A Contemporary History of Militaries in Southern Africa* edited by Rupiya, M. Pretoria: Institute for Security Studies, 2005. 235-268.

Liebenberg, I. & Malan, D. "Contrast and Irony: The Free, Fair and Festive Election in Namibia," *Democracy in Action* (December 1989): 16-17.

Liebenberg, I. "Apartheid's Military in Politics: Naked Power Revealed," *Journal for Contemporary History* 15, no. 1 (June 1990): 130-141.

Liebenberg, I., Dixon, T. & Zegeye, A. "Images: The Seesaw Haunting keeps Killing the Living," *Social Identities* 5, no. 4 (1999): 387-414.

Liebenberg, I. & Barnard, L. "Arms Acquisition and Procurement in South Africa: The Socio-History of Arms Deals with Reference to Attitudes, Strengths and Limitations in Decision-Making (1953-2004) (II)," *Journal for Contemporary History* 31, no. 1 (June 2006): 99-112.

Liebenberg, I. "Talking Small Wars in Far Away Lands: Three Incidences of Angola's 'Second War of Liberation'," in *Regions, Regional Organisations and Military Power* edited by Potgieter, T., Esterhuyse, A. & Liebenberg, I. Stellenbosch: Sun Media, 2008. 63-79.

Liebenberg, I. "Viewing the Other over a Hundred and a Score more Years: South Africa and Russia, 1890-2010." *The Journal for Transdisciplinary Research in Southern Africa* 6, no. 2 (December 2010): 482-460.

Liebenberg, I. "From racialism to authoritarianism: South Africa, militarised politics and the implosion of state legitimacy under apartheid." *Institul Pentru Studii Politice de Aparare Si Istorie Militaria* (ISPAIM), Occasional Papers, Vol. 10 no. 16 (2011): 64-93.

Liebenberg, I. "The Arms Industry, Reform and Civil-Military Relations in South Africa," in *South Africa and Romania: Transition to Democracy and Changing Security Paradigms* edited by Manganyi. C., Liebenberg, I. & Potgieter, T. Durban: Just Done Productions, 2012. 233-266.

Liebenberg, I. & De Wet, F. "Militarised Politics, Economic Consequences and the Implosion of State Legitimacy under Apartheid," in *Reflections on War: Preparedness and Consequences* edited by Potgieter, T. & Liebenberg, I. Stellenbosch: Sun Media, 2012. 65-90.

Liebenberg, I. "(Trans-)grense, Talighede, Boek- en Bloedrefleksies," *Tydskrif vir Letterkunde* 47, no. 1 (2010): 131-144.

Liebenberg, I., Du Plessis, T. & Van der Westhuizen, G. "Through the Mirage: Retracing Moments of a War 'Up There'," *Scientia Militaria, South African Journal of Military Studies* 38, no. 2 (2010): 131-149.

Lingle, C. "On the Real Costs of Military Conscription," *South African Journal of Economics* 57, no. 3 (1989): 178-183.

Lissoni, A. "The Implosion of the Pan-Africanist Congress: Basutoland, c. 1962-1965," in *Southern African Liberation Struggles: New Local, Regional and Global Perspectives* edited by Saphire, H. & Saunders, C. Claremont: UCT Press, 2013. 32-57.

Lodge, T. "The African National Congress in South Africa, 1976-1983: Guerrilla War and Armed Propaganda," *Journal of Contemporary African Studies* 3, nos. 1/2 (October 1983/April 1984): 153-180.

Lodge, T. "Soldiers of the Storm: A Profile of the Azanian People's Liberation Army," in *About Turn: The Transformation of the South African Military and Intelligence* edited by Cilliers, J. & Reichardt, M. Halfway House: Institute for Defence Policy, 1995. 105-117.

López Blanch, H.L. & Liebenberg, I. "A View from Cuba: Internationalists against Apartheid," in *Grensoorlog/Border War 1966-1989, Deel 2/Part 2* edited by Barnard, L. *Journal for Contemporary History* 34, no. 1 (February 2009): 81-112.

Lord, R.S. "Operation Askari (a Sub-Commander's Retrospective View of the Operation)," *Militaria* 22, no. 4(1992): 2-10

Lord, R.S. "SAAF Fighter Involvement in the Border War, 1965-1988," in *Grensoorlog/Border War 1966-1989* edited by Barnard, L. *Journal for Contemporary History* 31, no. 3 (December 2006): 251-266.

Louw, D.A. & Beyers, D. "Posttraumatiese Stresversteuring," in *Suid-Afrikaanse Handboek van Abnormale Gedrag* edited by Louw, D.A. Johannesburg: Southern Boekuitgewers, 1989.

Louw, C. "Boetman is die Bliksem in," in *Kruis en Dwars: 37 Nuwe Stories oor Suid-Afrika* compiled and edited by Ferreira, J. Cape Town: J.L. van Schaik, 2001. 136-141.

Luyt, N. "Veiligheidsraadsresolusie 435," *Journal for Contemporary History* 9, no. 2 (December 1984): 114-117.

Luyt, N. "The Accord of Nkomati," *Journal for Contemporary History* 9, no. 2 (December 1984): 117-121.

Luyt, N. "Hakkejagoperasies (*hot pursuit*): Volkeregtelike Perspektief," *Journal for Contemporary History* 10, no. 3 (December 1985): 165-168.

Luyt, N. "Suid-Afrikaanse Veiligheidsmag se Aanvalle in Zambië, Zimbabwe en Botswana," *Journal for Contemporary History* 11, no. 2 (August 1985): 91-96.

Macmillan, H. "Morogoro and After: The Continuing Crisis in the African National Congress (of South Africa) in Zambia," in *Southern African Liberation Struggles: New Local, Regional and Global perspectives* edited by Saphire, H. & Saunders, C. Claremont: UCT Press, 2013. 76-95.

ARTICLES & CHAPTERS

Malache, A., Macaringue, P. & Coelho, J-P.B. "Profound Transformations and Regional Conflagrations: The History of Mozambique's Armed Forces from 1975-2005," in *Evolutions & Revolutions: A Contemporary History of Militaries in Southern Africa* edited by Rupiya, M. Pretoria: Institute for Security Studies, 2005. 155-198.

Malan, M. "Die Aanslag teen Suid-Afrika." *ISSUP Strategiese Oorsig*, (November 1980): 3-16.

Manganyi, N.C. "The Baptism of Fire: South Africa's Black Majority After the Portuguese Coup," in *Southern Africa Since the Portuguese Coup*. Westview Special Studies on Africa, Boulder Colorado: Westview Press, 1980. 169-180.

Mankayi, N. "Race and Masculinities in the South African Military," *Scientia Militaria, South African Journal of Military Studies* 38, no. 2 (2010): 22-43.

Manning, P. & Green, R.H. "Namibia: Preparations for Destabilization," in *Destructive Engagement: Southern Africa at War* edited by Johnson, P. & Martin, D. Harare: Zimbabwe Publishing House for the Southern African Research and Documentation Centre, 1986. 111-138.

Marais, C. "War Games," *South African Sports Illustrated* (October 2011): 60-67.

Marchand, J. "French Foreign Policy towards Namibia 1981-85," in *Allies in Apartheid: Western Capitalism in Occupied Namibia* edited by Cooper, A.D. London: Macmillan Press, 1988. 79-90.

Marks, M. & Mckenzie, P. "Militarised Youth: Political Pawns or Social Agents?" in *From Defence to Development: Redirecting Military Resources in South Africa* edited by Cock, J. & Mckenzie, P. Cape Town/Ottawa: David Philip/ International Development Research Centre, 1998. 222-234; and in *Frontline Southern Africa: Destructive Engagement* edited by Johnson, P. & Martin, D. New York: Four Walls Eight Windows, 1988. 153-190.

Martin, D. & Johnson, P. "Mozambique: To Nkomati and Beyond," in *Destructive Engagement: Southern Africa at War* edited by Johnson, P. & Martin, D. Harare: Zimbabwe Publishing House for the Southern African Research and Documentation Centre, 1986. 1-42.

Marx, L. "Bodies and Borders: Vietnam/Namibia," *Safundi: The Journal of South African and American Studies* 8, no. 1 (January 2007): 91-102.

Mazrui, A.A. & Gordon, D.F. "Independent African States and the Struggle for Southern Africa," in *Southern Africa Since the Portuguese Coup*. Westview Special Studies on Africa, Boulder Colorado: Westview Press, 1980. 183-193.

McClure, D., Willers, D. & Barratt, J. "East Germans in Angola," *The South African Institute of International Affairs, Brief Report no. 10* (10 November 1978).

McFarlane, S.N. & Nel, P. "The Changing Soviet Approach to Regional Conflicts," *The Journal for Communist Studies* 5, no. 2 (1989): 148-172.

Mckenzie, P. "Reclaiming the Land: A Case Study of Riemvasmaak," in *From Defence to Development: Redirecting Military Resources in South Africa* edited by Cock, J. & Mckenzie, P. Cape Town/Ottawa: David Philip/ International Development Research Centre, 1998. 60-84.

McKenzie, P. "Weapons Testing: Its Impact on People and the Environment," in *From Defence to Development: Redirecting Military Resources in South Africa* edited by Cock, J. & Mckenzie, P. Cape Town/Ottawa: David Philip/International Development Research Centre, 1998. 85-96.

Melber, H. "Introduction II: Socio-Economic Interaction and Establishment of Colonialist-Capitalist Relations in Namibia before and during German Rule," in *Allies in Apartheid: Western Capitalism in Occupied Namibia* edited by Cooper, A.D. London: Macmillan Press, 1988. 8-38.

Melber, H. & Wellmer, G. "West German Relations with Namibia," in *Allies in Apartheid: Western Capitalism in Occupied Namibia* edited by Cooper, A.D. London: Macmillan Press,1988. 91-113.

Melber, H. "From Controlled Change to Changed Control," in *Limits to Liberation in Southern Africa: The Unfinished Business of Democratic Consolidation* edited by Melber, H. Cape Town: Human Sciences Research Council, 2003. 143-155.

Melber, H. "Limits to Liberation: An Introduction to Namibia's Postcolonial Political Culture," in *Re-examining Liberation Namibia: Political Culture since Independence* edited by Melber, H. Uppsala: Nordic Africa Institute, 2003. 9-24.

Melber, H. "'Namibia, Land of the Brave': Selective Memories on War and Violence within Nation Building," in *Re-examining Liberation Namibia: Political Culture since Independence* edited by Melber, H. Uppsala: Nordic Africa Institute, 2003. 306-327.

Melber, H. "Namibia's Past in the Present: Colonial Genocides and Liberation Struggle in Commemorative Narratives", in *South African Historical Journal*, 54, 2005, pp. 91-111.

Meskell, L. "Trauma Culture: Remembering and Forgetting in the New South Africa," in *Memory, Trauma and World Politics* edited by Bell, D. Basingstoke: Palgrave Macmillan, 2006.157-175.

Middlemas, K. "Independent Mozambique and Its Regional Policy," in *Southern Africa Since the Portuguese Coup*. Westview Special Studies on Africa, Boulder Colorado: Westview Press, 1980. 213-233.

Mills, G. "Armed Forces in Post-Apartheid South Africa," *Survival* 35, no. 3 (Autumn 1993): 78-96.

Mills, G. & Williams, D. "The Military Role in Political Victory: South Africa, Namibia and Apartheid," in *Victory among People: Lessons from Countering Insurgency and Stabilising Fragile States* edited by Richards, D. & Mills, G. London/ Marshalltown: Royal United Services Institute for Defence and Security Studies/Brenthurst Foundation, 2011. 203-217.

Minter, W. "Destructive Engagement: The United States & South Africa in the Reagan Era," in *Destructive Engagement: Southern Africa at War* edited by Johnson, P. & Martin, D. Harare: Zimbabwe Publishing House for the Southern African Research and Documentation Centre, 1986. 281-320; and in *Frontline Southern Africa: Destructive Engagement* edited by Johnson, P. & Martin, D. New York: Four Walls Eight Windows, 1988. 387-439.

Minter, W. "The US and the War in Angola," *Review of African Political Economy* 50 (March 1991): 135-144.

Minter, W. "Glimpses of the War in Angola: Three South African Accounts ... Review Article," *Africa Today* 39, no. 1/2(1992): 130-134.

Minter, W. "The Armoured Bubble: Military Memoirs from Apartheid's Warriors," *African Studies Review* 50, no. 3 (2007): 147-152.

Minty, A.S. "South Africa's Military Build-Up: The Region at War," in *Destructive Engagement: Southern Africa at War* edited by Johnson, P. & Martin, D. Harare: Zimbabwe Publishing House for the Southern African Research and Documentation Centre, 1986. 171-204

Minty, A.S. "South Africa's Nuclear Capability: The Apartheid Bomb," in *Destructive Engagement: Southern Africa at War* edited by Johnson, P. & Martin, D. Harare: Zimbabwe Publishing House for the Southern African Research and Documentation Centre, 1986. 205-220; and in *Frontline Southern Africa: Destructive Engagement* edited by Johnson, P. & Martin, D. New York: Four Walls Eight Windows, 1988. 283-304.

Monick, S. "An Original Approach to Regimental History: The Story of the Witwatersrand Rifles," *Militaria* 19, no. 4 (1989): 4-14.

Morris, J. "Namibia: The latest Round of Negotiations and the Continuing Struggle," *Review of African Political Economy* 9, (May-August 1977): 74-78.

Morris, Wendy. "Art and Aftermath in *Memórias Íntimas Marcas*: Constructing Memory, Admitting Responsibility," in *Beyond the Border War: New Perspectives on Southern Africa's Late-Cold War Conflicts* edited by Baines, G. & Vale, P. Pretoria: University of South Africa Press, 2008. 158-174.

Mostert, J.J.C. "Renamo: Die Stryd duur Voort," *Journal for Contemporary History* 12, no. 1 (April 1987): 123-132.

Mostert, J.P.C. "Die Angolese Konflik, 1975-1976," *Journal for Contemporary History* 5, no. 1 (December 1980): 49-63.

Motumi, T. "The Spear of the Nation – The Recent History of Umkhonto we Sizwe (MK)," in *About Turn: The Transformation of the South African Military and Intelligence* edited by Cilliers, J. & Reichardt, M. Halfway House: Institute for Defence Policy, 1995. 84-104.

Motumi, T. & Hudson, A. "Rightsizing: The Challenges of Demobilisation and Social Reintegration in South Africa," in *Dismissed: Demobilisation and Reintegration of Former Combatants in Africa* edited by Cilliers, J. Halfway House: Institute for Defence Policy, 1995. 112-129.

Motumi, T. & Mckenzie, P. "After the War: Demobilisation in South Africa," in *From Defence to Development: Redirecting Military Resources in South Africa* edited by Cock, J. & Mckenzie, P. Cape Town/Ottawa: David Philip/ International Development Research Centre, 1998. 181-207.

Mwase, N.R.L. "The Media and the Namibian Liberation Struggle," *Media, Culture and Society* 10 (1988): 225-237.

Nathan, L. "Resistance to Militarisation: Three Years of the End Conscription Campaign," in *South African Review 4* compiled and edited by Moss, G. & Obery, I. Johannesburg: Ravan Press & Southern African Research Service, 1987. 104-116. (Second impression 1989.)

Nathan, L. "Troops in the Townships, 1984-1987," in *War and Society: The Militarisation of South Africa* edited by Cock, J. & Nathan, L. Cape Town & Johannesburg: David Philip, 1989. 67-78.

Nathan, L. "'Marching to a Different Beat': The History of the End Conscription Campaign," in *War and Society: The Militarisation of South Africa* edited by Cock, J. & Nathan, L. Cape Town & Johannesburg: David Philip, 1989. 308-323.

Nathan, L. "The 1996 Defence White Paper: An Agenda for State Demilitarisation?" in *From Defence to Development: Redirecting Military Resources in South Africa* edited by Cock, J. & Mckenzie, P. Cape Town/Ottawa: David Philip/ International Development Research Centre, 1998. 41-59.

Nieuwoudt, C. "Relations between South Africa and the Communist World." *ISSUP Strategic Review*, (August 1980).

Nolutshungu, S.C. "South African Policy and United States Options in Southern Africa," in Bender, G., Coleman, J.S. & Sklar, R.L., eds. *African Crisis Areas and U.S. Foreign Policy.* Berkeley/Los Angeles/London: University of California Press, 1985. 49-63.

Nothling, C.J. "Kardinale Aspekte van Nasionale Diensplig met Spesifieke Verwysing na Suid-Afrika," *Scientia Militaria, South African Journal of Military Studies* 12, no. 3 (1982): 32-41.

Nothling, C.J. "Kort Kroniek van Militêre Operasies en Optredes in Suidwes-Afrika en Angola (1914-1988)," *Militaria* 19, no. 2 (1989): 5-18.

Nothling, C.J. & Meyers, E.M. "Chronicle of Military Service in South Africa/Kroniek van Diensplig in Suid-Afrika," in *Suid-Afrikaanse Weermag Oorsig 1990/South African Defence Force Review 1990* edited by De la Rey, A. Durban: Directorate Public Relations SADF/Walker-Ramus Trading Co, n.d. 255-283.

Nothling, C.J. "Bibliography of South African military History," in *South African Military Yearbook 1997*. Pretoria: South African Military History Consultants, 1997. 93-127.

Nzongo-Ntalaja. "United States Policy toward Zaire," in Bender, G., Coleman, J.S. & Sklar, R.L., eds. *African Crisis Areas and U.S. Foreign Policy.* Berkeley/Los Angeles/London: University of California Press, 1985. 225-238.

O'Brien, K.A. "South Africa's New Intelligence Environment," in *About Turn: The Transformation of the South African Military and Intelligence* edited by Cilliers, J. & Reichardt, M. Halfway House: Institute for Defence Policy, 1995. 172-193.

Ohlson, T. "The Cuito Cuanavale Syndrome: Revealing SADF Vulnerabilities," in *South African Review 5* compiled and edited by Moss, G. & Obery, I. Johannesburg: Ravan Press & Southern African Research Service, 1989. 181-190.

O'Neill, K. & Manslow, B. "Ending the Cold War in Southern Africa," *Third World Quarterly* 12, nos. 3/4 (1990/1991): 81-96.

Onslow, Sue. "The Cold War in Southern Africa: White Power, Black Nationalism and External Intervention," in *Cold War in Southern Africa: White Power, Black Liberation* edited by Onslow, S. London & New York: Routledge, Cold War History Series, 2009. 9-34.

Onslow, Sue. "The South African Factor in Zimbabwe's Transition to Independence," in *Cold War in Southern Africa: White Power, Black Liberation* edited by Onslow, S. London & New York: Routledge, Cold War History Series, 2009. 110-129.

Oosthuizen, G.J.J. "The Military Role of the Rehoboth Basters during the South African Invasion of German South-West Africa, 1914-1915," *Scientia Militaria, South African Journal of Military Studies* 28, no. 1 (1998): 91-110.

ARTICLES & CHAPTERS

Oosthuizen, G.J.J. "The Final Phase of South African Transborder Operations into Angola: Regiment Mooi River and Operations Modular, Hooper, Packer and Displace (Handbag), 1987-1988," *Journal for Contemporary History* 28, no. 2 (September 2003): 97-106.

Oosthuizen, G.J.J. "Regiment Mooirivier and South African Transborder Operations into Angola during 1975/76 and 1983/84," *Historia* 49, no. 1 (2004): 135-153.

Oosthuizen, G.J.J. "The South African Defence Force versus SWAPO and its Allies: Operation Askari, 1983-1984," *New Contree* 50 (November 2005): 3-14.

Oosthuizen, G.J.J. "Regiment Mooirivier, Potchefstroom: Grensdienservarings van 'n Pantserburgermageenheid, 1975-1989," in *Grensoorlog/Border War 1966-1989* edited by Barnard, L. *Journal for Contemporary History* 31, no. 3 (December 2006): 187-214.

Oosthuizen, G.J.J. "Operasies Chuva en Moduler (Fase 1): 'n Waardering van die SAW-Unita-Bondgenootskap, Mei tot Oktober 1987," *Historia* 57, no. 2 (2012): 378-415.[online]

Oudes, B.J. "Evolving American Views of South Africa," in Bissell, R.E. & Crocker, C., eds. *South Africa Into the 1980s.* Westview Special Studies on Africa, Boulder Colorado: Westview Press, 1979. 159-186.

Pahlavi, P. & Ali, K. "Institutional analysis and irregular warfare: Portugal's involvement in Angola, Guinea Bissau and Mozambique (1961-1874)," *Canadian Military Journal* 12 no. 2 (2012): 44-52.

Papp, D.S. "Angola, National Liberation and the Soviet Union," *Parameters, Journal of the US Army War College* 8, no. 1 (1978): 26-39.

Parsons, I. "Youth, Conflict and Identity: Political Mobilisation and Subjection in Angola," in *Invisible Stakeholders: Children and War in Africa* edited by McIntyre, A. Pretoria: Institute for Security Studies, 2005. 45-66.

Pearson, P. "The Rehoboth Rebellion," in *Working Papers in Southern African Studies* edited by Bonner, P. Johannesburg: Ravan Press, 1981. 31-51.

Pepler, E. "'n Inhoudsontledingstudie oor die Demografiese Eienskappe van Deelnemers aan die Boetman-persdiskoers," *Journal for Contemporary History* 26, no. 2 (December 2001): 125-147.

Philip, K. "The Private Sector and the Security Establishment," in *War and Society: The Militarisation of South Africa* edited by Cock, J. & Nathan, L. Cape Town & Johannesburg: David Philip, 1989. 202-216.

Phillips, M. "The Nuts and Bolts of Military Power: The Structure of the SADF," in *War and Society: The Militarisation of South Africa* edited by Cock, J. & Nathan, L. Cape Town & Johannesburg: David Philip, 1989. 16-27.

Pillay, V. "Rising Cost of Apartheid: The Economic Crisis," in *Destructive Engagement: Southern Africa at War* edited by Johnson, P. & Martin, D. Harare: Zimbabwe Publishing House for the Southern African Research and Documentation Centre, 1986. 221-244; and in *Frontline Southern Africa: Destructive Engagement* edited by Johnson, P. & Martin, D. New York: Four Walls Eight Windows, 1988. 305-338.

Pitswane, J. "Namibia: Challenges of the First Decade," in *Southern Africa at the Crossroads? Prospects for Stability and Development in the 1990s* edited by Benjamin, L. & Gregory, C. Rivonia: Justified Press, 1992. 105-123.

Ploeger, J. "Suid-Afrikaanse Staats- en Staatsondersteunde Militêre Geskiedskrywing, 1924-1987", *Militaria* 19, no. 4 (1989): 15-36.

Pollecut, L. "Unlocking South Africa's Military Archives," in *Paper Wars: Access to Information in South Africa* edited by Allan, K. Johannesburg: Wits University Press, 2009. 122-143.

Popescu, Monica. "Mirrorings: Communists, Capitalists and Voortrekkers of the Cold War," in *Beyond the Border War: New Perspectives on Southern Africa's Late-Cold War Conflicts* edited by Baines, G. & Vale, P. Pretoria: University of South Africa Press, 2008. 42-55.

Porto, J.G. "Contemporary Conflict Analysis in Perspective," in *Security and Surfeit: The Ecology of Africa's Conflicts* edited by Lind, J. & Sturman, K. Pretoria: Institute for Security Studies, June 2002. 1-49.

Posel, D. "A 'Battlefield of Perceptions': State Discourses on Political Violence, 1985-1988," in *War and Society: The Militarisation of South Africa* edited by Cock, J. & Nathan, L. Cape Town & Johannesburg: David Philip, 1989. 262-274.

Posel, D. "Symbolizing Violence: State and Media Discourse in Television Coverage of Township Protest, 1985-87," in *Political Violence and the Struggle in South Africa* edited by Manganyi, N.C. & Du Toit, A. Basingstoke: Macmillan, 1990. 154-171.

Potgieter, T.D. "Maritime Defence and the South African Navy, to the Cancellation of the Simon's Town Agreement," *Scientia Militaria, South African Journal of Military Studies* 30, no. 2 (2000): 159-182.

Potgieter, T. "Counterinsurgency in Africa: The Colonial Experience," in *South Africa and Contemporary Insurgency: Roots, Practices, Prospects* edited by Baker, D-P. & Jordaan, E. Claremont: UCT Press, 2010. 68-82.

Potgieter, T. "Guiding the Seafarers: The South African Hydrographic Office and the Contribution of the Three *Proteas*," *Scientia Militaria, South African Journal of Military Studies* 40, no. 3 (2012): 147-176.

Prah, K.K. "African Wars and Ethnic Conflicts – Rebuilding Failed States," United Nations Development Programme, Human Development Report Office. Background paper for HDR2004. Occasional Paper 10, 2004.

Preston, R. "Integrating Fighters after the War: Reflections on the Namibian Experience, 1989-1993," *Journal of Southern African Studies* 23, no.3 (1997): 453-472.

Price, R.M. "Creating New Political Realities: Pretoria's Drive for Regional Hegemony," in Bender, G., Coleman, J.S. & Sklar, R.L., eds. *African Crisis Areas and U.S. Foreign Policy.* Berkeley/Los Angeles/London: University of California Press, 1985. 64-88.

Prior, A. "South African Exile Politics: A Case Study of the African National Congress and the South African Communist Party," *Journal of Contemporary African Studies* 3, nos. 1/2 (October 1983/April 1984): 181-196.

Ramuhala, M.G. "Guerrilla Warfare from an MK Perspective," in *South Africa and Contemporary Insurgency: Roots, Practices, Prospects* edited by Baker, D-P. & Jordaan, E. Claremont: UCT Press, 2010. 125-135.

Rauch, J. "War and Resistance," in *War and Resistance: Southern African Reports* edited by Cawthra, G., Kraak, G. & O'Sullivan G. London: Macmillan Press, 1994. 1-15.

Reichardt, M. & Cilliers, J. "The History of the Homeland Armies," in *About Turn: The Transformation of the South African Military and Intelligence* edited by Cilliers, J. & Reichardt, M. Halfway House: Institute for Defence Policy, 1995. 63-83.

Reichardt, M. & Cilliers, J. "Swords and Business: The Past and Future of the South African Defence Industry," in *About Turn: The Transformation of the South African Military and Intelligence* edited by Cilliers, J. & Reichardt, M. Halfway House: Institute for Defence Policy, 1995. 249-270.

Rich, P. "Insurgency, Terrorism and the Apartheid System in South Africa," *Political Studies* 32 (1984): 68-85.

Robbertze, J.H. "Die Grondslae van Strategie," in *Konflik en Orde in Internasionale Verhoudinge* edited by Barnard, L.D. Johannesburg: Perskor-uitgewery, 1978. 164-181.

Roberts, A.R. "British Economic Involvement in South African-Occupied Namibia: 1845-1986," in *Allies in Apartheid: Western Capitalism in Occupied Namibia* edited by Cooper, A.D. London: Macmillan Press, 1988. 156-174.

Rogez, Mathilde. "'Borderline Cases': Madness and Silence in the Representation of the Border War in the Works of Select South African Novelists," in *Beyond the Border War: New Perspectives on Southern Africa's Late-Cold War Conflicts* edited by Baines, G. & Vale, P. Pretoria: University of South Africa Press, 2008. 120-136.

Roos, Henriette. "Writing from Within: Representations of the Border War in South African Literature," in *Beyond the Border War: New Perspectives on Southern Africa's Late-Cold War Conflicts* edited by Baines, G. & Vale, P. Pretoria: University of South Africa Press, 2008. 137-157.

Rotberg, R.I. "Namibia and the Crisis of Constructive Engagement," in Bender, G., Coleman, J.S. & Sklar, R.L., eds. *African Crisis Areas and U.S. Foreign Policy.* Berkeley/Los Angeles/London: University of California Press, 1985. 95-109.

Rotberg, R.I. "Political and Economic Realities in a Time of Settlement," in *Namibia: Political and Economic Prospects* edited by Rotberg, R.I. Lexington, MA: Lexington Books, n.d. 29-40.

Rothwell, P. "Introduction: 'Never again?' – Remembering Angola," *Portuguese Literary & Cultural Studies*, nos. 15/16 (2010): xii-xxiii.

Saul, S. & Leys, C. "SWAPO: The politics of exile," in *Namibia's Liberation Struggle: The Two-Edged Sword* edited by Leys, C. & Saul, J.S. London: James Currey, 1995. 40-65.

Saul, S. & Leys, C. "Lubango and After: 'Forgotten History' as Politics in Contemporary Namibia," *Journal of Southern African Studies* 29, no. 2 (June 2003): 333-353.

Sandler, D. "The Psychological Experiences of White Conscripts in the Black Townships," in *War and Society: The Militarisation of South Africa* edited by Cock, J. & Nathan, L. Cape Town & Johannesburg: David Philip, 1989. 79-89.

Saney, I. "African Stalingrad: The Cuban Revolution, Internationalism and the End of Apartheid," *Latin American Perspectives* 33, no. 5 (September 2006): 81-117.

Saphire, H. & Saunders, C. "Liberation Struggles in Southern Africa in Context," in *Southern African Liberation Struggles: New Local, Regional and Global Perspectives* edited by Saphire, H. & Saunders, C. Claremont: UCT Press, 2013. 1-29.

Sass, B. "An Overview of the Changing South African Defence Force," *South African Defence Review* 13 (November 1993): 13-22.

Sass, B. "The Union and South African Defence Force – 1914 to 1994," in *About Turn: The Transformation of the South African Military and Intelligence* edited by Cilliers, J. & Reichardt, M. Halfway House: Institute for Defence Policy, 1995. 118-139

Satchwell, K. "The Power to Defend: An Analysis of Various Aspects of the Defence Act," in *War and Society: The Militarisation of South Africa* edited by Cock, J. & Nathan, L. Cape Town & Johannesburg: David Philip, 1989. 40-50.

Saunders, C. "The Angola/Namibia Crisis of 1988 and its Resolution," in *Cold War in Southern Africa: White Power, Black Liberation* edited by Onslow, Sue. London & New York: Routledge Cold War History Series, 2009. 225-240.

Saunders, C. "Angola: From War to Peace," *Transformation* 69 (2009): 161-172.

Saunders, C. "The History and Historiography of Namibian Decolonisation," *South African Historical Journal* 31, no. 1 (November 1994): 221-234.

Saunders, C. "The United States and Namibian Independence, c. 1975-1989," *Journal for Contemporary History* 28, no. 1 (June 2003): 83-91.

Saunders, C. "South Africa's Role in Namibia/Angola: The Truth and Reconciliation Commission's Account," in *Beyond the Border War: New Perspectives on Southern Africa's Late-Cold War Conflicts* edited by Baines, G. & Vale, P. Pretoria: University of South Africa Press, 2008. 267-280.

Saunders, C. "Some Roots of Anti-Colonial Historical Writing about Namibia," *Journal of Namibian Studies* 3, (2008): 83-93.

Saunders, C. "Transition in Namibia 1989-1990: And the South African case," *Transformation* 17 (1992): 12-24.

Scholtz, L. "Cuito Cuanavale: Wie het Werklik Gewen?" *Scientia Militaria, South African Journal of Military Studies* 28, no. 1 (1998): 16-61.

Scholtz, L. "Die Ontwikkeling van die SA Leër in die Grensoorlog, 1966-1989," in *Grensoorlog/Border War 1966-1989* edited by Barnard, L. *Journal for Contemporary History* 31, no 3 (December 2006): 112-130.

Scholtz, L. "The Namibian Border War: An Appraisal of the South African Strategy," *Scientia Militaria, South African Journal of Military Studies* 35, no. 1 (2007): 19-48.

Scholtz, L. "'n Strategiese en Operasionele Beoordeling van die Suid-Afrikaanse Weermag (SAW) se Oorgrens-operasies in Angola, 1978-1988," in *Grensoorlog/Border War 1966-1989, Deel 2/Part 2* edited by Barnard, L. *Journal for Contemporary History* 34, no. 1 (February 2009): 57-80.

Scholtz, L. "Suid-Afrika se Strategiese Posisie en die 'Slag van Cuito Cuanavale', 1987-1988," *Journal for Contemporary History* 37, no.2 (December 2012): 165-190.

Scholtz, L. "The Air War over Angola, 1987-1988: An Analysis," in *Grensoorlog/Border War 1966-1989, Deel 2/Part 2* edited by Barnard, L. *Journal for Contemporary History* 34, no. 1 (February 2009): 237-265.

ARTICLES & CHAPTERS

Scholtz, L. "The South African Strategic and Operational Objectives in Angola, 1978-88," *Scientia Militaria, South African Journal of Military Studies* 38, no. 1 (2010): 68-98.

Scholtz, L. "The Standard of Research on the Battle of Cuito Cuanavale, 1987-1988," *Scientia Militaria, South African Journal of Military Studies* 39, no. 1 (2011): 115-137.

Scholtz, L. "Lessons from the Southern African Wars: A Counterinsurgency Analysis," *Journal for Contemporary History* 36, no. 2 (September 2011): 193-215.

Scholtz, L. "The Lessons of the Border War," *Scientia Militaria, South African Journal of Military Studies* 40, no. 3 (2012): 318-353.

Searle, C. "The Mobilization of Words: Poetry and Resistance in Mozambique," in *Marxism and African Literature* edited by Gugelberger, G.M. Trenton, New Jersey: Africa World Press, 1986. 150-164.

Seegers, A. "Extending the Security Network to the Local Level," in *Government by the People?* edited by Heymans, C. & Totemeyer, G. Johannesburg: Juta, 1988.

Seegers, A. "War in Southern Africa," *Africa* 62, no.2 (1992): 271-279.

Seery, B. "Security Council Resolution 435 and the Namibian Independence Process," in *South African Review 5* compiled and edited by Moss, G. & Obery, I. Johannesburg: Ravan Press & Southern African Research Service, 1989. 227-240.

Seiler, J. "South Africa's Regional Role," in *Southern Africa Since the Portuguese Coup*. Westview Special Studies on Africa, Boulder Colorado: Westview Press, 1980. 99-113.

Selfe, J. "South Africa's National Management System," in *War and Society: The Militarisation of South Africa* edited by Cock, J. & Nathan, L. Cape Town & Johannesburg: David Philip, 1989. 149-158.

Serote, M.W. "Freedom Park," *The Thinker* 7 (2009): 64-66.

Shange, V. "With the PAC in Exile," *Searchlight South Africa, A Marxist Journal of Southern African Studies*, no. 10 (April 1993): 31-33.

Shaw, M. "Biting the Bullet: Negotiating Democracy's Defence," in *South African Review 7: The Small Miracle – South Africa's Negotiated Settlement* edited by Friedman, S. & Atkinson, D. Johannesburg: Ravan Press, 1994. 228-256.

Shaw, M. "Negotiating Defence for a New South Africa," in *About Turn: The Transformation of the South African Military and Intelligence* edited by Cilliers, J. & Reichardt, M. Halfway House: Institute for Defence Policy, 1995. 9-34.

Shelton, G. & Magyar, P. "The War over Angola and Namibia: Factors of Prolongation," in *Prolonged Wars: A Post-Nuclear Challenge* edited by Magyar, K. & Danopoulos, P. United States of America: Department of Defense, July 2001. First published in October 1994. 259-289.

Shikangalah, S. "The Development Brigades: The Namibian Experience," in *Dismissed: Demobilisation and Reintegration of Former Combatants in Africa* edited by Cilliers, J. Halfway House: Institute for Defence Policy, 1995. 70-71.

Shubin, V. & Tokarev, A. "War in Angola: a Soviet Dimension," *Review of the African Political Economy* (ROAPE), no. 90 (2001): 607-619.

Shubin, G. & Shubin, V. "Relations between South Africa and Russia, 1898-2004," in *A Century is a Short Time: New Perspectives on the Anglo-Boer War* edited by Snyman, I., Liebenberg, I., Van der Westhuizen, G. & Roos, M. Pretoria: Nexus Publishers, 2005. 334-347.

Shubin, V. "Red Star over Southern African Skies," in *Regions, Regional Organisations and Military Power* edited by Potgieter, T., Esterhuyse, A., & Liebenberg, I. Stellenbosch: Sun Media, 2008. 29-50.

Shubin, V. "Unsung Heroes: The Soviet Military and the Liberation of Southern Africa," in *Cold War in Southern Africa: White Power, Black Liberation* edited by Onslow, Sue. London & New York: Routledge Cold War History Series, 2009. 154-176.

Sidaway, J.D. & Simon, D. "Geopolitical Transition and State Formation: The Changing Political Geographies of Angola, Mozambique and Namibia," *Journal of Southern African Studies. Special Issue: Namibia: Africa's Youngest Nation* 19, no. 1 (March 1993): 6-28.

Simpson, G. "The Politics and Economics of the Armaments Industry in South Africa," in *War and Society: The Militarisation of South Africa* edited by Cock, J. & Nathan, L. Cape Town & Johannesburg: David Philip, 1989. 217-231.

Simpson, T. "The ANC Underground in Swaziland, c. 1975-1982," in *Southern African Liberation Struggles: New Local, Regional and Global Perspectives* edited by Saphire, H. & Saunders, C. Claremont: UCT Press, 2013. 96-116.

Somerville, K. "Angola – Groping towards Peace or Slipping back towards War?" *Terrorism and Political Violence* 8, no. 4 (Winter 1996): 11-39.

Somerville, K. "Angola – Groping towards Peace or Slipping back towards War?" in *Violence in Southern Africa* edited by Gutteridge, W. & Spence, J.E. London: Frank Cass, 1997. 11-39.

Standard Bank of South Africa. "Angola: An Economic Survey." Johannesburg: Supplement to *Standard Bank Review* (September 1968).

Steenkamp, W. "'Rommel' in Angola," in *Beroemde Suid-Afrikaanse Krygsmanne* edited by Scholtz, L. Cape Town: Rubicon-Pers, 1984. 177-192.

Steenkamp, W. "The Commandos of South Africa" in *The Militia in 20th Century America: A Symposium* edited by Morgan Norval, Falls Church, Virginia: The Gun Owners Foundation, 1985. 127-141.

Steenkamp, W. "Politics of Power – The Border War," in *Challenge: Southern Africa within the African Revolutionary Context. An Overview* edited by Venter, A.J. Gibraltar: Ashanti Publishing, 1989. 183-223.

Steenkamp, W. "Armscor Today – Selling Arms to the Enemy," in *Challenge: Southern Africa within the African Revolutionary Context. An Overview* edited by Venter, A.J. Gibraltar: Ashanti Publishing, 1989. 470-500.

Steenkamp, W. "The Citizen Soldier in the Border War," in *Grensoorlog/Border War 1966-1989* edited by Barnard, L. *Journal for Contemporary History* 31, no. 3 (December 2006): 1-22.

Steenkamp, W.P. "The Shaping of the South African Soldier, 1510-2008," in *Grensoorlog/Border War 1966-1989* edited by Barnard, L. *Journal for Contemporary History* 34, no. 1 (February 2009): 207-222.

Stemmet, J-A. & Barnard, S.L. "P.W. Botha's Rubicon Speech of 15 August 1985: A River too Wide and a Bridge too Far," *Journal for Contemporary History* 27, no. 1 (2002): 119-135.

Stemmet, J-A. "Troops, Townships and Tribulations: Deployment of the South African Defence Force (SADF) in the Township Unrest of the 1980s," *Journal for Contemporary History* 31, no. 2 (September 2006): 178-193.

Stevens, C. "The Soviet Role in Southern Africa," in Seiler, J., ed. *Southern Africa Since the Portuguese Coup.* Westview Special Studies on Africa, Boulder Colorado: Westview Press, 1980. 45-58.

Strauss, A. "Die Betrokkenheid van Vroue in 'n Era van Oorlog," in *Grensoorlog/Border War 1966-1989* edited by Barnard, L. *Journal for Contemporary History* 31, no. 3 (December 2006): 370-398.

Sturgess, P., Katjihingua, M. & Mchombu, K. "Information in the National Liberation Struggle: Modelling the Case of Namibia (1966-1990)," *Journal of Documentation* 61, no. 6 (2005): 735-750.

Sturgess, P. "Information in the Namibian National Liberation Struggle (1966-1989): Applying a Model," *Proceedings of the American Society for Information Science and Technology* 41, no. 1 (2004): 45-53.

Swanepoel, J.J. "B.J. Vorster and South West Africa as International Question, 1966-1978 (III)," *Journal for Contemporary History* 10, no. 3 (December 1985): 92-109.

Swilling, M. & Phillips, M. "The Powers of the Thunderbird – Decision-Making Structures and Strategies in the South African State," in *South Africa at the End of the Eighties: Policy Perspectives 1989.* Johannesburg: Centre for Policy Studies, Graduate School of Business Administration, University of the Witwatersrand, 1989. 29-73.

Swilling, M. & Phillips, M. "State Power in the 1980s: From 'Total Strategy' to 'Counter-Revolutionary Warfare'," in *War and Society: The Militarisation of South Africa* edited by Cock, J. & Nathan, L. Cape Town & Johannesburg: David Philip, 1989. 134-148.

Tapscott, C. "War, Peace and Social Classes," in *Namibia's Liberation Struggle: The Two-Edged Sword* edited by Leys, C. & Saul, J.S. London: James Currey, 1995. 153-170.

Thompson, W.S. & Silvers, B. "South Africa in Soviet Strategy," in Bissell, R.E. & Crocker, C., eds. *South Africa Into the 1980s.* Westview Special Studies on Africa, Boulder Colorado: Westview Press, 1979. 133-158.

Titlestad, M. "My Defence Force," in *Load Shedding: Writing on and over the Edge of South Africa* edited by McGregor, L. & Nuttall, S. Johannesburg & Cape Town: Jonathan Ball Publishers, 2009. 31-43.

Tötemeyer, G. & Seiler, J. "South West Africa/Namibia: A Study in Polarization and Confrontation," in Seiler, J., ed. *Southern Africa Since the Portuguese Coup.* Westview Special Studies on Africa, Boulder Colorado: Westview Press, 1980. 79-96.

Trewhela, P. "The Kissinger/Vorster/Kaunda détente: Genesis of the SWAPO 'Spy Drama' - Parts I and II," *Searchlight South Africa, A Marxist Journal of Southern African Studies* nos. 5 and 6 (1990-91).

Trewhela, P. "SWAPO and the Churches: An International Scandal," *Searchlight South Africa, A Marxist Journal of Southern African Studies*, no 7 (July 1991): 65-88.

Trewhela, P. "Within the Secret State: The Directorate of Military Intelligence," *Searchlight South Africa, A Marxist Journal of Southern African Studies*, no. 8 (January 1992): 7-24.

Trewhela, P. "The ANC Prison Camps: An Audit of Three Years, 1990-1993," *Searchlight South Africa, A Marxist Journal of Southern African Studies*, no. 10 (April 1993): 8-30.

Trewhela, P. "Women and SWAPO: Institutionalised Rape in SWAPO's Prisons," *Searchlight South Africa, A Marxist Journal of Southern African Studies*, no. 11 (October 1993): 23-29.

Vale, P. "Pretoria and Southern Africa: From Manipulation to Intervention," in *South African Review I: Same Foundations, New Facades?* Southern African Research Service. Johannesburg: Ravan Press,1983. 7-22.

Vale, P. "The Botha Doctrine: Pretoria's Response to the West and to its Neighbours," in *South African Review II*, South African Research Service. Johannesburg: Ravan Press, 1984. 188-196.

Vale, P. "The Search for Southern Africa's Security," *International Affairs* 64, no. 4 (1991): 697-708.

Vale, P. "South Africa's New Diplomacy," in *South African Review 6: From 'Red Friday' to Codesa* edited by Moss, G. & Obery, I. Johannesburg: Ravan Press, 1992. 424-435.

Vale, P. "The Cold War and South Africa: Repetitions and Revisions on a Prolegomenon," in *Beyond the Border War: New Perspectives on Southern Africa's Late-Cold War Conflicts* edited by Baines, G. & Vale, P. Pretoria: University of South Africa Press, 2008. 22-41.

Van Coller, H.P. "Afrikaanse Literatuur oor die Gewapende Konflik in Suider Afrika sedert 1965. 'n Voorlopige Verslag," *Acta Academica* 22, no. 4 (1990): 74-91.

Van Coller, H.P. "Grensliteratuur," in *Literêre Terme en Teorieë* edited by Cloete, T.T. Pretoria: HAUM-Literêr, 1992. 153-156.

Van Coller, H.P. "'n Eietydse Afrikaanse Prosaterugblik op die Grensoorlog, Deel 1," *Tydskrif vir Letterkunde* 37, no. 2 (Mei 1999): 31-39.

Van Coller, H.P. "'n Eietydse Afrikaanse Prosaterugblik op die Grensoorlog, Deel 2," *Tydskrif vir Letterkunde* 37, no. 3/4 (1999): 31-39.

Van Coller, H.P. "'n Eietydse Afrikaanse Prosaterugblik op die Grensoorlog," *De Helende Kracht van Literatuur* 2 (2002): 131-162.

Van der Bijl, A. "Poetry as an Element of the Apartheid Military Discourse," *Scientia Militaria, South African Journal of Military Studies* 39, no. 1 (2011): 56-84.

Van der Waag, I. "The Writing of Military History in South Africa," in *South African Military Yearbook 1997.* Pretoria: South African Military History Consultants, 1997. 5-32.

Van der Waag, I & Visser, D. "War, Popular Memory and the South African Literature of the Angolan Conflict," in *Grensoorlog/Border War 1966-1989, Deel 2/Part 2* edited by Barnard, L. *Journal for Contemporary History* 34, no. 1 (February 2009): 113-140.

Van der Waag, I. & Visser, D. "Between History, Amnesia and Selective Memory: The South African Armed Forces, a Century's Perspective," *Scientia Militaria, South African Journal of Military Studies* 40, no. 3 (2012): 1-12.

ARTICLES & CHAPTERS

Van der Waag, I. "Military Culture and the South African Armed Forces: A Historical Perspective," in Vreÿ, F., Esterhuyse, A. & Mandrup, T. *On Military Culture: Theory, Practice and African Armed Forces*. Claremont: UCT Press, 2013, pp. 181-198.

Van der Westhuizen, G. "'n Oorlog wat te voet geveg is: Diensplig-infanteriesoldate in die Grensoorlog, 1973-1989," in *Grensoorlog/Border War 1966-1989, Deel 2/Part 2* edited by Barnard, L. *Journal for Contemporary History* 34, no. 1 (February 2009): 164-180.

Van Niekerk, I. "Laaitie tot 'n Man – Hoe die Weermag my van die Lewe Geleer het," in *Grensoorlog/Border War 1966-1989, Deel 2/Part 2* edited by Barnard, L. *Journal for Contemporary History* 31, no. 3 (December 2006): 349-369.

Van Wyk, Anna-Mart. "The USA and Apartheid South Africa's Nuclear Aspirations, 1949-1980," in *Cold War in Southern Africa: White Power, Black Liberation* edited by Onslow, Sue. London & New York: Routledge Cold War History Series, 2009. 55-83.

Vanneman, P. "Soviet Foreign Policy for Angola: The Brezhnev Doctrine Reconsidered," *ISSUP Strategic Review* (June 1985): 1-7.

Vaughan, M. "Literature and Populism in South Africa: Reflections on the Ideology of Staffrider," in *Marxism and African Literature* edited by Gugelberger, G.M. Trenton, New Jersey: Africa World Press, 1986. 195-220.

Velthuizen, A. "The Significance of the Battle for Cuito Cuanavale: Long-term Foresight of the Current Strategic Landscape," *Scientia Militaria, South African Journal of Military Studies* 37, no. 2 (2009): 107-123.

Venter, A.J. "Why Portugal Lost its African Wars," in *Challenge: Southern Africa within the African Revolutionary Context. An Overview* edited by Venter, A.J. Gibraltar: Ashanti Publishing, 1989. 224-272.

Venter, A. "Mededingende Politieke Paradigmas oor die Grensoorlog 1966-1988," in *Grensoorlog/Border War 1966-1989, Deel 2/Part 2* edited by Barnard, L. *Journal for Contemporary History* 34, no. 1 (February 2009): 36-56.

Vigne, R. "The Namibia File," *Third World Quarterly* 5, no. 2 (April 1983): 345-360.

Vigne, R. "SWAPO of Namibia: A Movement in Exile," *Third World Quarterly* 9, no. 1 (January 1987): 85-107.

Viljoen, M.J. "Die Ontstaan en die Ontwikkeling van die Skoolkadette-stelsel in die RSA: Grepe uit die Geskiedenis en 'n Oorsig oor die Huidige Stelsel," *Scientia Militaria, South African Journal of Military Studies* 15, no. 3 (2012): 38-49.

Vines, A. "Still Killing: Land-Mines in Southern Africa," in *From Defence to Development: Redirecting Military Resources in South Africa* edited by Cock, J. & Mckenzie, P. Cape Town/Ottawa: David Philip/International Development Research Centre, 1998. 148-162.

Vines, A. Angola: "40 Years of War," *Track Two Occasional Paper* 9, no. 2 (June 2000): 2-32.

Visser, D. "Namibiese Bosoorlog uit die Pen van 'n Deurwinterde Krysghistorikus (Review of Cas Bakkes' *Dagverhaal van 'n Grenssoldaat*)," *The Journal for Transdisciplinary Research in Southern Africa* 5, no. 2 (December 2009): 293-297.

Visser, D. "Accolades and Albatrosses: The South African National Defence Force's Centenary and the Commemoration of Milestones in South African Military History," *Scientia Militaria, South African Journal of Military Studies* 40, no. 3 (2012): 13-39.

Visser, G.E. "Militêre Professionalisme en die Onderrig van Krygsgeskiedenis in die Suid-Afrikaanse Nasionale Weermag: 'n Historiese Perspektief," *Scientia Militaria, South African Journal of Military Studies* 27, no. 1 (1997): 15-36.

Visser, W. "Afrikaner Anti-Communist History Production in South African Historiography," in *History Making and Present Day Politics: The Meaning of Collective Memory in South Africa* edited by Stolten, H.E. Uppsala: Nordiska Afrikainstutet, 2007. 306-333.

Warwick, R. "Operation Savannah: A Measure of SADF Decline, Resourcefulness and Modernisation," *Scientia Militaria, South African Journal of Military Studies* 40, no. 3 (2012): 354-397.

Weaver, T. "Namibian Review," in *South African Review II*, South African Research Service. Johannesburg: Ravan Press, 1984. 211-227.

Weaver, T. "The South African Defence Force in Namibia," in *War and Society: The Militarisation of South Africa* edited by Cock, J. & Nathan, L. Cape Town & Johannesburg: David Philip, 1989. 90-102.

Weideman, G. "Wat sê die Swygende Kubaan Vandag vir Ons? Oor Konflikliteratuur," *Acta Academica* 36, no. 1 (2004): 1-39.

Weiland, H. "Namibia: A Fresh Deal," *International Affairs Bulletin* 14, no. 1 (1990): 22-32.

Wessels, A. "South Africa's Grey Diplomats; Visits by South African Warships to Foreign Countries 1946-1996," *Scientia Militaria, South African Journal of Military Studies* 27, no. 1 (1997): 67-105.

Wessels, A. "Onwaarskynlike Ambassadeurs: Vlagvertoonvaarte deur Suid-Afrikaanse Oorlogskepe, 1922-2002," *Journal for Contemporary History* 27, no. 3 (December 2002): 54-81.

Wessels, A. "Die Suid-Afrikaanse Vloot se Eerste Fregat-era, 1944-1985 (1): Die 'Loch'-klas en SAS *Vrystaat*," *Journal for Contemporary History* 28, no. 3 (December 2003): 29-43.

Wessels, A. "Die Suid-Afrikaanse Vloot se Eerste fregat-era, 1944-1985 (2); Die 'President'-klas fregatte," *Journal for Contemporary History* 29, no. 1 (June 2004): 27-41.

Wessels, A. "Snelstormers: Torpedojaers in Suid-Afrikaanse Vlootdiens, 1950-1975," *Journal for Contemporary History* 29, no. 2 (September 2004): 25-42.

Wessels, A. "Buitelandse Vlagvertoonbesoeke aan SA Hawens: Vanaf die V.O.C.-tydvak tot 1961," *Journal for Contemporary History* 31, no. 1 (June 2006): 81-98.

Wessels, A. "Buitelandse Vlagvertoonbesoeke aan Suid-Afrikaanse Hawens (2): Die Periode van Fluktuerende Internasionale Betrekkinge, 1961-1994," *Journal for Contemporary History* 31, no. 2 (September 2006): 78-102.

Wessels, A. "The South African Navy during the Years of Conflict in Southern Africa, 1966-1989," in *Grensoorlog/Border War 1966-1989* edited by Barnard, L. *Journal for Contemporary History* 31, no. 3 (December 2006): 283-303.

Wessels, A. "Skout-admiraal (JG) André Burgers se Vlootherinneringe aan die Jare van die 'Grensoorlog', 1966 tot 1989," in *Grensoorlog/Border War 1966-1989* edited by Barnard, L. *Journal for Contemporary History* 31, no. 3 (December 2006): 304-325.

Wessels, A. "Veertig Jaar se Ondersteuning ter See. Gevegsteunskepe in die Suid-Afrikaanse Vloot, 1967-2007 (1): SAS *Tafelberg* en SAS *Drakensberg*," *Journal for Contemporary History* 32, no. 2 (December 2007): 164-182.

Wessels, A. & Marx, L. "The 1977 United Nations Mandatory Arms Embargo against South Africa: A Historical Perspective after 30 Years," *Journal for Contemporary History* 33, no. 1 (June 2008): 70-86.

Wessels, A. "Veertig Jaar se Ondersteuning ter See. Gevegsteunskepe in die Suid-Afrikaanse Vloot, 1967-2007 (2): SAS *Drakensberg* en SAS *Outeniqua*," *Journal for Contemporary History* 33, no. 1 (June 2008): 143-161.

Wessels, A. & Bredenkamp, I. "The Development of Military Chaplaincy, with Special Reference to South Africa (up to 1966)," in *Grensoorlog/Border War 1966-1989* edited by Barnard, L. *Journal for Contemporary History* 34, no. 1 (February 2009): 298-317.

Wessels, A. & Bredenkamp, I. "Military Chaplaincy in the South African Defence Force during the Namibian War of Independence, 1966-1989," in *Grensoorlog/Border War 1966-1989* edited by Barnard, L. *Journal for Contemporary History* 34, no. 1 (February 2009): 318-338.

Wessels, A. & Bredenkamp, I. "Suid-Afrikaanse Kapelane in 'n era van Militêre Konflik, 1966-1989: Enkele Persoonlike Ervarings en Perspektiewe," in *Grensoorlog/Border War 1966-1989* edited by Barnard, L. *Journal for Contemporary History* 34, no. 1 (February 2009): 339-360.

Wessels, A. "Sestig Jaar se Mynteenmaatreëlswerk in die Suid-Afrikaanse Vloot, 1947-2007 (2): Die 'oorlogsjare', 1966-1989," *Journal for Contemporary History* 34, no. 3 (December 2009): 190-206.

Wessels, A. "The South African Navy and its Predecessors, 1910-2010: A Century of Interaction with Commonwealth Navies," *Scientia Militaria, South African Journal of Military Studies* 38, no. 2 (2010): 109-130.

Wessels, A. "Hidrografiese Opmetingskepe in Diens van die Suid-Afrikaanse Vloot, 1922-2012," *Journal for Contemporary History* 37, no. 1 (June 2012): 232-250.

Wessels, A. "South Africa's Naval Forces, 1922-2012," *Journal for Contemporary History* 37, no. 2 (December 2012): 268-287.

Wessels, A. "The South African Air Force, 1920-2012: A Review of its History and an Indication of its Cultural Heritage," *Scientia Militaria, South African Journal of Military Studies* 40, no. 3 (2012): 222-249.

Wessels, A. "South Africa's Land Forces, 1912-2012," *Journal for Contemporary History* 37, no. 1 (2013): 229-254.

Wheeler, D.L. "Portuguese Withdrawal from Africa, 1974-1975: The Angolan Case," in Seiler, J. (ed.) *Southern Africa Since the Portuguese Coup.* Westview Special Studies on Africa, Boulder Colorado: Westview Press, 1980. 3-21.

Whittle, M. "OPS Medic – Operational Medical Orderlies during the Border War," in *Grensoorlog/Border War 1966-1989* edited by Barnard, L. *Journal for Contemporary History* 31, no. 3 (December 2006): 326-348.

Williams, C.A. "Living in Exile: Daily Life and International Relations at SWAPO's Kongwa Camp," *Kronos* 37, no. 1 (2011): 60-89. [online]

Williams, C.A. "'Remember Cassinga?' An Exhibition of Photographs on Histories," *Kronos* 36, no. 1 (2010): 213-251.

Williams, C.A. "National History in South Africa: Reflections on the 'Remember Cassinga?' Exhibition," *Kronos* 36, no. 1 (2010): 207-212.

Williams, R. "Demobilisation and Reintegration in Society: Human Resources Conversion," in *From Defence to Development: Redirecting Military Resources in South Africa* edited by Cock, J. & Mckenzie, P. Cape Town/Ottawa: David Philip/International Development Research Centre, 1998. 208-221.

Williams, R. "The Impact of 'Umkhonto We Sizwe' on the Creation of the South African National Defence Force (SANDF)," *Journal of Security Sector Management* 2, no. 1 (March 2004): 2-24.

Williams, R. "The Other Armies: Writing the History of MK," in *The Long March: The Story of the Struggle for Liberation in South Africa* edited by Liebenberg, I., Van der Westhuizen, G., Nel, F.B.O. & Lortan, F. Pretoria: Kagiso-HAUM, 1994. 22-34.

Williams, R. "A Comparative Overview of the Guerrilla Campaigns of the Boer Republics and Umkhonto We Sizwe," in *A Century is a Short Time: New Perspectives on the Anglo-Boer War* edited by Snyman, I., Liebenberg, I., Van der Westhuizen, G. & Roos M. Pretoria: Nexus Publishers, 2005. 59-88.

Windrich, E. "Savimbi's War: Illusions and Realities," in *Beyond the Border War: New Perspectives on Southern Africa's Late-Cold War Conflicts* edited by Baines, G. & Vale, P. Pretoria: University of South Africa Press, 2008. 195-206.

Winkler, H.E. & Nathan, L. "Waging Peace: Church Resistance to Militarisation," in *War and Society: The Militarisation of South Africa* edited by Cock, J. & Nathan, L. Cape Town & Johannesburg: David Philip, 1989. 324-337.

Wood, B. "Preventing the Vacuum: Determinants of the Namibia Settlement," *Journal of Southern African Studies* 17, no. 4 (1991): 742-769.

Wynchank, D.R.S.M. & Granier, S.K. "Opinions of Medical Students at the University of Cape Town on Emigration, Conscription and Compulsory Community Service," *South African Medical Journal* 79, no. 9 (May 1991): 532-535.

Young, C. The Portuguese Coup and Zaire's Southern African Policy," in *Southern Africa Since the Portuguese Coup.* Westview Special Studies on Africa, Boulder Colorado: Westview Press, 1980. 195-212.

Young, C. "The Zairian Crisis and American Foreign Policy," in Bender, G., Coleman, J.S. & Sklar, R.L., eds. *African Crisis Areas and U.S. Foreign Policy.* Berkeley/Los Angeles/London: University of California Press, 1985. 209-224.

Young, T. "Angola: Peace at Last," in *Southern Africa at the Crossroads? Prospects for Stability and Development in the 1990s* edited by Benjamin, L. & Gregory, C. Rivonia: Justified Press, 1992. 19-39.

Zartman, I.W. "The African States as a Source of Change," in Bissell, R.E. & Crocker, C., eds. *South Africa Into the 1980s.* Westview Special Studies on Africa, Boulder Colorado: Westview Press, 1979. 107-131.

ARTICLES & CHAPTERS

REPORTS

Centre for Conflict Resolution. Angola: 40 Tears of War. *Track Two*, 2000. Vol. 9(2).

Cronje, G. & Cronje, S. *The Workers of Namibia*. London: International Defence and Aid Fund (IDAF), 1979.

Human Awareness Programme. *Militarisation Dossier*. Johannesburg: South African Catholic Bishop's Conference (SACBC)/South African Council of Churches (SACC), 1984/1985/1986.

Van Zyl, M., De Gruchy, J., Lapinsky, S., Lewin, S. & Reid, G. *Human Rights Abuses of Gays and Lesbians in the South African Defence Force by Health Workers during the Apartheid Era*. The aVersion Project, Simply Said & Done for Gay and Lesbian Archives, Health and Human Rights Project, Medical Research Council, National Coalition for Lesbian and Gay Equality, Cape Town, 2009.

UNPUBLISHED THESES

Alexander, E.G.M. "The Cassinga Raid." MA thesis, University of South Africa, 2003.

Alheit, H.K.J. "'n Evaluasie van die Ontwikkeling van Maatskaplike Welsyn in die SAW." D Phil thesis, University of Pretoria, 1970.

Almer, M. "Remembering Angola – Cuban Internationalism, Transnational Spaces, and the Politics of Memories." D Phil thesis, University of Michigan, 2011.

Bissonnette, B. "The Angola Proxy War: A Study of Foreign Intervention and its Impact on War Fighting." MA thesis, US Army Command and General Staff College, Fort Leavenworth, Kansas, 2008.

Callister, G. "Compliance, Compulsion and Contest: Aspects of Military Conscription in South Africa, 1952-1992." MA thesis, University of Stellenbosch, 2007.

Connors, J.P. "Empowering Alternatives: A History of the Conscientious Objector Support Group's Challenge to Military Service in South Africa." M Com thesis, University of KwaZulu-Natal, 2007.

Cronjé, J.C. "Die Grens as Meerduidige Gegewe in die Kontemporêre Afrikaanse Prosa." D Litt thesis, University of Pretoria, 1989.

Correia, P.E.S.L.D-F. "Political Relations between Portugal and South Africa from the End of the Second World War until 1974." D Litt et Phil thesis, University of Johannesburg, 2010.

Craig, D. "The Viewer as Conscript: Dynamic Struggles for Ideological Supremacy in the South African Border War Film, 1971-1988." MA thesis, University of Cape Town, 2003.

Dempsey, M.C. "Die Militêre Konflik tussen die Suid-Afrikaanse Magte en SWAPO in die Operasionale Gebied, 1974-1980." MA thesis, University of the Orange Free State, 1984.

De Klerk, C.F. "Militêre Beriggewing in Suid-Afrika soos Gemanifesteer in *Beeld*." M Tec thesis, Tshwane University for Technology, 2007.

De Visser, L. "Winning the Hearts and Minds: Legitimacy in the Namibian Border War." MA thesis, Utrecht University, 2010.

De Vries, W. van W. "Die South West Africa People's Organisation." MA thesis, University of Pretoria, 1980.

Deysel, J.J.H. "The Subversive Afrikaner: An Exploration into the Subversive Stance of the Little Magazine *Stet* (1982-1991)." MA thesis, University of Pretoria, 2007.

Dorning, W.A. "A Historical Analysis of the Military Strategic Implications for the Republic of South Africa of Unita's Activities in Angola, 1976-1983." D Phil thesis, University of the Orange Free State, 1987.

Draper, C. "Psychological Experiences of Military Conscription in South Africa during the 1970s and 1980s." Honours thesis, University of Cape Town, 1999.

Du Plessis, H.D. "Resolusie 435: Agtergrond, Bepalings en Toepassing." MA thesis, University of Potchefstroom, 1988.

Eriksen, G.E. "Forged in Flames: The SADF Experience of the Battles of Cuito Cuanavale 1987-1988." BA Honours thesis, Rhodes University, 2010. With accompanying video documentary: Part 1: http://www.youtube.com/watch?v=fclRzi4E9TY; Part 2: http://www.youtube.com/watch?v=rdO1EM3Fpso; Part 3: http://www.youtube.com/watch?v=TsMmTDDUJYk.

Escandon, J.E. "Bush War: The Use of Surrogates in Southern Africa (1975-1989)." School of Advanced Military Studies, United States Army Command and General Staff College, Fort Leavenworth, Kansas, 2008-2009.

Goosen, C.P. "Die Toepassing van die Beginsels van Liggaamlike Opvoeding in die Opleiding van die SAW." D Phil thesis, University of the Orange Free State, 1970.

Graham, P. "The Response of African Societies in South West Africa to White Administration, 1915-1939." MA thesis, University of London, School of Oriental and African Studies, 1971.

John, N. "South African Intervention in the Angolan Civil War, 1975-1976: Motivations and Implications." MA thesis, University of Cape Town, 2002.

Labuschagne, B. "South Africa's Intervention in Angola: Before Cuito Cuanavale and Thereafter." MA thesis, University of Stellenbosch, 2009.

Liebenberg, I. "Truth and Reconciliation Processes and Civil-Military Relations: A Qualitative Exploration." D Litt et Phil thesis. Pretoria: University of South Africa, 2008.

Livhuwani, N.J. "The Role Played by the People's Liberation Army of Namibia (PLAN) during the Namibian Struggle, 1978 to 1989." MA thesis, University of Johannesburg, 1999.

Mathagu, R.V. "The Social Role of Militarism in Namibia with Specific Reference to Education, Health and Family Life, 1978-1988." MA thesis, University of Johannesburg, 1999.

McCrary, M.S. "Guerrilla Warfare in Namibia and Associated Implications for External Military Involvement." MA, Naval Postgraduate School, Monterey, Canada, 1979.

Moorcroft, H. "The Relationship between Experiences in the South African Special Forces and Current Levels of Well-being and Sense of Coherence." MA (Psychology) thesis, University of Pretoria, 2006.

Morris, M.I. "Back to the Front: Tracing Reverberations of the South West African Border Wars of the 1970s and 1980s." MA thesis, University of the Witwatersrand, 2006.

Munnik, V. "Confined to Base: A Psycho-Political Reading of "'n Wêreld Sonder Grense'." BA Honours thesis, University of the Witwatersrand, 1987.

Otieno, T.F. "Cuba's Revolutionist and Anti-Imperialist Foreign Policy in Southern Africa: The Case of Angola and Namibia." MA thesis, Rhodes University, 2000.

Phillips, M.W. "The End Conscription Campaign 1983-1988: A Study of White Extra-Parliamentary Opposition to Apartheid." MA thesis, University of South Africa, 2002.

Potgieter, J.F. "Die Militêre Kapelaan." DD thesis, University of Pretoria, 1971.

Ramabulana, R.I. "The US Brokered Settlement of the Namibian Dispute, 1988." MA thesis, University of Johannesburg, 1999.

Rochlin, J.F. "Cuban Intervention in Angola and Ethiopia, 1975-1980: The Question of Soviet Influence on Cuba." MA thesis, The University of British Columbia, 1980.

Rogers, S.A. "Fighting Tomorrow: A Study of Selected Southern African War Fiction." MA thesis, University of KwaZulu-Natal, 2005.

Rudham, C.B. "Lost Soldiers from Lost War: A Comparative Study of the Collective Experience of Soldiers of the Vietnam War and the Angolan/Namibian Border War." MA thesis, University of Cape Town, 2003.

Sandler, D. "Plucking the Wings of Butterflies: A Phenomenological Investigation of the Experiences of White SADF Conscripts in the Black Townships." BA Honours, University of the Witwatersrand, 1986.

Schaap, R. "State of Emergency: An Exploration of Attitudes towards Homosexuality in the SADF, 1969-1994." MA thesis, University of Stellenbosch, 2011.

Selfe, J. "The Total Onslaught and the Total Strategy: Adaptations to the Security Intelligence Decision-Making Structures under P.W. Botha's Administration." MA thesis, University of Cape Town, 1987.

Srinivas, C. "US Intervention in Sub-Saharan Africa since the Seventies: Case Studies of Angola and Ethiopia." D Phil thesis, University of Hyderabad, 1999.

Vale, P. "Remembering Koevoet. How South Africa has Come to Understand its Covert Military Operations in Namibia." Georgetown University, n.d.

Van der Merwe, J.C.K. "'n Ondersoek na die Ontstaan en Verloop van Insurgensie in Ovambo tot 1983." MA thesis, University of South Africa, 1985.

Van Heerden, A. "Die Suiderkruisfonds en die Mobilisering van die Suid-Afrikaanse Blanke Burgerlike Samelewing tydens die Grensoorlog, 1968-1989." MA thesis, University of Stellenbosch, 2014.

Van Wyk, J.L. "Die Geskiedenis van 1 Valskermbataljon, 1961-1984." MA thesis, University of the Orange Free State, 1986.

Velthuizen, A.G. "The Use of Military Force for Political Ends: The Case of South Africa in South-Western Africa." MA thesis, University of Pretoria, 1994.

Warwick, R. "White South Africa and Defence 1960-1968: Militarization, Threat Perceptions and Counter Strategies." PhD thesis, University of Cape Town, 2009.

Williams, C.A. "Exile History: An Ethnography of the SWAPO Camps and the Namibian Nation." D Phil thesis, University of Michigan, 2009.

INTERNET SOURCES

Ant's military notes. Accessed May 23, 2012. http://www.shantygoods.com/military/military_why.htm & http://shantygoods.com/military/camps.htm

Allport, R. "The Battle of Bridge 14." Accessed October 21, 2011. http://www.rhodesia.nl/bridge14.htm

Allport, R. "The Battle of Cuito Cuanavale: Cuba's Mythical Victory." Accessed October 21, 2011. http://www.rhodesia.nl/cuito.htm

Anonymous. "Days of glory: The Final Defeat of South Africa in Angola." Accessed June 26, 2013. http://www.sa-soldier.com/data/06_sadflinks/.../From_a_Cuban_perspective.pdf

Angola: African Giron. "Speech by Fidel Castro at the ceremony Commemorating the 15th anniversary of the victory at Playa Giron, Havana, April 19, 1976, Year of the 20th anniversary of the Granma." Accessed October 21, 2011. http://www.rhodesia.nl/giron.htm

Baines, G. "South Africa's Forgotten War," History Today, 59 (4), 2009. Accessed June 6, 2012. http://historytoday.com/gary-baines/south-africa%E2%80%99s-forgotten war

Bezuidenhout, A. "Roof op die Noot af: Hou my vas Korporaal ..." Accessed May 23, 2012. http://www.oulitnet.co.za/roof/roof2.asp

Castro, F. "Address to Cubans leaving for Angola, March 30 1977." Accessed June 26, 2013. http://www.cbsnews.com/stories/2005/03/07/world/main678582.shtml

Cherry, J. "A Disturbing Reminder: The Experiences of Conscripted Soldiers in South Africa's Border War," South African Journal of Science 108, no. 5/6 (2012). Accessed June 26, 2013. http://www.sajs.co.za

Fourie, T. "Vergete: 'n Artikel oor die vergete oud-stryders en die trauma wat hulle moes deurmaak." Accessed June 26, 2013. http://www.readabook.co.za/dl/system/books/58_full.pdf

Gear, S. "Wishing us Away: Challenges Facing Ex-Combatants in the 'New' South Africa." Centre for the Study of Violence and Reconciliation, no. 8, Johannesburg, 2002. Accessed June 26, 2013. http://www.csvr.org.za/papers/papvt8a.htm

Gleijeses, P. "The Massacre of Cassinga." Accessed June 26, 2013. http://amadlandawonye.wikispaces.com/ The+Massacre+of+Cassinga,+Piero+Gleijeses

Hammond, P. "South West Africa/Namibia and 435." Special Report. Frontline Fellowship. Accessed March 8, 2013. http://frontline-org-za.win03.glodns.net/news/namibia_special report.htm

Koekemoer, J. "TV-'dokumentêr' oor Grensoorlog is suiwer Kommunistiese Propaganda." Accessed January 27, 2012. http://praag.co.za/content/view/3690/402

Lotter, A. "Fighting the Last War." Accessed June 26, 2013. http://www.warinangola.com/portals/31/Fighting%20the%20last%20war%202.pdf

Malan, M.A. D-M. "Submission to the Truth and Reconciliation Commission." Accessed June 22, 2012. http://www.justice.gov.za/trc/hrvtrans/submit/malan.htm

REPORTS

THESES

INTERNET
SOURCES

Marquez, G.G. "Operation Carlota." Accessed October 21, 2011. http://www.rhodesia.nl.marquez.htm

Mitchell, N. H-Diplo Article Review: Piero Gleijeses. "Moscow's Proxy? Cuba and Africa, 1975-1988", in *Journal of Cold War Studies* 8, no.4 (Fall 2006). Accessed February 16, 2007. http://www.h-net.org/~diplo/reviews/PDF/Mitchell-Gleijeses.pdf

Morgan, M. "Refusniks down South," *Smokebox*, Issue 40. Accessed June 6, 2012. http://www.smokebox.net/archives/what/morga1206.html

Moss, R. "Castro's Secret War Exposed: How Washington Lost its Nerve and how the Cubans subdued Angola. Castro's Secret War 1." Originally appeared in *The Sunday Telegraph*, January 30, 1977. Accessed October 21, 2011. http://www.rhodesia.nl/moss1.htm

Moss, R. "How South Africa took on Castro's Invaders. Castro's Secret War 2." Originally appeared in *The Sunday Telegraph*, February 6, 1977. Accessed October 21, 2011. http://www.rhodesia.nl/moss2.htm

Moss, R. "Battle of Death Road. Castro's Secret War 3." Originally appeared in *The Sunday Telegraph*, February 13, 1977. Accessed October 21, 2011. http://www.rhodesia.nl/moss3.htm

Moss, R. *Moscow's next Target in Africa*. Originally appeared in *The Sunday Telegraph*, February 20, 1977. Accessed October 21, 2011. http://www.rhodesia.nl/moss4.htm

Nathan, L., Batchelor, P. & Lamb, G. "Submission to the Truth and Reconciliation Commission: Business Sector Hearing." Centre for Conflict Resolution, University of Cape Town, October 1997. Accessed June 5, 2012. http://ccrweb.ccr.uct.ac.za/archive/staff_papers/guy_trc.html

"Ons was Daar: 21 Februarie 2012. Sosiale Media-staptog teen die Eensydige oorvertelling van die Geskiedenis." Accessed February 24, 2012. http://www.afriforum.co.za/onswasdaar

Pederson, P. "Cubans who Fought in Angola 'Inspire Future Generations'," *The Militant* 74, no. 49, December 27, 2010. Accessed February 24, 2013. http://www.themilitant.com/2010/7449/744903.html

"Press Release: Nature and Extent of the SADF's Involvement in the Angolan Conflict." Accessed October 21, 2011. http://www.rhodesia.nl/sadfpress.htm

Rauch, J. "War and Resistance," in *War and Resistance: Southern African Reports* edited by Cawthra, G., Kraak, G. & O'Sullivan, G. London: Macmillan Press, 1994. Accessed May 23, 2012. http://www.csvr.org.za/wits/papers/papwarj.htm

Roodt, D. "Die Bosoorlog – 'n Verlore Saak Liefs Vergeet?" 12 November 2007. Accessed April 27, 2012. http://praag.co.za/?p=1073

SA Defence Force Contact Bureau. "Assessment of the Probable Results of Activities of the Truth and Reconciliation Commission (TRC) as Perceived by Former Chiefs of the SADF." Submission to the Truth and Reconciliation Commission, February 1988. Accessed October 21, 2011. http://www.rhodesia.nl/trurec1.htm

SANDF Nodal Point. "SA Defence Force Involvement in the Internal Security Situation in the Republic of South Africa." Submission to the Truth and Reconciliation Commission. Accessed June 8, 2012. http://www.justice.gov.za/trc/hrvtrans/submit/sadf.htm

Saney, I. "The Story of how Cuba Helped to Free Africa." Originally appeared in *Morning Star*, November 4, 2005. Accessed January 21, 2011. http://emba.cubaminrex.cu/Default.aspx?tabid=16014

Sassen, R. "Under Covers: South Africa's Apartheid Army – An Incubator for Artists' Books." Accessed June 26, 2013. http://www.theartistsbook.org.za/downloads/under_covers_sassen_essay.pdf

Senekal, B.A. "Grensoorlogstories nie Grensverskuiwend nie." Biebouw-reviews, Litnet. Accessed on September 28, 2012.http://www.litnet.co.za/Article/grensoorlogstories-nie-grensverskuiwend-nie/

Smiley, X. "Inside Angola," *The New York Review of Books*, February 17, 1983. Accessed October 21, 2011. http://www.nybooks.com/articles/archives/1983/feb/17/inside-angola/?page=2

Spence, J.E. "Southern Africa in the Cold War," *History Today* 49, no. 2. Accessed June 6, 2012. http://www.historytoday.com/je-spence/southern-africa-cold-war

Staff Reporter. "Hell, no, we won't go!" 25 August 2006. Accessed June 7, 2012. http://mg.co.za/print/2008-8-25-hell-no-we-wont-go

Strachan, A. "*Kopwond* deur Anthony Feinstein – die waarheid as fiksie beleef." LitNet Akademies-resensie-essay. Accessed April 27, 2012. http://www.litnet.co.za/Article/kopwond-deur-anthony-feinstein-die-waarheid-as-fiksie-beleef/

"SWATF/Koevoets not 'war veterans' – 'Over my dead body'," President Pohamba. Accessed March 8, 2013. http://www.swapoparty.org/swatf_koevoets_not_war_veterans.html

Truth and Reconciliation Commission. "Special Submission on Conscription." Cape Town, 23 July 1997. Accessed June 8, 2012. http://www.justice.gov.za/trc/special/conscrip/conscr01.htm

Van Eeden, J. "Somewhere on the Border – A Review." Accessed February 24, 2012. http://www.litnet.co.za/Article/somewhere-on-the-border-a-review-by-janet-van-eeden/

Venter, A. "Contending Paradigms regarding the South African Border War 1966-1989." Accessed June 26, 2013. http://www.inter-disciplinary.net/wp-content/uploads/2011/04/venterwpaper.pdf

Venter, G. "Kontaksport, Dinsdag 09 Desember 2008 09:48." Accessed January 27, 2012. http://praag.co.za/index2.php?option=com_content&do_pdf=1&id=3704

Venter, P.A. *Ek was daar*. Accessed June 27 2014. E-Book available at http://bookdir.info/?p=420853

Wall, D. "Operation Askari 1983-1984 Southern Angola." 2006. Accessed June 26, 2013. http://www.veridical.co.za/default.aspx?tabid=1173

Wilcox, S.S. "The South West Africa People's Organisation 1961-1991: A Guide to Archival Resources and Special Collections in the Western Cape, South Africa." UCT Libraries Occasional e-publications Series, Number 1, 2004.

WEBSITES

Africanactivist.msu.edu

Bethlehemssappers: www.bethlehemssappers.blogspot.com

Bezuidenhout, Leon. "Courage, Blood and Treachery: A Short Overview of Police Sergeant Herman Grobler's Involvement in the Namibian Bush War, 1982-1989", 2009. Available at http://tekkieraces.co.za/springbok/2009/inhoud/herman_grobler_e.pdf

Grensoorlog/Border War 1966-1989 Facebook Group: http://www.facebook.com/#!/groups/grensoorlog/

Just Done Productions. http://www.justdone.co.za

SADF Living History Facebook Group: http://www.facebook.com/#!/groups/5698430669

SADF Scrapbook: http://www.geocities.com/sadf_scrapbook/index.html

SA Magte Klub/SA Forces Club: http://www.samagte.co.za

Sentinal Projects: http://www.geocities.com/sadfbook/index.html

The South African Army Experience (The South African Soldier): http://www.sa-soldier.com/data/index.htm

South African Bush Veterans Association: www.sabwv.co.za

The South African Bush War 1966-1989: http://geocities.com/sa_bushwar/

South African History Online: http://sahistory.org.za

South African Roll of Honour Database: http://www.justdone.co.za/ROH/

The South African Veterans' Association (SAVA): http://www.veterans.org.za/

Suid-Afrikaanse Bosoorlog-veterane (SABOV). http://sabov.co.za

32 Battalion: http://www.32battalion.net

Unofficial SADF Information Page: http://www.geocities.com/Yosemite/Forest/1771/index.htm

The War in Angola (in Miniature): http://www.warinangola.com/

LITERATURE (NOVELS, SHORT STORIES, POEMS)

Akerman, A. "Somewhere on the Border," in *South African Plays* edited by Gray, S. London/Sandown: Nick Hern Books/Heinemann-Centaur, 1993.1-58.

Akerman, A. *Somewhere on the Border.* Johannesburg: Wits University Press, 2012.

Behr, M. *The Smell of Apples.* 2nd ed. London: Abacus, 1998.

Bezuidenhout, K. *Vryheidsvlug.* Kaapstad: Tafelberg, 1991.

"Boetie." *Vryval.* Wonderboompoort: Africa's Bowhunter, 2007.

Breytenbach, J. *The Plunderers.* Johannesburg & London: Covos Day, 2001.

Brooks, A.J. *The Border.* Johannesburg: 30 Degrees South Publishers, 2007.

Brown, T. *Doelwit Windhoek.* Johannesburg: Klub 707, 1982.

Coetzee, J. *Verby die Wit Brug.* Cape Town: Human & Rousseau, 1981. First published in 1978.

Couto, M. (Translated by Brookshaw, D.) *Under the Frangipani.* Cape Town: David Philip, 2001.

Donaldson, A. *Forces' Favourites.* Emmarentia: Taurus, 1987.

Dovey, J., ed. *Soldier's Verse: An Anthology of Poetry.* Durban: Just Done Productions, 2006.

Du Plessis, M. (With illustrations by Kruger, E.H.) *My Lang Soldaat.* Queenswood: Mara du Plessis, 1984.

Dymond, A. (Translated by Knoetze, T.) *Oor die Grens.* Pretoria: HAUM-Daan Retief Uitgewers, 1986.

Elsdon, A.D. *The Tall Assassin: The Darkest Political Murders of the old South Africa.* Cape Town: Umuzi, 2009.

Engelbrecht, E. *Kontak.* Cape Town: Human & Rousseau, 1981.

Eprile, T. *The Persistence of Memory.* Cape Town: Double Storey Books, 2005.

Ferreira, J., comp. and ed. *Grensoorlogstories.* Pretoria: Litera Publications, 2012.

Galgut, D. *The Beautiful Screaming of Pigs.* Johannesburg: Penguin Books, 2005.

Hiyalwa, K. *Meekulu's Children: A Tale of War and Survival in Northern Namibia.* Windhoek, Namibia: New Namibia Books, 2000.

Horn, T. *Droster.* Cape Town: Queillerie, 1996.

Joubert, E. *Ons Wag op die Kaptein.* Cape Town: Tafelberg, 1981. First published in 1963.

Joubert, E. *Die Laaste Sondag.* Kaapstad: Tafelberg, 1983.

Haasbroek, P.J. *Heupvuur.* Cape Town/Pretoria: Human & Rousseau, 1974.

Haasbroek, P.J. *Skrikbewind.* Cape Town/Pretoria: Human & Rousseau, 1976.

Haasbroek, P.J. *Verby die Wit Vlakte.* Cape Town/Pretoria/Johannesburg: Human & Rousseau, 1982.

Hugo, D. *Skeurkalender.* Cape Town: Tafelberg, 1998.

Kalmer, H. *X-Ray Visagie en die Vingers van God.* Kaapstad: Tafelberg, 1993.

Kalmer, H. *Vlieger en die Gevare van die Close Dance.* Cape Town: Queillerie, 2012.

Kellerman, G. *Swart Sendelinge.* Cape Town: Tafelberg, 1991.

Kellerman, G. *Wie de Hel het Jou Vertel?* Cape Town: Tafelberg, 1988.

Kilnsbay, B. *Seven Men in the Barrack Room.* Roosevelt Park: Bruce Kilnsbay, 1976.

Krüger, L. *'n Basis Oorkant die Grens.* Kaapstad: Tafelberg, 1984.

Krüger, L. *Gevaarlike Land.* Kaapstad: Tafelberg, 1990.

Liebenberg, I. "In Hoc Signo – In Hierdie Teken," *Perseel*, no. 31, pp.33-34, 1989.

Liebenberg, I. "Ik Had Een Wapen Broer," *New Contrast* 20, no. 4, December 1992.

Liebenberg, I. "Van 'n Ou Soldaat (of: Oor verraad)," *New Contrast* 20, no. 4, December 1992.

Liebenberg, K. "'n Storie vir Kersfees," *Stet* 20, no. 4, p. 20, 1989.

Liebenberg, K. "Oranje Blanje Blou," *Stet* 6, no. 4, p. 25, 1991.

Liebenberg, K. "'n Ware Verhaal," *Brul*, 1992.

Locker, B. *Starting Over.* Durban: Just Done Productions Publishing, 2008.

Louw, J.V. *Eric the Brave*. Cape Town: Umuzi, 2012.

Maartens, M. *Verste Grens*. Pretoria: Folio, 1987.

Maartens, M., Brinks, S.C., Engelbrecht, E., et al. *Ses Wenverhale*. Cape Town: Human & Rousseau, 1988.

Marnewick, C. *The Soldier Who Said No*. Cape Town: Umuzi, 2010.

Miles, J. *Blaaskans*. Johannesburg: Taurus, 1983.

Moolman, C. *Operasie Ché*. Cape Town: Human & Rousseau, 1997.

Opperman, D. *Môre is 'n lang dag en Die Teken*. Kaapstad: Tafelberg, 1986.

Opperman, D. (As retold by Breytenbach, K.) *Hartland*. Cape Town: Tafelberg, 2012.

Pieterse, F. *A War to Heal*. Durban: Just Done Productions - Publishing, n.d.

Potgieter, E.F. *Die Spinneweb*. Johannesburg: Perskor-uitgewery, 1974.

Pretorius, J. *So Lig soos Klip*. Cape Town: Tafelberg, 2012.

Prinsloo, K. *Die Hemel Help Ons*. Emmarentia: Taurus, 1988.

Retief, B. *Half Boom, Half Mens en Ander Grensstories*. Pretoria: J.L. van Schaik, 1986.

Retief, B. *Tweede Prys 'n Houtjas. Gresstories uit Wamboland*. Pretoria: J.L. van Schaik, 1983.

Rheeder, S. *Teardrops of the Waning Moon*. Knysna: Hedgehog Publishing, 2015.

Ryger, R.R. [Green, M.] *Dominatrix en Ander Stories*. Pretoria: Walkure Uitgewers, 2000.

Scheepers, R. *Die Heidendogters Jubel*. Kaapstad: Tafeldberg, 1995.

Steyn, J.C. *Op Pad na die Grens*. Cape Town: Tafeldberg, 1976.

Strachan, A. *Die Jakkalsjagter*. Kaapstad: Tafelberg, 1990.

Snyman, A. *Kruisvuur*. Pretoria: J.P. van der Walt, 1978.

Snyman, D. "Korporaal Fanie Venter, 1983," in *Op die Toneel: Stories, Reise, Stemme*. Cape Town/Pretoria: Human & Rousseau, 2009.

Snyman, D. "Die grammatika van 'n Verlore Jaar," in *Op die Toneel: Stories, Reise, Stemme*. Cape Town/Pretoria: Human & Rousseau, 2009.

Snyman, D. "Operasie Smokeshell," in *Op die Toneel: Stories, Reise, Stemme*. Cape Town/Pretoria: Human & Rousseau, 2009.

Sousa, J. *Patriots*. London: Viking, 1990.

Strachan, A. *'n Wêreld Sonder Grense*. Cape Town: Tafelberg, 1984.

Strachan, A. *Brandwaterkom*. Kaapstad: NB Uitgewers, 2015.

Torr, G. *Kill Yourself & Count to 10*. Johannesburg: Penguin Books, 2014.

Van der Merwe, C. *Moffie: A Novel*. Hermanus: Penstock Publishing, 2006.

Van Heerden, E. *My Kubaan*. Cape Town: Tafelberg, 1983.

Van Heerden, E. *Om te Awol*. Cape Town: Tafelberg, 1984.

Van Pletzen, J. *Liewe Ma: Briewe van Kleinjan*. Pretoria: J.P. van der Walt, 1982.

Van Pletzen, J. *Ma Weet Mos: Nog Briewe van Kleinjan*. Pretoria: Folio Publishers, 1982.

Van Pletzen, J. *"Ma, sê vir Sussie": Weer Briewe van Kleinjan*. Pretoria: Folio Publishers, 1984. Third printing 1985.

Van Vuuren, G. *Kanonvoer*. Johannesburg: Klub 707, 1980.

Venter, P.C. *Nagsprong*. Johannesburg: Voortrekker Boekklub, 1978.

Venter, W. *Falco*. Hartbees Uitgewers, Swellendam, 2008.

Viljoen, B. *'n Nuwe Wildernis*. n.p.: Human & Rousseau, 2013.

Wilhelm, P. *LM and other Stories*. Johannesburg: Ravan Press, 1975.

Wilhelm, P. *Some Place in Africa*. Craighall: Ad. Donder Publisher, 1987.

AUDIOVISUAL SOURCES

Documentary Films

Cuba: An African Odyssey. Directed by Jihan El-Tahri.

Cuba/South Africa after the Battle, 1990.

I have seen: Namibia. 1999.

Namibia: Africa's last Colony.1984. Video produced by Paul Hamann & Peter Salmon, BBC, distributed by California Newsreel.

Namibia – No easy Road to Freedom. 1988.

Films

Aanslag op Kariba. 1973.

Boetie gaan Border toe. 1984.

Boetie op Maneuvers. 1985.

Brug 14.

Forty Days. 1979.

Game for Vultures. SADF co-operation. 1979.

Grensbasis 13. 1979.

Jantjie kom Huis toe. 1985.

Kaptein Caprivi. 1972.

Mirage Eskader. 1975.

On the Wire. Director: Darrell Roodt.

Die Rebel. 1975.

Ses Soldate. 1975.

The Stick. Director: Darrell Roodt.

Terrorist. 1976. Appeal Board intervention.

'n Wêreld sonder Grense. 1987.

Wild Geese. 1978. (SADF cooperation.)

CDs, Records

Huisgenoot Troepie Treffers. Compiled by Gardner, D. & Strydom, J. Distributed by David Gresham Records, 2012.

Du Preez, V. *Totsiens Aufwiedersehen*. (Goosen/Esterhuizen, Jo'burg Records.)

Herholdt, S. *Jantjie* (Anton Goosen/EMI Music Publishing.)

Hugo, R. *Troepie Doepie*. (Reed, L./Dempsey, T. & Schuster, L. EMI Music Publishing.)

Schuster, L *Dis Lekker innie Army*. (Davis/Schuster, L., EMI Music Publishing/Gallo Music Publishers.)

Shaw, M. *Vasbyt, daar op die Grens*. (Hammond/Hazelwood, Copyright Control/David Gresham Music.)

ART EXIBITIONS

Memorias – Intimas – Marcas/Memory – Intimacy – Traces. Photographs by Fernando Alvim, Wayne Barker, Lien Botha, Carlos Garaicoa, Colin Richards, Jan van der Merwe and Gavin Younge. Contemporary Exhibition, Pretoria, 1999. Later published in *Social Identities: Journal for the Study of Race, Nation and Culture* 5, no. 4 (1999): 351-385. (Foreword by Bishop Desmond Tutu.)

Index